Dangerous Knowledge The JFK Assassination in Art and Film

Dangerous

The JFK Assassination in Art and Film

Knowledge

Art Simon

Temple University Press

Philadelphia

Temple University Press, Philadelphia 19122 ❡ Copyright © 1996 by
Temple University ❡ All rights reserved ❡ Published 1996 ❡ Printed
in the United States of America ❡ ☉ The paper used in this book
meets the requirements of the American National Standard for
Information Sciences – Permanence of Paper for Printed Library
Materials, ANSI Z39.48–1984.

Library of Congress Cataloging-in-Publication Data ❡ Simon, Art.
❡ Dangerous knowledge : the JFK assassination in art and film / Art
Simon. ❡ p. cm. — (Culture and the moving image) ❡ Includes
bibliographical references and index. ISBN 1-56639-378-7 (cloth). —
ISBN 1-56639-379-5 (paper) ❡ 1. Kennedy, John F. (John Fitzgerald),
1917 – 1963 — Assassination — Pictorial works. 2. Arts,
American. 3. Arts, Modern — 20th century — United States.
I. Title. II. Series.   NX652.K45S56 1996 ❡ 700 — dc20 95–24784

for Barbara and my father

Contents

ix

Acknowledgments

Many people have played important roles over the course of my work on this project. My greatest debt is to Robert Sklar. I have benefited immeasurably from his teaching and counsel, and my approach to history and film has been profoundly influenced by our friendship and dialogue over the years. I am grateful to Paul Arthur, my colleague at Montclair State University, not only for his input into this project, but for what he has taught me about the avant-garde cinema. Paul's casual remarks about film are generally more insightful than most people's concentrated efforts at critique. Teresa Podlesney has made an extraordinary contribution to my thinking about the cinema and, in fact, about anything worth having a passion for — politics, *Pat Garrett and Billy the Kid*, good scotch, Dean Martin. Ann Harris provided constant support, both intellectual and emotional, throughout the entire writing process. For their generous concern for my work and assistance with this project I want to thank William Simon, Peggy Phelan, Richard Allen, Melinda Barlow, and Fay Plant. Amber Hewins and Kevin Walter provided crucial help during the final stages. I am especially grateful for the support and consideration of Janet Cutler and Jim Nash. My thanks go to Janet Francendese at Temple University Press. I want to also acknowledge the editors of *Motion Picture*, *Women and Performance*, and *Cineaste*, who granted me space in their journals to work out some of the ideas in this book. For their assistance in providing illustrations or permissions I want to thank Bruce Conner, Chip Lord, Michael McClure, Beth Savage at the Warhol Foundation, and David Russick at the Phyllis Kind Gallery in Chicago.

Friends and family outside the university have been incredibly helpful and supportive. There is no way to adequately thank Neal Karlen. Since the days of Metropolitan Stadium, whether via short or long distance, he has provided me with nothing but encouragement and great humor. My work has been sustained by the camaraderie and patience of Jody Abramson, Jeff Cohen, Steve Burnham, Ed Markovitz, Craig Hunegs and Daniela Roveda, Carolyn Hunegs and Stuart Bloom, Harlan Berger, Sheila Berger, and Michael Rips.

Tom Simon first introduced me to the literature of the assassination; he and Vicki Simon have been as enthusiastic and supportive as any brother and sister could be. Melinda Peterson, Glen MacWilliams, Carrie Simon-

MacWilliams, and Saul Simon-MacWilliams all endured many hours of conversation about the Kennedy assassination.

I am most grateful for the love and loyalty of my father, Stan Simon, who taught me to keep my eye on the ball, take a level swing, and guard the plate when there are two strikes. I ask him to share the dedication with Barbara Berger. Barbara's patience and understanding never wavered, especially during those periods when I grew impatient and unsure. Without her extraordinary personal commitment, generosity, and love, this book would never have been written.

Dangerous Knowledge The JFK Assassination in Art and Film

In March of 1992, underground rock poster artist Frank Kozik created a dazzling and outrageous advertisement for the punk bands Helmet and L7. Silkscreened in fluorescent blue, green, and gold is a blown-up, grainy image of Lee Harvey Oswald, a closeup of the alleged presidential assassin at just the moment Jack Ruby pumped the deadly slugs into his stomach. Oswald's mouth open in anguish, his eyes closed tightly from the pain — we have seen this image countless times before. Yet in Kozik's poster, Oswald's face has been photomontaged with a hand holding a microphone so that now the open mouth appears to be screaming out a song, now the closed eyes appear to be lost in the rhythmic fury of punk rage.

Kozik's imagery is well chosen, for the poster advertises not just any rock performance, but the tour of two bands through Texas, their last stop being Dallas and a club located on Elm Street, the same street that runs through Dealey Plaza and on which JFK was assassinated. For thirty years a figure of fascination and attempted redemption for a subculture often on the margins, Oswald in Kozik's art finally gets the microphone and sings to his underground audience. For thirty years a political mystery and site of debate, the Kennedy assassination in this poster is imaged as entertainment, literally "on tour" — as it seems to have been since November 1963. Indeed, Kozik's silkscreen is but a more recent manifestation of work that appropriates and redefines assassination imagery, continuing a process inaugurated by pop art and underground film during the sixties, carried on by experimental video, and sustained by the Hollywood cinema. Its presentation of alleged assassin as angry young rock star (he was, after all, only twenty-four when he died) not only continues the persistent reidentifications of Oswald — lone gunman, government agent, conspiracy patsy — but continues an assault on the "official" framers of assassination discourse, those supports of mainstream culture whose legitimacy was assailed by assassination skeptics.

Imaging the Assassination

Perhaps no set of imagery has toured the cultural landscape as much as that referring in some way to the death of JFK. Since Kennedy and Oswald were

1

killed, the photographic evidence of their deaths and the accompanying narratives have circulated through government commissions and investigative agencies, the print and televised press, museums of high culture and strange collections of camp, the research of assassination critics and the products of commercial filmmaking. It is an increasingly familiar imagery — for many, still intriguing, occasionally shocking, and often frustrating; for others, banal, even tiresome. Yet this imagery remains at the center of a political dispute which has not ended and which, during the sixties and seventies, contributed to a culture of dissent that struck at a wide array of social institutions and psychic structures. Unlike the resistance to the war in Southeast Asia and the battle for civil rights, surely the period's defining political struggles, the debate over who killed JFK was fought not in the streets but over an ever-widening discursive field. That field was dominated by visual representation and characterized by a complex struggle over access to and interpretation of film and photographic imagery. The debate raised crucial questions about who should assume the authorship of history: the state's voice in the Warren Commission, the commission's critics, (or) the press. The assassination debates (as I will refer to them) manifested quite publicly Michel Foucault's ideas about the often-invisible politics of looking: "Power has its principle not so much in a person as in a certain concerted distribution of bodies, surfaces, lights, gazes."[1] Here Foucault is speaking specifically about Jeremy Bentham's Panopticon, a physical structure for discipline and punishment, but his understanding of power in terms of the visible aptly characterizes the political contests found in the assassination debates. How those debates became the focal point for a protracted struggle over camera vision and historical authorship and how the images and issues stemming from the case have been inscribed in art and film over the last thirty years is the subject of this book.

The "distribution of bodies" — Foucault's phrase is nearly perfect in its applicability to the authorial and interpretive struggles that characterize this subject: various bodies, their positioning in a black Lincoln convertible before, during, and after the impact of bullets shot from one or more high-powered rifles, their location in windows or on a grassy knoll. The location of these bodies on various dates in New Orleans or Mexico City or Dallas or the Soviet Union or Atsugi, Japan. Further, the construction and reconstruction of bodies through tampered photographs and bungled autopsies. And "surfaces, lights, gazes": the publication and censoring of film evidence, the constant and obsessive study of photographs, the endless replay of a twenty-six-second film shot by a Dallas dressmaker, images of a plaza or of a face enlarged or computer enhanced, appearing suddenly as if excerpted from some structural film, transformed into grain or shadow, and returned in some minimalist way to pure surface and light. Combined with the "distribution of bodies, surfaces, lights, gazes," and fully implicated in their dispersion into society, were the operations of narrative, the multiple efforts by the government and its critics to make the evidence cohere in a stable and legible story. Roland Barthes's understanding of narrative — that it is constructed out of a need "to end, to fill, to join, to unify . . . as though it were prey to some obsessive fear: that of omitting a connection" — describes the impulse behind efforts to reconstruct a coherent account out of the events surrounding the president's death.[2]

A Structure for Study

A consideration of three separate yet related sites for the combination of image and narrative make up this project: (1) the central image-based texts and the discursive practices that informed the government's investigations and media reportage; (2) a series of nonmainstream texts, works associated with the American avant-garde cinema or with sixties' pop art which refigure assassination issues through alternative stylistic strategies; and (3) a small group of commercial films inscribed by the discourses of the assassination which in turn contributed through their values and narrative formats to the persistent rearticulation of those discourses.

The structure of this study follows two trajectories: one tries to maintain a chronological discussion; the other separates texts according to their mode of production and formal characteristics. The chronological sequence is crucial to my efforts at placing this diverse and increasingly mobile imagery within a discursive context that built up unevenly but decisively through a process of accumulation. It is precisely this sense of chronology that I will be trying to construct so that linkages between various journalistic practices, films, and artwork can be brought into relief. Yet it is also important that art forms be discussed within a framework that positions them next to their textual kin, whether that relationship springs from a shared method of production or of exhibition.

Although my organization might appear to make the case, I am not prepared to argue that the avant-garde is always the first field of culture to confront current or newly emerging historical topics. Certainly, pop art and underground film absorbed assassination discourses before the commercial narrative cinema. But one easily recalls moments when Hollywood moved relatively quickly to image a contemporary subject, whether World War II or the plight of the returning vet. With the breakdown of the classic studio system, that kind of production efficiency has shifted to television, the electronic medium becoming increasingly swift in its transformation of news story into docudrama. It may well be that this tendency in television programming is the result of a late sixties' and seventies' cinema that was not just interested in topicality but also conveyed a cynicism toward society not witnessed in the popular arts since film noir. Undoubtedly, the new broadcasting technologies and more portable equipment that changed the nature of television news and forced public confrontation with images of war, whether in Southeast Asia or on American campuses, accelerated the process by which television in all its formats would come to deal with contemporary historical events.[3] If in the mid-sixties the industrial story-telling culture did lag behind the plastic arts in responding to events, this gap seems to have closed during the period of political contestation that framed the assassination inquiries.

The point of examining these three sites of textual practice is not to rerun the facts and speculations of the assassination mystery. Although certain details of the oft-repeated evidence will resurface here, my purpose is not to weigh in on one side or the other, for or against the findings of the Warren Commission. My point, especially with respect to the government's investigations and the media's reporting, is to theorize the status of the film and photographic image as it developed amid one of the period's defining and intriguing political debates, and then to register its impact on and incorporation within various image-making arts. With each anniversary of Kennedy's death, artifacts and images of the event continue to surface along the channels of mainstream and marginal culture. Image bites of the motorcade or of Lee Harvey Oswald are rerun on television news programs. Postmodern publications, from underground comics to the seriously semiotic, create or explore the once-scandalous imagery. In part, this book is an attempt to tether these seemingly free-floating signifiers of assassination imagery in the context of a history of representational practice. But I do not intend a comprehensive survey of all the ways in which some aspect of the assassination has been incorporated in pop culture. Its presence in, say, punk rock or science fiction will go undiscussed here, although any subsequent study of these might find a companion in my analysis. The presence of assassination imagery in diverse social locales is not a recent phenomenon. My discussion of these sites — the mainstream and alternative press, pop art, soft-core pornography, the collectibles of camp, the underground and commodity cinema — seeks to elaborate an epistemological setting for these practices.

In his essay "Periodizing the Sixties," Frederic Jameson suggests that the JFK assassination functioned as a crucial detonator for the decade, one that undermined the faith of a new generation and may have meant "the dramatic defeat of some new spirit of public or civic idealism."[4] I would suggest that this erosion of civic spirit resulted not only from Kennedy's shocking and untimely death but in great measure as a response to the post-Dallas investigations — given the inadequacy of the government's inquiry and the diversity, ferocity, and potentially scandalous character of the government's critics. In other words, something beyond a loss of idealism made the assassination a detonator for its own decade as well as the decades to follow, something that can be registered only when the focus shifts from the event in isolation to the full-blown critique of the state that developed around its interpretation. This critique of the state must, of course, be viewed in the larger context of sixties' social unrest; I do not mean to suggest that the assassination debates alone be credited over all other social and political processes with erosion of the state's power to control public debate. The overriding factor on this point remains the contestation around the definition and waging of the Vietnam War. Indeed, the arguments generated by many assassination critics were severely limited by the frequently narrow scope of their analysis, by their overinvestment in solving the Dallas mystery, and by their subscription to Camelot mythology. Efforts by Warren Commission critics must be read within the wider context of debate. The critics gave the assassination the appearance of a defining cultural signifier because its solution seemed to require a no less persistent (if far less visible) questioning of the government. Indeed, the political accusations and scandalous imagery that informed the assassination debates often shadowed, in a sinister, uncanny fashion, those other well-known and more visible movements that challenged the legitimacy or activities of the state.

Commenting on the sense of historical rupture occasioned by the killing of JFK, Christopher Lasch has written:

His murder plunged the country into a time of troubles, or at least coincided, more or less, with the beginnings of a turbulent era. The United States has had a long history of political assassinations; but it is only in the last generation that assassinations have come to serve as one more piece of evidence— interpreted in conformity with already existing beliefs about history and politics—that things are falling apart.[5]

Lasch's comment that only within the last generation have assassinations been read in conformity with other widespread political and social problems begins to address my point: John Kennedy's death may not be the most significant aspect of his assassination. What was of crucial importance was the struggle over its framing. The evidence that something was "falling apart," to use Lasch's phrase, was the government's inability to author(ize) a coherent and believable account of the assassination and of the events surrounding that day in Dallas. What made the assassination political, then, beyond the subtle change in power and its possible ideological motives and execution, was its textual encoding, its telling and retelling, the very struggle over its transformation into history.

The *assassination debates,* more strictly defined, refers to those texts and activities devoted to the study, investigation, or interpretation of the events related to and surrounding Kennedy's death. It is not limited to a set of books or articles or imagery, although it obviously includes these and other textual matter, but refers also to a set of practices or social relations through which investigative or reportorial texts were produced and circulated. With the release of Oliver Stone's *JFK* in December 1991, the debate reemerged on the national agenda with a force it had not known since the years immediately following the release of the report of the House Select Committee on Assassinations in July 1979. In response to the public dialogue reignited by the conspiracy theory presented in Stone's film, the federal government once again focused energy on the case, most specifically through efforts to make public the remaining secret files on its investigations. Beyond these "official" actions, Stone's film reanimated questions about the relationship between film and the writing of history. The thirtieth anniversary of the assassination witnessed a flurry of new texts, both print and televised, which sustained the dialogue. Subsequent anniversaries may well bring more of the same. Despite efforts by the mainstream press, fueled by its own backlash against Stone's film, to celebrate Gerald Posner's 1993 book and declare along with its title, *Case Closed,* the debate over the assassination continues.[6] The writing of the assassination's various histories seems a long way from an end.

Two methodological problems are worth noting here. First, in what temporal mode should my analysis be fashioned? Since the issues, images, and narratives being discussed are constantly being rearticulated, should the historical account be referred to in the past or the present tense? Ideally I should suggest that, whereas most of the events and discourses discussed in this book are placed in the past, their social meanings are subject to revision by still-active investigatory practices, both reportorial and artistic. Related to this is a second problem, one that is certainly not specific to my project. I am thinking of what Dominic LaCapra has termed *transference* — what is, in his words, "at play, in history, that is, in the very relation of the historian to the 'object' of study. Transference in this somewhat more indirect and attenuated sense refers to the manner in which the problems at issue in the object of study reappear (or are repeated with variations) in the work of the historian."[7] Assassination critics' "obsessive fear of omitting a connection" to use Barthes's phrase, is difficult to resist, as the encyclopedic (yet often one-dimensional) character of some of their work would seem to testify. The myriad "facts" and multiple scenarios cannot help but overwhelm studies of this material, and the question of how much background detail to supply the reader poses a persistent dilemma. Much of what follows in this introduction attempts to respond to this problem. The case of JFK's death is complex enough for those who have worked with it for many years. Rather than make yet another all-inclusive gesture, I will attempt to assemble some of the events in a narrative chronology of the significant assassination literature. For those who have followed the case closely, this section will no doubt be familiar. It is provided here so that the in-depth analyses in the following chapters can be free of the obsessive concerns implied in Barthes's phrase and so that the analysis can move less hesitatingly between survey and specificity.

At the outset note the recurring centrality of the assassination case for the period under discussion. It resonated far beyond the much-discussed psychological imprint, the widespread testimony by individuals as to where they were and what they were doing when they heard the news of Kennedy's death. At least six government investigations or studies — five at the federal level and one state/local — were conducted into or as a result of the assassination:

- The Warren Commission's investigation initiated on November 29, 1963, and completed with the public release of its report on September 27, 1964. (The Warren Report was itself founded in part on a five-volume FBI report delivered on December 9, 1963.)
- An inquiry by a panel of pathologists appointed by Attorney General Ramsey Clark in February 1968 who examined the available autopsy photographs and x rays.
- The 1968 conspiracy trial of Clay Shaw brought by New Orleans District Attorney Jim Garrison.
- The report of the National Commission on the Causes and Prevention of Violence issued in October 1969, in large part initiated in response to the assassinations of JFK, Robert F. Kennedy, and Martin Luther King, Jr.
- The Rockefeller Commission's investigation of the CIA, begun in March 1975, which devoted a section of its report to possible links between the assassination and various CIA operatives.
- The report of the House Select Committee on Assassinations, begun in 1976 and issued on July 22, 1979.[8]

Even when it was not the subject of government inquiry, the assassination was continually on the nation's journalistic agenda. Between 1963 and 1979 over 2,300 articles and books were devoted to some aspect of the assassination or the ongoing inquiry.[9] The national television networks returned to the subject throughout the thirty years following the assassination, CBS being the most interested. The CBS coverage included at least one program each year from 1963 to 1965, a four-part series in June 1967, a two-part inquiry broadcast in November 1975, and a two-hour report marking the thirtieth anniversary in November 1993. Pollsters inquired as to the people's faith in the Warren Commission's conclusions nearly every year. Before the House assassinations committee convened in 1976, at least three public interest groups — the Citizens' Commission of Inquiry, the Assassination Information Bureau, and the Committee to Investigate Assassinations — were established to disseminate information and spearhead efforts to launch a new federal investigation.[10] Numerous inquiry groups were formed after the assassination's twenty-fifth anniversary.[11]

As I've suggested, the assassination debates went beyond some notion of resonance. They were more than an echo rebounding in the press every couple of years. They contributed directly to a growing culture of skepticism and to a critique of the affirmative ideology of what officially took place in November 1963, an ideology that now seems even more distant than the years might suggest.[12] More specifically, the assassination inquests took part in multiple efforts to disrupt the political hegemony of the federal government; to expose and condemn the war in Southeast Asia, CIA activities, the FBI's infiltration of domestic organizations, and the state's overall abuse of power.

Perhaps most important was the attack leveled against the federal government's control of discourse and the state's claim to authoring (and authorizing) contemporary history. One of the defining characteristics of the period was the effort by disenfranchised individuals or marginalized groups to take control of activities generally carried out by the centralized government. The popular interventions by women or students or blacks succeeded, at points, in transgressing "the boundaries of power," and some of these interventions offered compelling challenges to established interpretations of history.[13] The assassination debates directly addressed this form of contestation, marking a process whereby the state lost authority and whereby its power to control public debate suffered a disruption, even a disintegration. At the same time, and closely related to this disruption, was a similar crisis for the "official" media and their role as legitimators, their function as supports for the government's claim to interpreting history and current events.

A History of Assassination Literature

Long before the release of the Warren Report in September 1964, the history of JFK's assassination was being constructed by the media, especially the print media.[14] Although occasional questions were raised about the commission's procedures, doubts as to the level of involvement of its celebrated members or concerns about possible links between Lee Harvey Oswald and agencies of the U.S. government, the vast majority of mainstream news reports conformed to a story originally circulated by the Associated Press and United Press International. That story, constructed within an hour of the assassination, parts of which would remain intact in the official government version, maintained that three shots were fired at the presidential motorcade, all three coming from the Texas School Book Depository building to the right and behind the president and all three fired by a single assassin named Lee Harvey Oswald. The alleged assassin was apprehended one hour and twenty minutes later in the Texas Theater. However, the account given in early press reports, stating that the first shot hit Kennedy, the second hit Governor John Connally, and the third hit Kennedy again, would be changed in the version offered by the Warren Commission in September of the following year. Forced to account for one bullet's totally missing the motorcade and for the time constraints imposed on Oswald's alleged firing time by the evidence contained in the Zapruder film, the commission amended the initial accounts and concluded that one bullet passed through the bodies of both Kennedy and Connally. This would come to be known as the magic bullet.

Media attention then quickly shifted for a time from the logistics of the shooting to the background of the alleged assassin. Oswald was labeled a Marxist and a psychopath whose brief residence in the Soviet Union and alleged political affiliations with pro-Castro Cuban organizations were promoted as signs of implicit guilt. In December 1963 and January 1964 the FBI report on its investigation, as well as the work-in-progress of the Warren Commission, were leaked to elements of the mainstream press, and it was duly reported that both official groups were concluding what had so far been put forth as the correct version of events: the lone assassin theory. *Time* magazine declared there was "little doubt of Oswald's guilt," and in February 1964 *Life* magazine pictured Oswald on its cover with the tag "Lee Oswald with the weapons he used to kill President Kennedy and Officer Tippit." Indeed, three months earlier, on the very day that Lyndon Johnson appointed the Warren Commission, *Life* published in its November 29 issue a photograph taken from the window on the sixth floor of the School Book Depository. Under the photograph, the magazine's text declared that this was the site from which the assassin had fired the fatal shots. *Life* seemed in a particularly good position to construct a history of the event, for it had in its possession the best photographic evidence: Abraham Zapruder's twenty-six seconds of film. The magazine had purchased the film from Zapruder for an estimated $150,000 and thus had exclusive publication rights to it.[15] It had taken only a couple of months for the journalistic community to convict Oswald despite the lack of any thorough or coherent reconstruction of events.

This conviction, however, did not go totally uncontested. Two books released in 1964, Joachim Joesten's *Oswald: Assassin or Fall Guy?*[16] and Thomas Buchanan's *Who Killed Kennedy?*[17] were the first book-length studies of the case issued prior to the release of the Warren Report. Perhaps more important from the long-range standpoint of commission criticism was a series of articles which began appearing in liberal or left-wing publications during 1965. Vincent Salandria's articles for the January and March issues of the magazine *Liberation* raised serious questions about the medical evidence reported by the Warren Commission. Also in March of 1965 Harold Feldman's article "Fifty-Two Witnesses: The Grassy Knoll" appeared in *Minority of One*. Analyzing eyewitness accounts of the shooting found in the Warren Report's twenty-six volumes of evidence and testimony, it produced quite a different account of what happened in Dealey Plaza. Witnesses told of shots from in front of the president and of smoke, possibly gunsmoke, rising from an area near the grassy knoll. A year later, also writing in *Minority of One,* Salandria revealed that the FBI's departmental investigation had reported, contrary to the commission's conclusion, that the nonfatal bullet that had struck Kennedy had in fact not exited his body. Within a year, the government's investigation had been soundly criticized, its investigation made to appear a composite of contradictory reports.

These and other early alternative analyses reveal several crucial aspects of the assassination debates. First, many of the initial counterinquests to critique the government's version had to rely solely on the government's published evidence as a source for their own investigatory work. It soon became clear that the massive *Warren Report* was a text that critics would have to construct and simultaneously deconstruct. The report ran to almost 300,000 words — only a summary of twenty-six volumes containing some 20,000 pages of testimony — yet it was still an incomplete record, its immensity standing as a bulky monument to the elusiveness of historical experience. It thus fell to independent investigators to complete the government's work. The twenty-six volumes of evidence and testimony had no index until 1966 when Warren Commission critic Sylvia Meagher constructed one, a task that took her over a year.[18] Prior to her work, much of the evidence, especially that which contradicted the commission's conclusions, was buried in the narrative chaos of the unindexed volumes.

Much of the assassination critics' early work was thus absorbed in textual analysis of the government's documents. From this they learned that, of the over four hundred persons present in Dealey Plaza the day of the assassination, only around ninety were asked to give testimony. Their first look at the Zapruder film, as reprinted in Volume 18 of the commission's exhibits, suggested to them that Kennedy's head had been thrown violently backwards upon impact of the fatal bullet, a reaction that might point to shots coming from the front rather than the rear of the limousine. Critics further discovered that, as published in Volume 18, the two Zapruder frames immediately following the head wound had been printed out of sequence. That is, frame 315 had been printed as coming before frame 314, thus possibly giving the wrong impression as to which direction the president's head had moved following impact. These points only begin to hint at the problems uncovered by the first generation of critics, but they suggest the areas of inquiry in which persons without any official investigatory status engaged.

The people doing the digging were not, for the most part, experienced in working with government records, but ordinary folk who simply wanted to know what had happened. Perusing the twenty-six volumes, we found accounts of what was seen and heard in Dealey Plaza mentioned nowhere in the Warren Report.

The process was slow and laborious, like learning the names and locations of numerous extras on a huge movie set. Though the FBI could easily have made a complete compilation while memories were still fresh, this was not done. Consequently, the historical record was pitifully incomplete.[19]

Motivated by a range of factors — grief, skepticism, confusion — a network of unofficial investigators, journalists, and what would become known as assassination buffs began collecting newspaper articles pertaining to the assassination. As contradictions and complexities grew, so did their research into the case. In a June 1967 article on "The Buffs" for the *New Yorker*, Calvin Trillin wrote:

By the first week in February [1964], Shirley Martin, a housewife who then lived in Hominy, Oklahoma, had driven to Dallas with her four children to interview witnesses. Lillian Castellano, a Los Angeles book-keeper who thought that reports on the wounds indicated that the President must have been hit from the front, had studied a picture of the Dealey Plaza area, discovered what seemed to be a strategically placed storm drain in front of the motorcade, and called that fact to the attention of a local news commentator, The Los Angeles Times, the Warren Commission, and anyone else she could think of who might be investigating what had happened.[20]

Within months, this circuit of critics had privately assumed the responsibilities of the federal government in a series of independent and concerted efforts which ultimately resulted in a full-scale attack on the official account of the president's death. In the process, the role of author and interpreter of history became the focus of a protracted struggle. Certainly this struggle was not new. Certainly individuals — among them, historians and journalists — had long before constructed historical texts outside of or in conflict with state practices. But rarely had such a debate over issues of historiography — questions of method or claims to authorship or problems of interpreting evidence — been waged so publicly, nor had its ideological tenor been so dramatically demonstrated across a diverse range of public media. The assassination debates forced into the nation's headlines the crucial questions later articulated by Michel Foucault: "what is an author? what are the modes of existence of this discourse? where does it come from; how is it circulated; who controls it?"[21]

An inquisition into the government's methodology was an immediate by-product of the earliest independent research. In this category the most notable works were Edward Jay Epstein's *Inquest*[22] and Harold Weisberg's *Whitewash.*[23] The former, begun as a master's thesis at Cornell University, conducted a study of the Warren Commission's procedures and argued convincingly against the image of a thorough and efficient official investigation. A number of mainstream publications were moved to credit *Inquest,* and their sanctioning of Epstein's work appeared to signal improving conditions for Warren Commission critics. Yet the mild acceptance of Epstein's book can probably be attributed to its limited scope. Epstein was, for the most part, content to critique the processes of the commission and did not seek to indict the integrity of its members or argue for any countertheory of assassination. Indeed, in his introduction to *Inquest,* journalist Richard Rovere commended Epstein for not taking part in the "shabby 'demonology'" of the other critics who argued that the commission had intentionally suppressed evidence.

Weisberg's *Whitewash* can be neatly juxtaposed to Epstein's book. Weisberg was clearly one of those "demonologists" to whom Rovere referred. Employing the commission's records against itself, Weisberg argued in this, the first of his many books on the assassination, that Oswald could not have committed the crimes of which he was accused. But, unlike Epstein, Weisberg could find no one to publish his research, no one to confer upon it even the look of scholarship. After a fourteen-month period and rejection from sixty-three U.S. publishers, Weisberg produced the book himself, admitting in its preface that the work appeared in "the least desirable of all forms." He was referring to the typewritten appearance of the manuscript, a form that, however undesirable, aptly characterized the marginalized status of Weisberg's work.

The alternative voices were indeed marginalized during the two years following the assassination, for despite the development of the buff network and the appearance of articles in left-leaning journals, the overwhelming tendency of the mainstream press was to support the Warren Commission's conclusions. Support came in many forms. As mentioned, periodicals with a wide circulation hammered home the lone gunman theory months before the Warren Report was released.[24] When the report was released, *Life, Newsweek, Time* and the *New York Times* hailed its findings. In its issue of September 28, 1964, the *New York Times* printed a forty-eight-page supplement carrying the report and subsequently collaborated with two other publishers to issue it in both hard and soft cover. In the introduction to these editions, journalist Harrison Salisbury wrote: "No material question now remains unresolved so far as the death of President Kennedy is concerned. The evidence of Lee Harvey Oswald's single handed guilt is overwhelming."[25] In December, the newspaper copublished an edition entitled *The Witnesses,* a selection of testimony from the commission hearings. For its part, *Life* turned over editorial space to state authorship in its issue of October 2, 1964, running a story entitled "How the Commission Pieced Together the Evidence — Told by One of Its Members," Congresssman Gerald Ford. Like Salisbury, Ford concluded that the commission's case was airtight: "there is not a scintilla of credible evidence to suggest a conspiracy to kill President Kennedy. The evidence is clear and overwhelming. Lee Harvey Oswald did it."[26]

For roughly three years the politics of affirmation held out over the politics of critique. But it is important to note that the historiographic struggle that had been launched, the public debate over the politics of interpretation, was not confined to contest between the mainstream powerhouses of American publishing, in concert with the government, and the occasional leftist muckraker. Rather, the details of the assassination debates permeated every journalistic genre, its subject matter appropriated by a range of specialty publications. The debate over the conduct and findings of JFK's autopsy was sustained in the *Journal of the American Medical Association* and the *American Journal of Physics.* The psychology of the case was considered in such periodicals as *Journal of Personality* and *Psychiatric Quarterly,* the latter reporting on the reactions of "emotionally disturbed adolescent females."[27] Warren Commission procedures and conclusions were analyzed in scores of university law reviews, supermarket tabloids, and local newspapers throughout the country. And the various print media accounts were constantly tracked in *Editor & Publisher* and *Publishers Weekly.*

Then in late 1966 and throughout 1967 the public print debate underwent a transformation, a crucial phase in its history characterized by growing public interest in the arguments of the Warren Commission critics. The general acceptance of Epstein's efforts in *Inquest* played a role in this, as did the appearance of Mark Lane's *Rush to Judgment* in 1966.[28] By this time Lane had been on the case for three years, and much of his public exposure (and self-promotion) had come by way of the campus lecture circuit. His book, in essence a defense brief for Lee Harvey Oswald, relied heavily on interviews with eyewitnesses who were either never called before the commission or whose testimony about possible gunmen on the grassy knoll contradicted the evidence privileged by the Warren Report. Though widely criticized by the popular press at the time and subsequently assailed by other critics for its own omissions and contradictions, Lane's book was enormously influential, staying on the *New York Times* bestseller list for six consecutive months.

1967 brought the publication of the two most thorough attacks on the commission until that time: Sylvia Meagher's *Accessories After the Fact* and Josiah Thompson's *Six Seconds in Dallas*.[29] Meagher had been carrying out a sophisticated attack on the commission for several years, primarily in *Minority of One*, and her book's meticulous refutation of commission findings became a model for subsequent critics. Thompson's work, much of it devoted to a detailed analysis of the physics and logistics of the shooting in Dealey Plaza, came from a somewhat more inside position. As a consultant for *Life*, Thompson had access to the magazine's original print of the Zapruder film as well as to the color transparencies produced from it. Over the course of repeated viewings, he began to construct an alternative theory of assassination. Thompson's hypothesis of a three-assassin conspiracy found a trace of mainstream acceptance when an excerpt of his book ran as a cover story for the December 2, 1967, *Saturday Evening Post*. Its cover headline declared: "Major New Study Shows Three Assassins Killed Kennedy."

The *Post*'s declaration was perhaps not as daring as it might seem, for at the end of the previous year *Life* claimed to have had a radical change of opinion. Its cover story for November 25, 1966, called out: "Did Oswald Act Alone? A Matter of Reasonable Doubt." *Life* had asked John Connally to review the Zapruder film, and the then-governor of Texas repeated his claim that he and Kennedy, contrary to the commission's findings, had been hit by separate bullets. The magazine did allow a rebuttal in the same issue from commission member and magic-bullet author Arlen Spector, but the editors now appeared little convinced by his defense of the Warren Report. The article concluded with the magazine suggesting that a "new investigating body should be set up, perhaps at the initiative of Congress."[30] In fact, *Life* had planned to undertake new research efforts of its own, and the November 25 issue was to be but the first of a series of investigative reports. Ironically, the editors of *Life*'s sister publication, *Time*, chose their issue of the same date to question the efficacy of further assassination probes. Noting "there seems little valid excuse for so dramatic a development as another full-scale inquiry," *Time* referred unflatteringly to commission critics as "hawkshaws," "amateur Sherlocks," "cocktail party dissenters," and a "cult of parlor detectives."[31] The two magazines eventually found common ground, and the planned *Life* series was killed.

The *New York Times* began and then aborted its own investigation in late 1966 under the direction of Harrison Salisbury. Permission to travel to North Vietnam to report on the war in Southeast Asia took Salisbury from the assignment, and the project was scrapped by the beginning of 1967. However, the *Times* saw fit to comment on the emerging skepticism surrounding the Warren Commission's work. Its remarks warrant a close reading because they aptly characterize a position staked out by elements of the mainstream press at the time. In an editorial headlined "Unanswered Questions," also from November 25, 1966, the paper commented:

There are enough solid doubts of thoughtful citizens, among the shrill attacks on the Warren Commission, now to require answers. Further dignified silence, or merely more denials by the commission or its staff, are no longer enough.

We have come to this conclusion not because of any of the specific charges brought by the dozens of books, TV shows and articles about President Kennedy's assassination but because of the general confusion in the public mind raised by the publication of allegations and the many puzzling questions that have been raised.

Since the whole purpose of the commission's appointment and mission is being eroded a little at a time by the clamor, it would seem the commission itself has the most to answer. Certainly, it should be given a chance.

Its members and staff, in varying degrees, of course, have full knowledge—or should have—of the investigations, evaluations and decisions that went into the report. Until they have spoken, the demands for special Congressional committees, foundation studies and inquiries by prestigious people seem premature.[32]

The dual position straddled by much of the press is captured in the extraordinary second paragraph of this editorial. The *Times,* reluctant—indeed unwilling—to give credit or credence to commission critics or assassination buffs, nonetheless articulated a position clearly persuaded by the accumulated strength of their arguments. The paper was quick to draw a distinction between the so-called public mind and the dreaded "books, TV shows and articles" that had been instrumental in the construction of the "public mind." Published allegations and puzzling questions appear to have an invisible source, one that the paper was unable to recognize amidst the "general confusion." The editorial called not for a new investigation, that being the cry of the "shrill attacks," but for a clarification from the commission as to its decision-making procedures. But a curious phenomenon accompanied this call. In a chronological breakdown, the editorial was written as if the Warren Commission were still at work, as if the investigation were ongoing. The last paragraph cited above ended: "The Warren Commission itself is composed of leading members of Senate and House and responsible citizens, headed by the respected Chief Justice." Yet the commission had released its report to the public over two years earlier, its official investigation long since ended. It might thus be argued that in a rather strange way the commission critics had been so successful at perpetuating what had (and perhaps should have) been the government's investigatory efforts that the *Times* unconsciously legitimized the critics' work by speaking of the commission's investigation in the present tense. Effacing the critics by denying them any role in their viewpoint, the editors succeeded at becoming lost in their own ellipses; 1964 and 1966 become, if not interchangeable, then at least somewhat collapsible. The editorial's demand for answers combined with its reservations about the premature nature of a new inquiry amounted to a call for procedural closure. As the assassination case grew more complex during 1966 and 1967, this was perhaps the only kind of stopgap request that was at all fit to print.

Although a Louis Harris poll taken in 1967 found that 70 percent of Americans still believed Lee Harvey Oswald was guilty, 54 percent now thought the Warren Commission had left "a lot of unanswered questions about who killed Kennedy."[33] Amid growing public skepticism and increasing criticism of the *Warren Report* in mainstream publications, William Manchester's *The Death of a President* was serialized in *Look* and sold as a Book-of-the-Month Club selection. Manchester was the only assassination author to have access to and approval of the Kennedy family, and the conclusions he offered essentially agreed with the Warren Commission's findings.[34]

Far more important to the course of the assassination debates, however, was the news of an emerging investigation being undertaken by the district attorney of New Orleans, Jim Garrison. Garrison charged Clay Shaw, a prominent businessman and director of the New Orleans International Trade Mart, with taking part in an assassination conspiracy with several anti-Castro Cubans who were former CIA agents. Although the trial did not get under way until February of 1969, Garrison had as early as 1967 set about publicizing his investigation and enlisting the eager assistance of assassination critics. His efforts were accorded some sympathetic press coverage, most notably *Ramparts'* issue of January 1968. But as media scrutiny increased, the flimsy nature of Garrison's case and the questionable legal tactics he employed were slowly revealed. Attacks on the New Orleans investigation came from traditional Warren Report defenders like *Time* and *Newsweek* as well as from critics Meagher and Epstein.[35] Garrison succeeded in getting the Zapruder film exhibited in the courtroom, and his Cuban conspiracy leads would be pursued by subsequent researchers. But Shaw's acquittal, after the jury deliberated just fifty minutes, along with the overall ineptness of Garrison's investigation, for the most part succeeded in undermining the general credibility of assassination conspiracy theorists, setting back efforts to renew either state or federal government inquiries. The New Orleans debacle continued for some time as both an embarrassment and a cautionary reminder for commission critics. Garrison, himself subsequently acquitted on federal bribery charges, helped perpetuate the media-manufactured image of the assassination buff as paranoid self-promoter in search of political ghosts. In the shadow of the Garrison trial, the early 1970s contributed little in the way of assassination literature, and what quiet dialogue did continue circulated through more specialized publications. Magazines such as *Computers and Automation* applied computer technology to the photographic evidence, and information was regularly published for the buff network, such as the list of the secret Warren Commission documents deposited in the U.S. Archives.[36]

However, this retreat did not signal wholesale retirement for assassination critics. Indeed, the murders of Robert F. Kennedy and Martin Luther King, Jr., served to fuel the passion and frustration of critics displeased with the official government handling of both cases. One direction they took was to organize the loosely connected network of part-time investigators, writers, and researchers who had independently amassed files of documentation. In 1968 attorney and former Senate committee counsel Bernard Fensterwald formed the Committee to Investigate Assassinations (CTIA). Intended as an agent for the pooling of assassination research, the interviews and randomly collected clues, the leading theories and thousands of press clippings, CTIA also sought to lobby for new congressional action.[37]

More grassroots in its formation and activities was the Assassination Information Bureau (AIB). Officially incorporated in 1974, the AIB had its origins several years earlier in the activities of journalist Bob Katz. Katz, working through correspondence with Richard Sprague, a New York computer analyst, and with graphics assistance by Robert Kutler, initiated a set of presentations entitled "Who Killed Kennedy?"[38] After some successful local appearances in the Boston/Cambridge area and through the arrangements of a Boston booking agency, Katz, now joined by several other Cambridge-area researchers, delivered his presentation at college campuses across the country. When not on the road, the AIB outlined a political agenda for citizen action, a program designed to pressure a new congressional investigation, which included information packets with text and slides for community organization around the topic of political assassination. Despite their investment in grassroots efforts, the AIB saw political success in terms of federal government action. In an article from 1975, the AIB stated: "It was, and remains, the contention of the AIB that private citizens could not themselves answer in full the question of who killed JFK—and indeed we should not be in a position where it is even our responsibility."[39] Among the AIB's most significant achievements was "The Politics of Conspiracy," a three-day conference held at Boston University in January 1975 where over 1,500 people heard presentations from some of the most well known assassination critics.

The Skeptics Revived

By the time of the B.U. conspiracy conference, the question of who killed JFK had reemerged on the national agenda, and commission critics had gained new momentum. Indeed, a number of factors mark 1975 as a watershed year for the investigation. Commenting on a three-day assassination seminar at the University of Hartford, the *New York Times* noted that critique of the Warren Commission "is said to be the hottest topic on the college lecture circuit." The topic had most definitely returned to the newsstand and bookstore. The most significant titles were Robert Sam Anson's *They've Killed the President* and the paperback edition of Thompson's *Six Seconds in Dallas*. Anson had been writing about the assassination for several years, his most important articles appearing in *New Times,* for which he was a national political correspondent. His book both neatly summarized the salient features of the case up to his writing and argued for consideration of a Cuban/CIA/Mafia conspiracy. The release of Thompson's book was significant for the legal victory it represented. In 1967 *Life* had sued Thompson, Bernard Geis Associates, and Random House to prevent publication of the book with reproductions of the Zapruder film, charging that Thompson had in fact stolen parts of the film. Denying the charge, Thompson had his book published that year with charcoal reconstructions of the key Zapruder frames.[40] Eight years later, after a victorious suit against Time-Life, Thompson saw his book reissued with reproductions from the Zapruder film.

A number of magazines also turned their attention back to the case. Detailed studies appeared in *Rolling Stone* and *New Times,* and many of the arguments pro and con conspiracy were briefly summarized in an issue of *Skeptic.*[41] In its September 1975 issue, the *Saturday Evening Post* devoted its cover story to the commission critics, profiling nineteen of the leading assassination researchers and printing a brief "Bibliography for JFK Buffs." It was at this time also that assassination literature found its way increasingly into soft-core pornographic magazines. The interconnections between the assassination debate and issues of pornography will be taken up in a subsequent chapter. For now it is worth noting the appearance of numerous articles, both multipart series and forums, in magazines such as *Penthouse, Playboy, Swank, Gallery,* and *Playgirl.*

The Zapruder film's appearance in Thompson's reissue and Anson's book was accompanied by widespread screenings elsewhere. AIB college presentations had been supplemented by fifth- and sixth-generation bootleg prints. But in 1975 Robert Groden, a New York photo optics expert, completed years of working with Zapruder's film, producing a high-quality, image-enhanced print with crucial sections, primarily frames of Kennedy's head wounds, slowed and magnified. Groden's print was exhibited at the AIB Boston conference in January 1975 and then on March 6 and March 27 of that year, for the first time to a national audience, on the ABC broadcast "Goodnight America" with Geraldo Rivera. Groden would later show his print to federal lawmakers, testify before the Rockefeller Commission, and serve as a consultant to the House assassinations committee.

The exhibition of Groden's print aided researchers and intensified calls for a new investigation. In October 1975, the *New York Times* reported that Senator Richard Schweiker of Pennsylvania had publicly declared that the Warren Report was "like a house of cards; it's going to collapse."[42] The paper then noted that two congressional committees, the Senate's Schweiker-Hart Select Committee on Intelligence and the House's Edwards Committee, would be opening inquiries into federal intelligence and law enforcement agencies' performance during the Warren Commission's investigation. The *Times* piece was characteristically schizophrenic on the subject, labeling critics a "curious mixture" of dignified doubters and an "irrational enclave." Nonetheless, by December 1, 1975, the *Times* was again moved to editorialize on the persistent skepticism concerning the commission's findings. Hoping for a "restoration of the government's reputation," the paper called for a congressional investigation to lay "out all the now-sequestered evidence" and to "establish the extent of the cover-ups." As with its editorial of November 25, 1966, cited above, the *Times* withheld credit from commission critics: "The most powerful arguments for doing so [reopening the case] come not from any of the veteran assassination buffs, but emerge from the secret recesses of the FBI and the CIA themselves."[43]

In fact, the House, Senate, and Rockefeller Commission inquiries into the activities of the FBI and CIA reflected, if not directly followed, the broadening focus of Kennedy assassination critics. Furthermore, these inquiries marked various points where the overlapping terrains of the assassination debates and other political debates became especially obvious. Clearly the JFK inquests always shared a relationship with adjacent political issues, most notably the cold war questions circulating around Oswald's identity and his ties to Cuban interests, the Soviet Union, and various FBI contacts. But whereas during the early and mid-1960s the government sought to suppress these questions, by the mid-1970s, it sought at least in part to expose the connections between conspiracy speculations surrounding the assassination and the more widespread activities of American intelligence organizations.

Indeed, three years prior to the new congressional action and prompted in no small measure by the revelations of Watergate, writers who had focused primarily on an alleged Dallas cover-up expanded their research and widened the scope of their critique. Staking out this broader arena, the AIB noted in one of its position papers:

The discoveries set in motion around Watergate and the great aftershocks of Chile and Cointelpro have crystallized public awareness of the realities of power politics in the United States. We are at one of those moments when a providential convergence of events opens a window and shows us the treacheries involved in the struggle for state power. It is more possible today for masses of Americans to understand the need for a new framework of political thought which coherently situates these murders in an overall perspective on American politics during the Cold War. "Who killed JFK?" ought to be a leading slogan of the whole Bicentennial period.[44]

Some critics saw in the Watergate cover-up a reflection of the same explanations used to defend the commission's work a decade earlier. The refrain of concerns about national security and the sensitive operations of intelligence were once again raised to guarantee federal silence about possible government wrongdoing. Assassination theorists thus began to see their efforts against the wider backdrop of conspiracy and state-sanctioned criminality. Their public discussions began to include the deaths of Martin Luther King, Jr., and Malcolm X and scrutinized the FBI's Cointelpro operations, the secret counterintelligence programs mounted to undermine the Black Panthers and the work of the New Left. Moreover, attention turned toward elaborating the perhaps conspiratorial interrelationships between covert government operations, foreign politicos, and organized crime. These investigations repeatedly revealed the joint involvement of CIA or former CIA operatives, former members of the Batista government ousted by Castro in Cuba, and figures prominent in the world of organized crime. What slowly emerged was a bureaucracy of criminals whose activities included foreign and domestic narcotics sales, campaign financing, money laundering (in Cuban exile–owned Florida banks through which funds for the Watergate break-in were funneled), and the attempted overthrow or assassination of foreign heads of state. The result, a criminal musical chairs with the same players — E. Howard Hunt, Frank Sturgis, Bebe Rebozo, Richard Nixon, and a score of top and second-echelon mob figures — with a twenty-year history of covert activity, led assassination critics to argue that the conspiracy and cover-up they identified with the Dallas killing was not some phantasmagoric exception to government affairs but conduct more like business as usual.

The House Select Committee on Assassinations (HSCA) was established in September 1976 with a four-part prescription for investigation:

1. Who killed Kennedy and Martin Luther King, Jr.?
2. Was there evidence of a conspiracy in either assassination?
3. What was the performance of government agencies in protecting each man?

4. With respect to cooperating with earlier investigations, was there a need for new legislation regarding assassinations?[45]

In his introduction to the HSCA, Chief Counsel G. Robert Blakey, while noting the lobbying efforts of assassination critics, credited the Senate Select Committee on Intelligence and its report of April 1976 with supplying the impetus for creating the HSCA. But the thirteen years of persistent investigation by the private network of assassination critics was in large part responsible for this new congressional probe. The critics' efforts, combined with the general criticism of American policies and institutions and the erosion of public confidence in government affairs fueled by the antiwar movement and the Watergate scandal, had served as catalysts for the government-sponsored self-critique of the mid-seventies.

What, then, were the critics' major accomplishments? Assassination critics did not solve the case or uncover incontrovertible evidence pointing to the guilty parties. They did, however, call into serious question the efficacy of the government's work, exposing its imprecise methods and the general negligence of its investigation. They democratized the inquiry through demands for access to classified material and forced the most powerful news media to reconsider their blanket endorsement of the state's findings. In the process, they challenged the legitimacy of the government's discourse, whether cloaked in the rhetoric of national security, the authorial privilege of those sitting on the commission, or the sanctity of federal law enforcement agencies. Assassination critics wondered in print and on the airwaves whether sectors of the government were not in fact the *source* of criminality—either through obstruction of justice or, according to some, through orchestrating the assassination itself.

More specifically, commission critics appeared to create reasonable doubt about the guilt of Lee Harvey Oswald. They made a strong case that three bullets could not have been fired by one man in the firing time established by the Zapruder film and still account for the wounds and the bullet that missed. They established a range of contradictions and errors in the official autopsy. They gave voice to dozens of eyewitnesses who were not granted space in the Warren Report and whose observations did not corroborate the commission's findings. They brought forth evidence of Oswald's contact with the FBI prior to the shooting, as well as his possible links to anti-Castro Cubans, and linked Jack Ruby with key organized crime figures who had both motive and means to assassinate the president.[46] Amid these and many other questions, the HSCA undertook its study with the eager assistance of some of the most visible assassination researchers.

Yet the mild government self-critique sustained by the HSCA and the pronouncements of its *Final Report* hardly suited most critics. That report, issued on July 22, 1979, offered a contradictory interpretation of the considered evidence, one that both affirmed much of the Warren Report yet took issue with its primary conclusions. On the one hand, the HSCA concluded that "the Warren Commission conducted a thorough and professional investigation into the responsibility of Lee Harvey Oswald for the assassination." But it also stated: "The Warren Commission failed to investigate adequately the possibility of a conspiracy to assassinate the President."[47] Indeed, despite the overwhelming degree to which its report supported the Warren Commission's findings, the HSCA concluded that, based on the available evidence, "President John F. Kennedy was probably assassinated as a result of a conspiracy."[48] The crucial evidence for the HSCA, uncovered by three Dallas-based assassination buffs, was a recording of Dallas police radio transmissions in Dealey Plaza the day of the shooting. Acoustics experts called in by the committee conducted recordings during a reconstruction of the assassination in Dallas and compared their results with the tape from November 22, 1963. They concluded that four shots were recorded on the original police dictabelt and that the third shot most likely came from the grassy knoll in front of the presidential limousine.[49] However, the HSCA was unable to identify any of Oswald's alleged coconspirators. Furthermore, it sought to counter other conspiracy theorists by concluding that the available evidence negated suggestions that anti-Castro Cubans, organized crime, or elements within the U.S. government were involved in the assassination.[50]

The House Select Committee on Assassinations was the last of the government-sponsored probes into JFK's death, but it did not mark closure for the debate. Warren Commission critics continued their research in two directions: one focusing on the alleged involvement of organized crime, the other on complicity of U.S. agencies, the FBI and Secret Service. G. Robert Blakey and Richard Billings's *The Plot to Kill the President*[51] in 1981 and then David Scheim's *Contract on America*[52] in 1989 put forth the mob thesis. Blakey, who had been chief counsel and staff director for the HSCA, and Billings outlined the government's covert employment of major crime figures in various plots to overthrow Castro. Involved were kingpins Sam Giancana, John Roselli, Santos Trafficante, and Carlos Marcello. The theories vary somewhat, but the general outline follows this pattern: the mob had worked in various ways for John Kennedy during his run for office and then during his administration. It had rigged the election results in Chicago and in Texas to assure his victory, and it believed he was an ally in mob efforts to oust Castro. By some accounts, the most important factor was that his friends in organized crime had afforded the president a steady supply of women, many of them Hollywood hopefuls. What angered mob bosses was that the president had paid these favors back with a weakening commitment to Cuba and a full-scale Justice Department attack on organized crime led by Attorney General Robert Kennedy. Lee Oswald, whose bizarre life had brought him into contact with various New Orleans racketeers, was set up to take the fall, his silence guaranteed by a contract with long-time petty hood Jack Ruby.[53]

Criticism of government law enforcement agencies, especially the FBI, had been part of the anticommission literature since the assassination. David Lifton's *Best Evidence* culminated this critique with a sincere yet bizarre and frequently confusing indictment of the Secret Service in 1981. Lifton laboriously detailed the development of his investigation over a fifteen-year period, which focused on the president's autopsy. Examining the evidence supplied by doctors' testimony, the autopsy and x rays of Kennedy's body, and reports compiled by various government bureaus, Lifton argued that the president's body had been surgically altered sometime between his arrival at Parkland Memorial Hospital in Dallas and the official autopsy conducted at Bethesda naval hospital in Washington, D.C. This alteration, he suggested, was the most efficient way for a Secret Service–engineered conspiracy to cover up the "best evidence" and lead all subsequent investigations down the wrong path.

The Thirty-Year Debate

For the most part, then, the assassination literature of the eighties turned away from the mechanics of Dealey Plaza to consider other aspects of the alleged conspiracy. The evidence of photos, acoustics, and eyewitnesses had for now been exhausted of their capacity to supply researchers with anything new. Perhaps, believing that logistical analysis of the shooting either had been sufficiently discussed in other works or had reached an impasse, assassination critics focused on those aspects of the case that, even twenty years later, were still unfolding.

Yet the release of Oliver Stone's *JFK* in December 1991 returned attention to the specifics of the shooting while simultaneously insisting on a theory of conspiratorial motive. What is ironic about the impact and the overwhelming public discussion generated by *JFK* is that its narrative put forth the six-shot "secret team" thesis, long believed by some critics to be the least credible of propositions.[54] Furthermore, its story centered on Jim Garrison and the New Orleans conspiracy trial, perhaps the single most undistinguished moment in the history of the investigation. Stone's film resuscitated interest in critiques of the magic bullet theory and, as Chapter 10 will discuss, returned to a reliance on the epistemological certainty of filmic evidence. Moreover, it presented JFK as dove rather than as cold warrior, a reading of Kennedy's foreign policy to which liberal conspiracy theorists clung, insisting that escalation in Vietnam was a product of the assassination and the work of Kennedy's successor. *JFK* served to introduce yet another generation to many of the issues surrounding the assassination debate. It is significant within the scope of this chronology because it is the only commercial film to propel the investigation further and to highlight, if not generate, additional critical literature.[55]

Stone's film also generated considerable backlash; the mainstream press met its release by telling readers that the film was not to be believed.[56] Indeed, while breathing new life into assassination inquiries, *JFK*'s all-encompassing conspiracy theory brought sharp skepticism back upon itself. By the thirtieth anniversary of JFK's death, a curious situation had come to characterize the assassination debates. Warren Commission critics found themselves working together in an atmosphere of renewed energy, an atmosphere of well-attended semiannual conferences, a growing list of new publications, and the release of previously classified government files.[57] And yet their public identity was coming under renewed indictment from the airwaves and pages of the major media, in large part due to the publication of Gerald Posner's *Case Closed*. Touted as the book that "Finally Proves Who Killed Kennedy," *Case Closed* relied less on brilliant analysis than on shrewd timing. With its release conveniently coinciding with the media-saturated anniversary, Posner's book was granted breakthrough status when in fact it frequently reiterated analysis that had circulated for years. Posner summarized various interpretations of the Zapruder film, arguing that, contrary to the readings offered by conspiracy critics, the visual evidence showed that Lee Harvey Oswald had ample time to fire three shots and inflict all the wounds. Posner attempted a theory-by-theory rebuttal of thirty years' worth of anti–Warren Commission literature and was granted considerable media approval for his efforts.[58] Armed with Posner's book, the mainstream press could strike an investigatory pose while embracing the Oswald-as-lone-assassin theory.

Indeed, the nineties' version of the critical duality articulated during the sixties by the *New York Times* editorials was enunciated most clearly by *Newsweek* in its issue of November 22, 1993. There had been a cover-up, the magazine told its readers, but not the one Warren Commission critics had suggested. "The real cover-up," to borrow the article's headline, was that "the U.S. government did not try very hard to unearth the truth about the assassination of JFK."[59] Implying that this was somehow an original thesis produced after considerable research by themselves, the *Washington Post,* and CBS, the magazine suggested that it was the "frenzied week" of high-level government scrambling that "led to 30 years of conspiracy theories."[60] As for the arguments generated by Warren Commission critics, the magazine psychoanalyzed these as the products of children in search of "a grander design" to compensate for the notion that one man could force such tremendous "historical transformation."[61] Although assassination critics could take heart that the case remained on the national agenda, not since the days of their earliest efforts had they also been subjected to such widely circulated ridicule.[62]

The recycling of imagery and arguments occasioned by the release of *JFK* and the thirtieth anniversary of the assassination draws attention to a crucial characteristic of this subject matter: its cell-like quality, its propensity to be transformed and constantly reconfigured. This quality has constantly, and perhaps ultimately, frustrated critics and the wider public in their attempts to narrativize and lend coherence to these historical events. Let me be more specific. The assassination debate has expanded and contracted throughout its thirty years as texts of all kinds have become available for analysis. Myriad factors have contributed to the sense of flux surrounding the assassination debates: the release of the Warren Commission's documents to the public, the sealing of evidence donated to the National Archives by the Kennedy family; the purchase and limited publication of the Zapruder film by *Life* magazine, the sale and exhibition of bootleg copies of the film, the report issued in 1968 by a special medical panel appointed by Attorney General Ramsey Clark to review the sealed autopsy photos, the revelations concerning secret government activities reported by various congressional committees, and perhaps most importantly, the steady release of classified government materials made possible by commission critics' persistent use of the Freedom of Information Act.[63]

And there is more: the untimely deaths, especially within the first five years, of a number of potentially crucial witnesses or interested parties, the discovery of the Dallas Police's dictabelt with the recording of the shots; the circulation and analysis of the hundreds of photographs taken just before, during, or after the shooting; and the ever-mounting and often contradictory personal testimony of a variety of individuals, from autopsy doctors to hospital personnel to sources within organized crime.[64] As the years passed and the assassination texts multiplied or were resituated, subsequent critical studies were forced to summarize (or attempt to summarize) the debate's ever-shifting signifiers. Approaching various books and articles about the case became a matter of wading through a network of direct or implicit cross-references to other significant texts, both literary and photographic. By the late seventies, a general index to the assassination literature was almost needed even for initiated readers to engage with the discussion. This complexity perpetuated a process that seemed to take critics further and further from the assassination itself, such that much of the literature ultimately appeared to map not so much the event itself as the surface of its representation.

This persistent yet haphazard development of the investigation reflects one of its fundamental tensions: its simultaneous movement toward and denial of closure. Both defenders and critics of the Warren Report sought a solution to the crime and an end to the debate; they sought the kind of narrative closure that could transform the assassination into a coherent event and a knowable history. But for commission critics this desire was complicated by efforts to deny closure. They refuted arguments that insisted the murder had been solved, even resisting while building upon the alternative conclusions put forth by other critics. Their repeated scrutiny of the photographic evidence and their constant struggle with the government over the declassification of documents, while ultimately aimed at closing the case, engendered a position that was suspicious of endings and encouraged postponement.

The investigation's tendency to expand and contract, as well as its internal tensions around closure, demand a self-consciousness with respect to my own work. This chronology of assassination literature is already a slip in the direction of seamlessness. My account is constructed as a partial map because the assassination debates are so densely layered that some contours need to be sketched at the outset. But even these contours are too distinct; the mapping process is at once accurate and misleading. Somehow the reader needs to keep this in mind: the ebb and flow of critique and defense, of investigation and analysis, was neither smooth nor precisely patterned, and the topic I am isolating was not made up entirely by the public appearance of various texts.

Indeed, the debate circulated and intensified in private, the range and complexities of the literature matched by the scope and varied involvement of its readers. Individuals came to these works at different times, through softcover editions years after the release of the hardcovers, for example. The appearance of certain books or articles at a certain time did not mean that public opinion or involvement ran parallel to these publications. It is essential to any elaboration of the assassination debates to note the debates' more private components, their life among the unpublished, their impact on individuals for whom the aftermath of the assassination became everything from a weekend hobby to a full-time obsession.[65]

Like other groups engaged in acts of social contestation during the 1960s, assassination critics and buffs established and worked through local channels, challenging and appropriating roles traditionally left to official public agencies. Some left the professions for which they were trained or modified their occupations to study the assassination full or part time.[66] Others became amateur researchers into the activities of government agencies or trained themselves in media analysis so as to better critique the government's version of events. In so doing, these individuals and groups struggled along different fronts than other political movements during the period. Yet, like those other movements, assassination critics did seek a reversal of forces, did struggle over the positions that underwrote political power. The assassination debates, defined once again, appear as more than the sum of a set of texts, verbal or imaged, but as something less stable or unified; they are a series of shifting arrangements and positions, textual, personal, temporal, political. My own language here is clearly influenced by Foucault's discussion of "effective" history, and it is useful at the end of this introduction once again to consider the assassination in the context of his remarks:

An event, consequently, is not a decision, a treaty, a reign, or a battle, but the reversal of a relationship of forces, the usurpation of power, the appropriation of a vocabulary turned against those who had once used it, a feeble domination that poisons itself as it grows lax, the entry of a masked "other."[67]

The active quality of Foucault's language — *reverse, usurp, appropriate, turn against* — should condition our understanding of the assassination debates. So, too, should his shift in focus from single agent — decision, treaty, battle — to wider fields of activity, such as forces, power, and the uses of vocabulary. The debates cover an ever-growing range of practices and histories. Had the government's account of the assassination gone uncontested and all the subsequent questions never been raised, the case would still have involved a complex process; multiauthored not only by various individuals but by competing government agencies; multilayered in its codification in image and narrative; still constituted by gaps and silences; circulated by the entire field of ideological state apparatuses. The commission critics, however, splintered the forces that mediated the event and the government's account of it. They elevated this process to a level at which its mechanisms of construction, its gaps, silences, contradictions, and representational strategies, became acutely visible. They thereby subjected this history to a radical re-visioning.

When I came to print the negative, an odd thing struck my eye. Something standing in the cross street and invisible to me was reflected in a factory window and then reflected once more in the rear view mirror attached to the truck door. It was only a tiny detail. Since then I have enlarged this small section of my negative enormously. The grain of the film all but obliterates the features of the image. It is obscured. By any possible reckoning it is hopelessly ambiguous. Nevertheless, what I believe I see recorded in that speck of film fills me with such fear, such utter dread, and loathing, that I think I shall never dare to make another photograph. Here it is. Look at it. Do you see what I see?[1]

Over the course of three decades, the visual representations produced around the JFK assassination have proven fundamentally unstable. Indeed, to theorize the epistemological status of such imagery is not just to insist on its instability but to register its shifting movement, its negotiation between legibility and ambiguity. Traced through the assassination case is both a faith and a crisis in representation. On the one hand was a belief in the powers of photographic evidence to legibly transcribe events, primarily the logistics of the Dealey Plaza shooting. This faith held that sufficiently close scrutiny of images could tell patient investigators how the crime was committed, that the photographic apparatus could yield knowledge as a result of a precise and expanded vision. On the other hand, the steady construction of assassination counter-theories and the slow accumulation of varying interpretations of the photographic evidence, although produced independently by individual theorists' attempting to put forth a single, coherent account, resulted in a general crisis of representation, a heterogeneity of interpretations that frustrated any confidence in the visual evidence. Faith in the powers of camera vision, initially located in the investigative efforts of the government and its supporters, ultimately came to characterize both sides of the debate. Both Warren Commission advocates and critics have spoken in definitive terms when analyzing the film and photographic evidence. However, as the debate expanded and multiple interpretations were generated, these definitive readings of the image became increasingly challenged by an epistemological anxiety which frequently undermined interpretive coherence.

31

This crisis of representation affected the narrative as well as the photographic. The state's version of historic truth relied heavily on the revelatory powers of the image — but not wholly. For the state reinforced the visual evidence with a faith in the structuring power of narrative. If a coherent account was possible, closure could be genuine because the disparate details of the case were manageable within a traditional form.

Part One of this book focuses primarily on three sets of representation: the Zapruder film, the JFK autopsy materials, and images of Lee Harvey Oswald. The epistemological status of each is situated within the forms that framed its public exposure and interpretation — primarily government publications and the books and articles authored by Warren Report critics. As noted in the Introduction, my elaboration of the inquests into Kennedy's death does intend to uncover new leads or contribute to the still-growing literature probing for solutions. I am interested foremost in establishing a context for the various art practices discussed in Parts Two and Three, in laying out a textual terrain so that I can later map its contours onto the films, silkscreens, assemblages, and videos produced during this same thirty-year period.

My discussion opens, then, with the journalistic forms produced around the investigation rather than with the visual arts that took the assassination as their central subject matter. Of course, it would be wrong to characterize this network of representations as a one-way channel leading from mainstream and marginal journalistic inquiries to experimental representations and then to the commercial cinema. The activities of institutions or individuals involved with the case obviously cannot be separated from the historical and social context in which they operated, a context that includes the cinema and is constructed by its conventions of narrative and imaging. One certainly can argue that the assassination inquiries of the late sixties and seventies were influenced in various ways by the commercial and perhaps noncommercial exploitation of the assassination. Hollywood's mediation of the issues — through genre conventions, star identities, narrative tropes — while reaching an audience far greater than other assassination texts, also served to marginalize or compartmentalize the investigators' efforts. The movies suggested that anti–Warren Report speculations were the stuff of fiction, more appropriate for screen fantasies than for serious political debate. Thus, to position the commercial cinema as if it were a response would only be to simplify the complex matrix of relations operating here. Furthermore, it is most definitely the case that studying these art works has constantly forced me to reconceptualize the images and tropes used by assassination critics.

Still, it is necessary first to identify the journalistic texts, their deployment, and their commentary on the visual evidence. On their pages the debate was publicly initiated and most thoroughly developed. They manifest better than other texts—letters of correspondence between critics, Warren Commission memoranda—the plight of representation within the dynamics of the multilevel investigation. These publications can often claim the priority of having come first and, throughout the next three decades, continued to carry the heaviest weight of advancing arguments or mapping investigative terrain. The crucial terms, the most acutely contested issues, the array of pro- and antigovernmental positions were all first laid out and then most technically articulated in the journalistic texts to which I now turn for a more specific analysis. The epistemological struggle that they illustrate forms the essential backdrop for any subsequent readings of the art forms created around the death of JFK.

Chapter 1 **The Zapruder Film**

The fluctuating status of photographic imagery in the assassination debates is best illustrated by the history of the Zapruder film. It is a history punctuated by faith in the film's revelatory power and by a crisis of interpretation, by movement between epistemological certainty and anxiety over not only readings of the film but also the narratives constructed to accompany its social exposure. So central is Zapruder's film footage that it loops continuously over this entire project. Even where not explicitly discussed, the film retains a privileged position, just as it did throughout the three decades following the assassination: a central yet marginalized piece of film, scandalous and long sequestered for its content, prized as vérité, dissected for its narrative, a thinly veiled subject for the commercial movie industry (Brian De Palma's *Blow Out* after Antonioni's *Blow-Up*), and a structuring absence for the film avant-garde (Bruce Conner's *Report*). Its points of contact with an array of social and political institutions and its subjection to a variety of formal analyses endow it with a richly telling history, for the Zapruder film registers, perhaps better than any other single film text, the shifting status of film representation over the last thirty years.

The Zapruder Story

Assassination critics are fond of telling how the Zapruder film was something of a near accident, a last-minute idea. Abraham Zapruder, a dress manufacturer whose downtown Dallas office was adjacent to Dealey Plaza, left his 8mm Bell and Howell at home on the morning of November 22 because the skies were overcast. The story has it that, as midday approached and the sun broke through, Zapruder, at his secretary's prompting, returned home to retrieve the camera, then took up a position on a concrete pedestal on the north side of Elm Street to film the presidential motorcade as it drove by en route to the Dallas Trade Mart.[1] As the leading wedge of police motorcycles turned off Houston Street and onto Elm, Zapruder began shooting and for the next twenty-six seconds recorded the most famous amateur footage in the history of cinema.

The complex public and private circulation of Zapruder's film began immediately after the assassination, and the ambiguity of the narrative within the film came to be mirrored by narratives about the film. Stories varied as to the path the film traveled the afternoon of the 22nd. Early accounts had it that Zapruder was approached by a police reporter for the *Dallas Morning News* who, after unsuccessfully trying to confiscate the film, found a Secret Service agent to accompany both men to the Kodak film lab.[2] Subsequent accounts trace the film from Zapruder to the Kodak lab to the Jamison Film Company, although it remains unclear exactly where the first-generation copies were made. Three such copies were produced the day of the assassination, two of which were handed over to the Secret Service. One of these Secret Service copies was then sent on to Washington so that the FBI could produce its own copies. Whether the CIA also received a copy has been a matter of question, because records made public through Freedom of Information Act suits suggest that a copy of the film was at the agency's National Photo Interpretation Center within days of the assassination.[3] Meanwhile, it appears that Zapruder wound up retaining the third of the first-generation copies after relinquishing the original film in a deal with Richard Stolley of *Life* magazine. Stolley learned of the film from a stringer correspondent, reached Zapruder by phone around midnight, and had him sign a handwritten contract the next day. Some confusion also surrounded Zapruder's deal with the magazine: $40,000 was the purchase price as reported the week of the assassination; Zapruder told Warren Commission counsel that he was paid $25,000; his contract with *Life* revealed that $25,000 was only the first installment on a total of $150,000.[4]

It was of profound importance that Zapruder's images first found public exposure in Henry Luce's picture magazine. Here it was implied that images nearly spoke for themselves, that knowledge, perhaps truth, was ensured by the camera's expanded vision. The defining concept for the magazine, its own enabling fiction, asserted that the photograph, not the word, was the privileged signifier.[5] In the introduction to his history of *Life,* long-time editor Loudon Wainright articulates this faith in the magazine's deployment of camera vision:

For those who shaped it, Life's treatment of an event somehow transcended the event itself. In a long and curious jump of thinking (or of feeling) whatever happened to make the photograph possible took place now and then, again and even better, in the pages of the magazine. The production in light and shadow seemed bigger than the reality it came from.[6]

The mystifying word in Wainright's remarks is *bigger.* In fact, the "production in light and shadow" takes part in a new construction of reality, using its materiality and its imaged object, in a new discursive chain. The event becomes focused around a particular production of imagery, and a narrowing set of perspectives is distributed. Thus, when Zapruder sold his film to *Life,* public access to the most crucial moments of the murder (more precisely the crucial moments of its representation, mediated first by Zapruder's perspective) was limited to what the magazine chose to reveal. With the purchase of the film by *Life* began a tacit alliance between the government investigation and the mainstream press which would last for the next two years.

In its issue of November 29, coincidentally the same day that LBJ's executive order established the Warren Commission, *Life* published, in black and white, thirty-one frames taken from Zapruder's film. Since the magazine neglected to identify these images by their proper frame numbers and omitted the image of the president's head wound, the film's chronology, so fundamental to the ensuing investigation, was effectively eliminated, its efficacy as transparent evidence undermined. Anyone really interested in seeing stills from the film in sequence would have to wait ten months and then obtain a copy of Volume 18 of the Warren Commission exhibits. Of course in November of 1963 the magazine was not interested in supplying counterevidence to the public or in contradicting the statements of various federal and local law enforcement agencies. Rather it accepted and immediately turned to selling the earliest accepted version of events: the lone assassin theory. Exclusive ownership of the film allowed *Life* to deploy it alongside other imagery in the service of Lee Harvey Oswald's posthumous prosecution. Thus it made sense that, when the Warren Report was released to the public, the magazine not only turned over its space to state authorship, but republished excerpts of the Zapruder film in support of that text. *Life* accompanied Congressman Gerald Ford's account of the official findings with eight enlarged color images. Once again there were no corresponding frame numbers, but this time the magazine printed the graphic frame 313 which depicts the president's head exploding. The revelation of the horrifying secret image in this issue seemed to signify *Life*'s reendorsement of the government's case. So, too, did its editorial decision to accompany each of the eight frames with an interpretive description of what that image showed. The headline read: "Color sequence shows how the President was killed."

Yet there was a problem. The editors, it turned out, were not at all clear on what that sequence should be or how to read its imagery. Apparently believing that their first arrangement of text and photo was not a proper match, the editors changed their original layout of images from Zapruder frame 323, depicting Kennedy slumped to the side after being struck in the head, to frame 313 with its orange explosion of head wound. However, this second version was printed with no corresponding change in the caption. Then, in a second revision, it was decided that, although frame 313 would remain, a new caption was necessary to explain it. Thus three different combinations of image and text went to press, a confusion that required the unorthodox practice of breaking and resetting plates twice. The third version of this issue (and some home subscribers received issues different from those sold on newsstands) came no closer to delivering on its headline. But *Life*'s editorial confusion did suggest early in the debate how resistant to definitive interpretation representation was to become.[7]

Warren Report critics were quick to argue that *Life*'s exploitation of the Zapruder film proved little. The sequence did not "show how the president was killed," as its headline declared, because the magazine had not really provided a sequence. The meaning of Zapruder's film rested not only within the content of individual frames but in the relationship between frames. Only by returning to the film as film and not as a series of stills could productive research continue. But even this commonsense methodology seemed complicated by the government's attempt at film analysis.

The Government Interpretation

To begin with, multiple copies of the Zapruder film floated around Washington during the months following the assassination, as the FBI and Secret Service analyzed it for their reports to the Warren Commission. However, although government officials appear to have screened the original, the investigative agencies based their work on detailed scrutiny of inferior copies. What the FBI termed its "official" version of the film, the print it worked from, was in fact a copy made not from *Life*'s original but from a copy of it. In a Warren Commission memorandum from January 28, 1964, its assistant counsel noted: "the FBI film of the assassination is a copy of a Secret Service copy of the original colored film taken by Zapruder. . . . FBI Agent [Lyndal] Shaneyfelt [the agent in charge of the analysis] felt that with a more clear film print it could give a more precise determination of the data we are endeavoring to obtain."[8] Assassination critics who, while preparing their own studies, got access to a print made from *Life*'s original, would subsequently note the qualitative differences between the print they saw and that examined by the FBI and then stored at the National Archives. On February 25, 1964, a representative from *Life* exhibited the original to Agent Shaneyfelt and, according to one source, to members of the commission as well. However, as late as June of 1964 Shaneyfelt testified that he was still basing his inquiry and thus the conclusions offered to the commission on a second-generation copy.[9]

The government's exploitation of the film did not end with the FBI's analysis. On May 24, 1964, the Warren Commission conducted a reconstruction of the assassination. Using another limousine and stand-ins, the crucial moments of the motorcade were reenacted based on the Zapruder imagery. A camera mounted behind the telescopic sight on the alleged murder rifle photographed the point of view from the sixth floor of the School Book Depository, Oswald's alleged line of vision, each frame intended to correlate with the position of the limousine as recorded in the Zapruder film. A parallel set of photographs was made of the reconstruction from Zapruder's filming position. It was hoped that the photos from the window would supply information about bullet trajectories and the probability of Connally's and Kennedy's being hit by the same one. In this way, the government went *Life* one better: when confronted with a film (or multiple copies of a film) that could not supply the necessary answers, it made a new film, supplemented by a series of stills.[10] Based on the film reenactments, the commission concluded that between frames 207 and 225 Kennedy and Connally were aligned such that a single bullet could have wounded both of them.

Some faith in the truth-bearing powers of camera vision could thus be maintained, its conclusions confirmed by the potency of the photographic image. The reenactment's production as representation thus came to substitute for the real event but was used in a process that rewrote the event. Kennedy's assassination does not become replaced by the simulation, but its subsequent encoding becomes inseparable from representation, from the films and still photographs and conclusions drawn from the reenactment. The suggestion here is that, when reconstructing the past, history as a series of past events cannot be understood merely as a set of texts (image based or otherwise) but must also be seen as occurrences that almost immediately assume a dialogic relationship to the present.[11] Among contemporary events, the assassination could perhaps be isolated as a privileged moment, a special case in which the array of relevant signifiers has over the years been severed from the original contexts, where the profusion of images has put notions of the real into full crisis. However, I would argue that it is crucial to preserve the category of the real in this case; that the forces at work exert a political influence whose very existence would be radically underestimated if the label of real were denied. The wholesale dispersion of assassination imagery on television, in cinema, on posters, in the underground press, in academic conferences no doubt testifies to a condition peculiar to the age of electronic reproduction, a condition perhaps best termed the *postmodern*. But the widespread existence of such imagery does not explain, nor should it efface, questions of its production or reproduction. Rather, in each specific context the dissemination of assassination imagery must be met with questions concerning its modes of existence and control of its circulation.

As long as the Zapruder film remained privately held, whether by the government or by *Life*, a relatively unified reading of the film dominated its status as evidence. (Even within secret channels, however, alternatives uses could be found for the film. In December of 1964, after the release of the

Warren Report, J. Edgar Hoover sent a letter to the commission's general counsel explaining that the CIA had asked for a copy of the Zapruder film to be used "solely for training purposes."[12] Hoover did not explain what these purposes might be, but the role of Zapruder's images in the Kennedy case begins to seem most perverse when one imagines the CIA's own film-inspired "reenactments.") Control over the discussion surrounding the film changed dramatically, however, with the release of the Warren Report.

A Matter of Doubt

As its mode of existence changed so, too, did the boundaries of its meaning. The government's efforts at textual analysis were confronted with a series of detailed critiques. Relying for the most part on material evidence made available by the government, assassination critics seized access to historical authorship, challenging the government's legitimate authority to function as interpreter of the assassination. Eventually, of course, not only would the state be criticized for its performance as investigator, judge, and jury, it would also be suggested that the government's rightful claim to these roles had been jeopardized by its cover-up efforts.

The breakdown in the state's power to control discourse centered first around its handling of the Zapruder film. Listed as Commission Exhibit 885, the film was not reprinted in its entirety in the volume devoted to testimony and exhibits.[13] Crucially, and to the critics' minds suspiciously, frames 208 through 211 were omitted despite the fact that the commission had identified frame 210 as the one in which Kennedy was first struck. As printed in Volume 18 of the commission's exhibits, frame 212 appears quite obviously as a splice of 207 and 212. Perhaps the commission figured no one would notice. *Life* would later admit to accidentally damaging these frames of the Zapruder original, although complete copies had been produced prior to this accident.[14]

In their reprinting of the film, the commission also reversed the two frames immediately following frame 313, the image depicting the precise moment of the president's head wound. In 1965 commission critic Ray Marcus discovered that frames 314 and 315 were printed out of order, giving the impression that the president was initially thrown forward after the bullet's impact rather than backward as the film appeared to reveal. J. Edgar Hoover would eventually concede there had been a printing error, but by this time attention had focused on Kennedy's reaction after the head wound — what would later come to be known as the "head snap." That same year, three other commission critics in Philadelphia obtained sketches of frames 313 and 316 from the Zapruder film as drawn by an artist at the National Archives. After making 35mm slides of these sketches, they inserted them into side-by-side projectors and observed Kennedy's movements as they alternated from one frame to another. In the October 1966 issue of *Liberation,* one of these critics, Vincent J. Salandria, wrote, "In failing to address a single word to this problem of why President Kennedy did not fall on his face as a consequence of the head hit, the Warren commission fell on its face as a fact-finding body and revealed itself to be the fact-concealing body which it was."[15] For Salandria, as well as a growing number of critics, the Zapruder film not only held the key to the assassination, its handling was now evidence of crimes being perpetrated by the government. Whereas it was believed that x rays and photographs of the president's autopsy could have been subject to government forgery, the Zapruder film still retained its authority as evidence because of the number of researchers who had viewed it over the preceding three years. Commission critics also held to some notion that the film could speak for itself. Salandria conveys this faith in some of the most fractured prose to be found in the assassination literature:

When the Zapruder films are shown to the public every adult and every child over six years of age, will upon viewing them, know that the Warren Commission and its staff wore no clothes. They will realize that the dead thing which immediately before the head hit was a President, since it was pounded leftward and backward, had to be hit by an assassin situated to the right and in front of it. . . . Our people will understand these films.[16]

Salandria concluded by calling on *Life* to release the Zapruder film for public screening, but by the end of 1966 even *Life* was expressing doubts as to how the government had interpreted Zapruder's footage.

A Matter of Reasonable Doubt

Two years of persistent criticism of the Warren Report led to the resurfacing of the Zapruder film in *Life*'s November 25, 1966 issue, but whereas earlier it had served as "clear and overwhelming" evidence, a comprehensible transcription of the spectacle which supported the commission's findings, it now lent itself to "a matter of reasonable doubt." The magazine had asked John Connally to review the film and, alongside photos of the Texas governor examining color slides, printed his repeated claim that he and Kennedy, contrary to the magic-bullet theory, had been struck by separate shots. Here *Life* chose to reprint a segment of the film in sequence, frames 222 through 244 clearly labeled. The result was not only a slightly less mediated look at the evidence, but the suggestion on the part of the editors that "a new investigating body should be set up, perhaps at the initiative of Congress."[17] Yet despite their recognition of alternative readings and the fact that just two years earlier the film evidence had appeared "unimpeachable," the magazine's editors clung to a rhetoric that insisted upon the epistemological currency of camera vision:

Of all the witnesses to the tragedy, the only unimpeachable one is the 8-mm movie camera of Abraham Zapruder, which recorded the assassination in sequence. . . . By studying individual frames one can see what happened at every instant and measure precisely the intervals between events.[18]

Much of the assassination literature portrays the film apparatus as somehow independent of the context of investigation. The photographic image presents the only "inviolable form of evidence." As the debate over the assassination grew more intense, access to the Zapruder film became an even more crucial point of contestation. Critics insisted that a public screening would "instantly democratize the research."[19] At the conclusion of a CBS News Inquiry from June 1967, Walter Cronkite told watchers: "*Life*'s decision [not to allow CBS to show the film] means you can not see the Zapruder film in its proper form, as motion picture film. We believe that the Zapruder film is an invaluable asset, not of Time, Inc. — but of the people of the United States."[20]

Then, with the 1967 publication of Josiah Thompson's *Six Seconds in Dallas,* the issue went to court. *Life* had asked for an injunction against Thompson's book because it used detailed charcoal sketches made from the Zapruder film to illustrate the author's theory that three assassins killed Kennedy. The magazine alleged that a "deliberate appropriation" had taken place, one executed by way of "night-time activities." The U.S. district court judge found, however, that, although *Life* did have a valid copyright on the film, the doctrine of "fair use" protected Thompson's "appropriation." The public's right to "a free dissemination of information," and what the court decided was minimal competitive damage done by the book to the magazine, compelled the court to rule that there had been no infringement on the part of Thompson and his publisher.[21] Of special note, however, is the claim made by Thompson and his codefendants that, since in their words "the pictures are simply records of what took place," *Life* had no legitimate copyright on the news. Here again the debate surrounding the film positions it outside its specific conditions of production. In some Bazinian sense, the representation becomes indistinguishable from the original event, and the Zapruder film is characterized as "simply records of what took place." But the court challenged this notion and argued that, although the news is indeed not subject to copyright, what *Life* had in its possession was Zapruder's specific representation of the event.

Life claims no copyright in the news element of the event but only in the particular form or record made by Zapruder. . . . The Zapruder pictures have . . . many elements of creativity. Among other things, Zapruder selected

the kind of camera (movies not snapshots), the kind of film (color), the kind of lens (telephoto), the area in which the pictures were to be taken, the time they were to be taken, and (after testing several sites) the spot on which the camera would be operated.[22]

Thus, while finding in favor of Thompson and his publisher, the court did not fully agree with their argument about the nature and function of the apparatus and its use.

A Crisis of Legibility

By the end of 1967, the flurry of renewed interest in the case and the importance of Zapruder's film within the controversy set a central, perhaps defining feature of the assassination debates in place. The mobile and often contradictory status of the photographic image, the shifting position of representation, the way that film imagery shifted between epistemological certainty and ambiguity, legibility and a crisis of legibility, would continue to characterize the debates. Over the next twenty years the film evidence came to appear both "unimpeachable" (*Life*'s term) and highly suspect, at times unreadable, and constantly open to multiple interpretations. The flux of film's currency did not stem only from the government's analysis. Indeed, from the Warren Report's release until the congressional investigations of the mid- to late seventies, the government was at least officially off the case. Researchers and buffs sustained the debate. Like the government's approach to the assassination, their independent inquests were driven by a belief that an accurate account of the past was within the power of representation.

For the most part, the conspiracy theorists put their faith in the film record, in the accessibility of knowledge through images, through multiple looks that would yield a master perspective and a full explanation. While more comfortable with the idea that some questions appeared unanswerable, the critics still testified to the superiority of camera vision, insisting that the photographic evidence, sometimes in isolation as with the Zapruder film, could speak conclusively to questions about the number of rifle shots, their points of origin, and their precise timing. They could be read for answers about the location of gunmen in buildings or hiding behind fences and could pinpoint the arrangement of bodies in the motorcade at the moments of impact.

Consider what real professionals can do with such evidence. It is possible to build a time phased chronological moving panorama of all events on Dealey Plaza from five minutes before the murder to ninety minutes after it.[23]

Supplied with "a time phased chronological moving panorama," researchers tested their faith in the image with a series of optics experiments which they believed would enhance the vision of the apparatus. On the day of the assassination, Robert Hughes filmed the motorcade from his position at the southwest corner of Main and Houston streets, photographing the limousine as it turned onto Elm Street just below Oswald's alleged shooting perch, the sixth-floor corner window of the School Book Depository. The Hughes film thus contained images of that window just before the shots were fired. In 1967, at the request of *Life,* the Hughes film was subjected to computer studies by the Itek Corporation, in particular an enlargement of frames that appeared to show figures moving in the alleged Oswald window. The results, according to Itek, established a shape or figure appearing to move in the right side window under consideration, but it could not be determined exactly what was in motion. Commission critic Thompson interpreted the Hughes frames as showing the presence of figures in the window next to that allegedly used by Oswald. In 1975, this time at the request of CBS, Itek returned to the Hughes footage with more advanced optical technology but again concluded that, although movement was detectable in the window, further identification was impossible. When the government returned to the case, the House assassinations committee employed the Aerospace Corporation to study these images of the School Book Depository. According to Aerospace, their own computer analysis suggested that apparent motion in the window was due to properties of the photographing process and not to figures moving in the window.[24] However, commission critics continued to highlight the claims of human movement in the window, one of them going so far as to suggest in an HSCA memo that he could detect the color of the shirts worn by men on the sixth floor.

Perhaps the most influential experiments carried out on the Zapruder film were conducted by assassination critic and optics technician Robert Groden. Groden spent years working on the film, enhancing the image quality of the bootleg copy he had obtained in 1968. In particular, Groden enlarged those images depicting the head wound so that Kennedy's body filled a larger portion of the frame. This version quickly became the quintessential print of the Zapruder film for conspiracy theorists as it made the college lecture circuit and was exhibited in 1975 at the Politics of Conspiracy conference sponsored by the Assassination Information Bureau.[25] For Groden this enhanced view of the shooting provided "absolute, incontestable proof of cross-fire and conspiracy."[26]

CBS News weighed in with its own analysis in November of that year with a four-part inquiry series called "The American Assassins," anchored by Dan Rather.[27] In the first two hours of the series, CBS reviewed the JFK assassination, in essence extending the thesis it had put forth in its inquiry of the Warren Commission in 1967. Citing the war in Southeast Asia, Watergate, and the revelations of congressional probes into CIA and FBI activities, Rather told a national audience that the murders of JFK, RFK, and Martin Luther King and the attempted murder of George Wallace had combined to form "a national nightmare." One result of this crisis was an emerging sense of conspiratorial politics such that, according to a CBS poll, 46 percent of those questioned believed that the four shootings were in fact connected.

The network turned to the Itek Corporation to perform their optical investigation, this time claiming to use the original Zapruder footage, not a copy. Of the many questions Rather posed over the course of the program, two were of crucial importance with respect to the imagery: in what direction did JFK move after the head shot, and could Connally's reactions be read in such a way that the magic-bullet theory could be verified? The show's rhetorical strategy was clear: cite a theory put forth by an assassination critic and then look to Itek for confirmation or rebuttal. Thus we see Carl Oglesby lecturing at the Boston AIB conference, and then we see Robert Groden screening his version of the Zapruder film as he tells his audience that the film depicts a double hit to the president's head. Back at the Itek lab, Rather tells John Wolf, head of the company's optical systems division, that just looking at the film does indeed give one the impression that Kennedy is thrown backward, perhaps suggesting a shot from the front. Wolf responds that this is exactly why one must rely on the superiority of the apparatus, "to get away from the subjective impressions that are developed by looking at a blurred motion picture." Itek's analysis shows JFK propelled rapidly forward for three frames before he begins falling backward. Amidst shots of an Itek employee looking into the microscope lenses of a piece of high tech photographic equipment, Rather states the conclusion: both shots fired from behind the limousine.

With the issue of Connally's reaction, the eye is again positioned against the apparatus. This time Josiah Thompson sets forth the alternative theory. When we see Groden and Thompson, they are sitting next to an 8mm projector or a slide machine while Itek technicians are shown working the dials and gauges of expensive equipment. Claiming that he can pinpoint the moment Connally is struck, Thompson concludes that the governor was hit some eighteen frames after JFK or about 1.1 seconds later. This was too much time for both men's wounds to be inflicted by the same bullet, but too little time for a single shooter to get off two shots. For Thompson, this is evidence of at least two gunmen. On this point CBS both acknowledges the illegibility of the visual evidence and still uses it to refute Thompson's theory. "We cannot tell when precisely Connally was hit," Rather tells his audience. "Frankly, we do not believe anyone can." But the last word is really left to Itek who, we are told, asked "five trained photo interpreters" to study the original Zapruder positive. Although the instant of impact cannot be pinpointed, these "interpreters" suggest that Connally's apparent wrist movement might indicate the beginning of a reaction to a bullet, a reaction they see as early as frames 223 to 226. This would mean he is wounded just one-sixth to one-third of a second after JFK, timing consistent with both men being hit by the same bullet. Rather states the CBS News conclusion: "the single bullet theory is at least possible, that's the most that can be said."

Optical enhancements of the evidence thus continued to be a source of contradictory readings. In *Pictures of the Pain,* his survey of the photographic material produced the day of the assassination, Richard Trask articulates a crucial point: that the sophisticated imaging technologies posed the difficult problem "that you can't believe what you see, but only what you can measure."[28] The move from film image to computerized display produces a new piece of evidence modeled on but in a different register than the original Zapruder footage. In the search for new forms of knowledge, the 8mm images of the death are subjected to a second articulation, one that simultaneously fuels a faith in optical machinery and confesses to its limitations. Trask concludes by suggesting, "And thoughtful laymen who at first blush found fascinating the apparent wizardry of modern scientific technology, when confronted with various seemingly contradictory scientific findings, could only question just how exact current science can be."[29] Yet amid such questions, the assassination debates continued to be informed by a commitment to the powers of the photographic apparatus.

In fact, the critics' faith in the revelatory potential of the film evidence drove them to interrogate the image in a way that now appears synchronous with (if not sometimes anticipatory of) the efforts of structural filmmakers of the American avant-garde cinema. Their recourse to repetition, their multiple viewings of the same film fragments shot in Dealey Plaza, their strategies of looping and image enhancement, their reduction of film to still frames, their alternating projection of slides, not only rehearsed the tropes of structural film but resulted in the same "internal tensions" identified by David James: "part against whole; presence against discourse; materials against representation; object-text against meta-text; motion against stasis."[30] Indeed, several critical analyses of Ken Jacobs's *Tom, Tom, The Piper's Son* make apt characterizations of the Zapruder film and the analytical dissection to which it was subjected. In Jacobs's film, James sees the discovery of "not a stable meaning, but only multiplicity and change, a text centrifugally dispersed, constantly reformulating itself in new configurations."[31] In their reading of *Tom, Tom,* Lois Mendelson and Bill Simon note:

Because Jacobs subjects the images to so many radical alterations, they frequently lose their recognizability and attain varying degrees of abstraction. The point of reference both to the outside world and to the original film, disappears. A human body becomes patterns of lines, forms and light and dark.[32]

Much the same could be said of the Zapruder film's transformations. Groden's and other critics' detailed manipulations of the image through rotoscoping, rephotography, and frame enlargement, in search of some hidden truth, ultimately achieved abstraction rather than precision. Indeed, one could argue that these manipulations negated the Zapruder film while using it, as they discarded aspects of the original in pursuit of maximum visibility of JFK. Several critics, of course, insisted otherwise, arguing that the blurry and grainy blowups only enhanced the investigator's vision. Groden, for example, identified in Zapruder frame 413 the head and rifle of a fourth assassin concealed behind branches and claimed that frame 454 revealed the face of the first assassin.[33] But as the experiments of structural filmmakers suggested, "radical alterations" of the film could have a destabilizing function, and image legibility could be put into crisis in at least two ways: by eclipsing sense-making perception, undermining registers of reception so that the viewer is confused about what he or she is looking at; or by expanding possible interpretations, whose variability would eliminate anything like consensus among researchers. Unlike structural filmmakers, of course, assassination critics did not set out to study the parameters of the apparatus or of the filmstrip, but the formal extremes to which their work at times drove them often limited their investigative efforts.

This is not to say, however, that the intense scrutiny of the film evidence always resulted in crisis. The formal experiments, the image enhancement, the rephotography, the transformation of, say, the Zapruder film into the Groden-Zapruder film contributed significantly not only to the critique of the government's methods of investigation but to a more detailed reconstruction of the event. Its very existence prevented the government (or other researchers) from constructing its own, unverifiable sequence for the gunfire.[34] The film allowed investigators to establish a rough time frame for the shooting, albeit one that subsequent writers would seek to modify, and to pinpoint precisely the moment of impact of the fatal head shot. The film became the focal point for a dense, amorphous intertext, the record against which so much other evidence was measured. Despite being only twenty-six seconds long, itself only a fragment, the Zapruder film established the time clock, became the dominant point of reference, and its perspective was invisibly back-projected on all the other film evidence: the Nix film and the Moorman and Altgens photos, among others.[35] Indeed, the structural limitations discussed above may have been in part compensated for by the centering of the Zapruder film within a larger montage of film evidence, within a collage macrotext. Groden, for example, not only enhanced the Zapruder imagery but cut it together with other available motorcade clips in order to establish a longer film with visual continuity. An organization working out of Canada, the Collector's Archive, marketed a videotape in which the Groden-Zapruder film became part of an extended collage, ostensibly edited in sequence, depicting Kennedy's visit to Dallas from his arrival at Love Field to his arrival at Parkland Memorial Hospital.[36]

The insertion of the Zapruder footage into larger filmic chains once again suggests the shifting status of imagery within the debate, its insufficiency despite and in the midst of its efficacy. This quality comes to the fore when we see the tendency to suture the Zapruder footage with other clips, along with a reverse tendency to constantly fragment the film. Its use as a master was thus balanced by its repeated segmentation, the propensity of critics to split the film into microtexts: black-and-white prints, four-by-five-inch color enlargements. Warren Commission Volume 18 printed two frames to a page taken from 35mm black-and-white slides. At one point frames 301 to 330 were subjected on their own to an optics analysis to determine the three-dimensional motion of the limousine and the president's head upon impact.[37] What I have referred to as the critic's panoptic impulse was thus characterized by macro and micro tendencies contingent on each other. In fact, the status of Zapruder's imagery as evidence hinged on an irrevocable contradiction: the simultaneous demand that it be film and stop being film. Put simply, the film must be slowed down to be legible; its twenty-two seconds go by too fast for its vital content to be adequately studied. As a result, it speaks its own impossibility as film. Yet the precise temporal measurements it has to offer concerning the logistics of the shooting demand that it also always speak at 18.3 frames per second. Its status as evidence relies simultaneously on duration and its arrest, film and still frame.

Unimpeachable . . . Unintelligible

When, by the end of the seventies, the inquiry into JFK's death reached a temporary point of impasse, it may have come to rest at the limits of film representation, limits to which the Zapruder film had repeatedly testified. Not only had researchers encountered the contradiction embedded within analyses of the film, they had spawned such a diverse set of interpretations that the investigation became plagued by an acute epistemological crisis. The powers of camera vision, poised plausibly within many of the alternative theories, authoritatively supported interpretations refuting the government's case. Yet taken collectively and read as a singular though infinitely plural text, the counterinquests (combined with the government's account) resulted in a general crisis of knowledge, a critique of the truth-bearing capacities of film.

And so Groden, working with the film for many years, sees in it evidence of six shots plus a warning shot, arguing that the first one aimed at the president comes some twenty-one frames before the government's assigned first-shot frame. Thompson, working for three years with the film and with access to the original purchased by *Life,* sees evidence of four shots, concurring with the Warren Commission as to the first located at frame 210, but disagreeing with it (though agreeing this time with Groden) that Connally is hit between frames 236 and 238.[38] In the course of its investigation between 1978 and 1979, the House Select Committee on Assassinations (HSCA) read four shots from the Zapruder film. Unlike the Warren Commission, Groden, or Thompson, it located a first shot miss at frame 160; agreed with Groden but not with the Warren Commission or Thompson about a second shot (first hit) around frame 190; saw a third shot which no one else saw located between frames 295 and 296, which it theorized came from the grassy knoll; and a fourth and fatal shot at frame 313.[39]

As with other researchers, the HSCA augmented its reading of the Zapruder film with eyewitness testimony and cross-referencing with other images. But more important was its reliance on another form of representation, an audiotape taken from a Dallas police dictabelt which had recorded the sounds of the motorcade and what two teams of acoustics experts concluded were four shots. Now not only was the Zapruder film cut into a working montage, either literally or in collage fashion, but it was synched up with a sound track. The antidote for the image's epistemological crisis was thus discovered in nonvisual representation. Seemingly conscious of the interpretive paralysis engendered by the photographic image, the committee privileged the acoustical evidence and used it to reread the Zapruder film in a somewhat unconventional way. Relying on studies of the dictabelt, the committee identified shot one at frame 160. Furthermore, as noted above, contrary to the observations of all the critics, the committee located a third shot at frames 295 and 296. And yet, unlike its thorough treatment of shots one, two, and four, nowhere in the text of its final report does the committee discuss visual evidence for its claims about shot number three.

Various critics have also used the Zapruder film as a register of the shots, but not only by scrutinizing the image for reactions to wounds being inflicted. Rather, postulating that Zapruder's camera could be understood as an extension of his body, these critics have studied the footage for jiggles or blurs that might register Zapruder's reaction to gunshots. In studies he began in the mid-sixties, which have been cited primarily by pro–Warren Commission researchers, University of California physicist Luis Alvarez read the film for shockwaves that might then function as a time clock for the number and frequency of shots. Alvarez's analysis suggested shots being fired at Zapruder frames 177, 215, and 313. What he understood as minor streaks or blurs Alvarez considered either imperfections resulting from the film-developing process or Zapruder's reaction to the start of a siren.[40] In one of the more curious attempts to read the film for the timing of shots, one critic took note of Governor and Mrs. Connally's testimony about what they said in the automobile at the time shots were being fired. Two expert lip readers were then shown the film on tape, as well as slides of individual frames, in an attempt to pinpoint where in the Zapruder sequence Connally's verbal reactions might have been spoken. The researcher acknowledged that little came of this experiment, but the effort testifies to the analytical extremes to which some tried to push the filmic record.[41]

This notion of crisis with respect to the Zapruder film emerges only after a cumulative account of the inquiries and noting each individual theory's persistent faith in the powers of the apparatus. Whereas it was impossible for researchers to determine exactly the location of the first shot (or shots), due to Zapruder's view being momentarily obstructed by the Stemmons Freeway sign on Elms Street (the motorcade passed behind it at a crucial moment), Zapruder had a clear angle of vision for the fatal head shot. Kennedy's head is torn open at frame 313 where an orange halo of blood and brain matter sprays the limousine. And yet multiple interpretations have convincingly challenged any single reading of even this and the surrounding frames.

The Warren Commission pinpointed the location and position of Kennedy's body by cross-referencing the Zapruder, Nix, and Muchmore films, all three of which recorded the head shot but paid little attention to the movement of Kennedy's body after impact. It simply stated that the films showed the bullet striking from the back and exiting "through the upper right portion of the skull."[42] As has been mentioned, commission critics seized on this point to dispute the official account, finding in the film record of the president's postimpact movements the kind of evidence ensured by camera vision. Referring to slides of the Zapruder frames depicting the head shot, Sylvia Meagher told readers, "The resultant diagram constitutes conclusive and irrefutable proof that the bullet that sent the President violently backward and to his left was fired in front of and to the right of the car and not from the book depository."[43]

However, this interpretation was not accepted by all Warren Report critics. Groden and Thompson developed strikingly similar readings which remained radically different from other critics'. Thompson sought to verify his predecessors' "head snap" theories and made what he thought was a major discovery: a double movement by the president's head, a distinct pitching forward in frame 312 lasting one-eighteenth of a second, followed by the body's abrupt backward movement toward the rear of the car. The magnitude of this forward movement would have to be measured to determine whether it resulted from the impact of a bullet or simply showed Kennedy leaning forward at frame 312. Using 8 × 10 enlargements with a dissecting microscope in the offices at *Life,* Thompson found:

Its magnitude is substantial. Measured parallel to the axis of the car the President's head has been given a forward acceleration of 69.6 feet per second per second between frames 312 and 313. One-eighteenth second later, this movement has been reversed and the head has been given an acceleration backward and to the left of 100.3 feet per second per second. These accelerations are quite large (a falling body at the earth's surface, for example, accelerates at a rate of 32 feet per second per second), and what is even more striking is the brevity of the interval in which the movement is reversed.[44]

After disqualifying a number of possible explanations for this — a neuromuscular reaction by Kennedy, the rapid acceleration of the limousine, Mrs. Kennedy pulling him back — Thompson concluded that the film clearly reveals "a simultaneous double impact on the President's head. One shot was fired from the rear, and the other from the right front."[45] Groden moves one step beyond Thompson by suggesting the directions of origin for these two shots. He sees in frame 313 a "glancing blow" to the right temple coming from the Book Depository, with an impact that throws Kennedy "slightly forward." Then he sees in frame 314 a shot from the grassy knoll which strikes "with such force it actually lifted him out of his seat."[46] As noted above, the HSCA read the Zapruder film differently, arguing that the grassy knoll shot that was picked up on the police dictabelt missed Kennedy completely and that the wound inflicted in frame 313 came from the Book Depository.[47]

These varying interpretations and the contradictory conclusions that issued from them seemed to put in doubt any singular and coherent account of the shooting. Yet remarkably, at the thirtieth anniversary of the assassination, the axis of insistence and its faith in the powers of camera vision returned to inform the debate once again, this time in a work that defended the Warren Commission's findings but spoke with the kind of epistemological guarantee that had often characterized its critics. And again the Zapruder film was the focus of analysis. For throughout Gerald Posner's *Case Closed,* interpretations of the visual evidence were invested with the language of certainty. Indeed, Posner declared to Dan Rather and a national television audience: "We can look at the Zapruder film and with new enhancements and new technology that film can answer exactly what took place on November 22nd."[48] Thus, like those who came before him, Posner's claims rested on technological refinements, advancements that endowed camera vision with a power that could clear away thirty years of interpretive struggle and contradictory readings. Denying any constructive role to the government's critics, Posner implied that the technology available to the Warren Commission and the HSCA limited their analysis of the photographic record.

However, scientific advances within the past five years allow significant enhancements of the Zapruder film, as well as scale re-creations using computer animation, which were unavailable to the government panels. As a result, it is now possible to settle the question of the timing of Oswald's shots and to pinpoint the moment when both Kennedy and Connally were struck with a precision previously unattainable.[49]

Posner's faith in the film approximated that of *Life* from the early sixties. The "scientific advances" to which he referred allowed him to argue, with the same rhetoric of finality that has echoed throughout the case, that Oswald's first shot came near Zapruder frame 160; that is, just after the presidential limousine turned onto Elm Street. Among the significant details revealed by the image enhancements and noted by Posner in defense of this reading is the reaction of a ten-year-old girl who, after running alongside the limousine, appeared to turn to look back toward something or someone behind her.[50] Citing with approval the young girl's own subsequent testimony, Posner claimed she was reacting to a rifle shot. But despite the fact that the Zapruder film does not contain even a glimpse of the building from which Oswald allegedly fired, Posner concluded "the enhancement clearly shows she . . . was staring back at the School Book Depository." In fact, the film only shows her looking back; it does not tell us what she was looking at. Posner's faith in the "enhanced" film authorizes an interpretation not based on the denotation of the image. Posner commits a similar, minor slippage when he is analyzing Kennedy's movements just after Zapruder frame 160: "He looked to his right toward the crowd, and then back to his left to Jacqueline, as if to be reassured that everything was alright."[51] The film does appear to show Kennedy moving his head toward the left, but it does not reveal him looking for reassurance. Posner's qualification with the words "as if" shows some restraint, but the result is still an insistence that the image offers conclusive information that it does not contain.

More telling than these details of interpretation is the way Posner's analysis was framed in the language of the new. His observation about the young girl running beside the limousine is introduced with the phrase "New Zapruder enhancements, however, confirm the ear-witness testimony that early shot missed the President and the Governor," and two sentences later Posner again implied the freshness of his reading with the phrase "the enhancement clearly shows."[52] And yet the photographic evidence panel convened by the House assassinations committee took note of this young girl and her reaction nearly fifteen years before Posner observed her off his "new Zapruder enhancements." On the CBS broadcast of November 1993 on which Posner appeared, Dan Rather reinforced the false impression by telling viewers, "That film discovery of a possible early miss shot and a longer time to fire three shots is new." Perhaps all one had to do now to guarantee the certainty of one's film analysis was to attach the words "new enhancements" and thus tap into the collective and long-sustained faith in the powers of the movie camera.

Armed with such certainty, Posner claimed he could now conclusively answer all remaining questions about the logistics of the shooting. From the position of Kennedy's arms, elbows out and hands toward the throat, Posner read something called Thorburn's position, a physiological reaction to a spinal injury, taken as proof of a shot at frames 223 to 224.[53] Second, the enhanced frames "reveal exactly when the Governor was hit," because they depict the lapel on his suit flipping up at frame 224 and the hat held in his right hand rising just a couple of frames later.[54] Posner saw further confirmation of a shot at this point in Mrs. Connally's turning to her right, toward the governor, at frames 227 and 228, despite her recollection that she turned after the first shot. This interpretation of the film, contrary to critics who assigned Connally's wounds to frames 235 through 238, allowed Posner to argue that Kennedy and Connally were struck, in his words, "almost simultaneously" and thus by one bullet. Furthermore, Posner's enhanced Zapruder film was put in the service of two computer experiments: one that sought to determine whether Kennedy and Connally were aligned in the limousine such that a single bullet could inflict their wounds and one that constructs a bullet trajectory back to a firing location for the gunman. In both cases, Posner claimed, these new tests confirmed the Warren Commission's most important conclusion: that Oswald was the lone gunman firing from the sixth floor of the Depository.[55]

For thirty years assassination researchers on both sides of the magic-bullet theory insisted that the film evidence, primarily the Zapruder film, could explain the killing. For the editors at *Life* in 1966, the camera was the only "unimpeachable" witness. Many critics concurred with Josiah Thompson in 1967 that, if the film "is studied with the utmost care and under optimum conditions, it can yield answers to enormous questions. Where did the shots come from, and when were they fired?"[56] At the New Orleans trial in 1969, Jim Garrison had the Zapruder film screened ten times, telling the court, "This film, which has not been shown to the public, will clearly show you the effect of the shots striking the President."[57] For Groden in 1975 the film provided "absolute, incontestable proof." And in 1993 Posner told readers, "Conspiracy buffs have yearned for thirty years for a witness able to supply conclusive evidence about what happened in Dealey Plaza. We now have that witness, thanks to technological advances."[58] That witness was the Zapruder film, new and improved. And yet, the "unimpeachable" witness could be made to speak in several voices. In 1964 the film showed, after "painstaking analysis," how JFK was shot from the rear.[59] In 1967 the film testified to a "double impact on the President's head. One shot was fired from the rear, and the other from the right front."[60] When aired on network television for the first time in 1975, it was interpreted for the national audience as proof of a crossfire in Dealey Plaza. In 1993 that same film was once again the prosecution's star witness in the case against Oswald.

Thus the multiple forms of image enhancement and the critics' textual analyses hardly resulted in a unanimity of interpretation. Public frustration with assassination researchers and skepticism regarding conspiracy theories were in part products of this epistemological crisis. The impassioned claims of each researcher and his or her faith in the film evidence constantly clashed with the tangled and ever more confusing accounts of the imagery already on record. The various films and photographs exposed in the sun of Dealey Plaza were all produced at a distance from the president's body. The work of optics experts and investigators struggled to turn long shots into closeups so as to narrow the gap between witness and wound. But what of the images made from a more direct encounter with the body? If intense scrutiny of the photographic evidence resulted in a form of collective ambiguity, certainly the facts obtained directly from the president's corpse would be irrefutable.

If the assassination debates were challenged by the shifting legibility of the film evidence, they were in fact haunted by a further, perhaps more troubling crisis of representation: the problems posed by Kennedy's autopsy. In the years immediately following the assassination, both the Zapruder film and the images produced in connection with the president's autopsy remained sequestered texts, yet not in the same way. The government had chosen to make the infliction of wounds public, if only through the printing of black-and-white Zapruder stills in Volume 18 of the Warren Commission's exhibits. But it chose to keep the images of death private, for the commission refrained from publishing any of the photographs taken during the autopsy.

Access to the Autopsy

Perhaps the subsequent bootlegging of the Zapruder film, which challenged *Life* magazine's private possession, ultimately made sense in light of the film's public production as the work of an amateur, made outdoors at a political function. The photographs and x rays exposed during the autopsy, on the other hand, were the work of medical professionals. These indoor pictures of a corpse were to be viewed and analyzed by a limited number of government-sanctioned officials. Although both the Zapruder film and the autopsy images lay at the center of a struggle over public access, they were embedded in different discursive networks. Those networks that demanded public access to the film (and to other motorcade footage) occupied a more visible forum. Since the Zapruder film was held by Time-Life, requests for access to it came, not surprisingly, from its extremely visible competition in the journalistic community. In the name of democratizing the evidence, the press could attempt to wrest monopoly of the scene from *Life*.

The struggle over the autopsy was less visible. The graphic and explicit nature of its imagery certainly would have restricted its publication in mainstream periodicals or appearance on network television. Publishers and networks thus had far less incentive to fight with the government for access. Moreover, this type of representation demanded a level of interpretive expertise that the buffs did not generally possess. Making the medical evidence public would not instantly democratize the research because its images would first have to be translated by the forensic pathologist or radiologist. During the seventies and eighties, when autopsy photos and reproductions of the x rays slowly became available for public inspection, defenders of the government's conclusions were extremely critical of those who sought to interpret the evidence with a layman's knowledge of medicine. Throughout the assassination debates, the few medical experts who were critical of the Warren Commission and who had access to the classified materials served as conduits for the critics whose research depended on the sequestered evidence.[1]

While demanding access to the autopsy imagery, commission critics continued their struggle for historical authorship by challenging the legitimacy of the government's discourse — in this case the qualifications of the doctors who performed the official autopsy at Bethesda naval hospital in Washington on the night of the assassination. The commission's findings relied heavily on the report submitted by these doctors, but its members, with the exception of Earl Warren, never looked at the images produced at the autopsy. Critics pointed out that commission members had not examined this evidence and that the Secret Service had immediately taken custody of the autopsy photographs, preventing even the doctors who wrote the official autopsy report from seeing the crucial evidence. Critics argued further that the autopsy was inadequate because the hospital pathologists who conducted the procedure lacked adequate previous experience with the kind of medicolegal diagnosis required by the case.[2]

The Meaning of Autopsy

The competing voices in the assassination debates believed that medical records of JFK's body, like the footage shot by Zapruder, could offer unequivocal testimony about the logistics of the shooting. In fact, their faith in this evidence tapped into a science of the corpse that was some two centuries old. In his chapter "Open up a Few Corpses" from *The Birth of the Clinic,* Michel Foucault, discussing the meaning of death and the role of pathological anatomy in the discourses of clinical knowledge, isolates the epistemological status of the autopsy. He quotes from a medical treatise by J.-L. Alibert: "When philosophy brought its torch into the midst of civilized peoples, it was at last permitted to cast one's searching gaze upon the inanimate remains of the human body, and these fragments, once the vile prey of worms, became the fruitful source of the most useful truths."[3]

Foucault uses this passage in laying out the traditional argument for why autopsies were rarely undertaken openly prior to the Enlightenment, an argument he quickly characterizes as historically inaccurate. It is a rhetorical strategy that Foucault commonly uses. And yet the chronological argument he is making, that autopsies were in fact common during the mid-eighteenth century, does not disqualify the important content found in the Alibert citation: the implication of the corpse in the search for truth, its centrality to medical knowledge. Foucault's interest in the corpse follows from his discussion throughout the book on discourses around disease, but his comments on the function and efficacy of the autopsy are relevant to my case regarding representation and the body of JFK. Foucault writes: "Hence the appearance that pathological anatomy assumed at the outset: that of an objective, real, and at last unquestionable foundation for the description of diseases."[4]

Foucault explains that, prior to "the technique of the corpse," death had an ambiguous status for eighteenth-century medicine. "But if the traces of the disease happened to bite into the corpse, then no evidence could distinguish absolutely between what belonged to it and what to death; their signs intersected in indecipherable disorder."[5] The autopsy conferred on clinical medicine a temporal efficiency, the ability to open up the body immediately after death to distinguish between the organic effects belonging to the category of illness and those arising from decomposition. In other words, the autopsy was seen as the guarantor of two truths: that belonging to the body and that belonging to death. Indeed, for clinical discourse, the autopsy redefines death:

Instead of being what it had so long been, the night in which life disappeared, in which even the disease becomes blurred, it is now endowed with that great power of elucidation that dominates and reveals both the space of the organism and the time of the disease. The privilege of its intemporality, which is no doubt as old as the consciousness of imminence, is turned for the first time into a technical instrument which provides a grasp on the truth of life and the nature of its illness. . . . Analysis, the philosophy of elements and their laws, meets its death in what it had vainly sought in mathematics, chemistry and even language: an unsupercedable model, prescribed by nature; it is on this great example that the medical gaze will now rest.[6]

An Unstable Body of Evidence

And yet, for the assassination debates, the body and clinical representations of it did not offer access to truth but became one more site of illegibility and contradiction, another set of texts posited as the best evidence, subjected to secrecy and charges of tampering, the center of so many narrative explanations and medical interpretations. Not until the nineties was there anything near consensus about the autopsy. In the preceding years an unstable body of evidence had resulted first from two medical procedures' having been performed on JFK: one in Dallas at Parkland Memorial Hospital moments after the shooting and the official autopsy performed later that night at Bethesda naval hospital. In Dallas the body appeared to show evidence of a frontal neck wound, which in the opinion of at least two doctors was an entrance wound. Their "unofficial" opinion was widely quoted throughout the press that weekend of the assassination, initiating a confused narrative process that would continue throughout the debate.[7] The doctors at the official autopsy in Washington, however, did not take notice of the neck wound because the Dallas doctors had obscured it with a tracheotomy incision while performing emergency surgery on Kennedy. Rather, the Bethesda doctors observed a back wound which the Dallas doctors had not seen. Finding no corresponding exit wound for the back wound, the Bethesda doctors concluded that this bullet had not transited the president's body. Indeed, their examination determined that the back wound was quite shallow, as the end of its opening could be felt by probing with a finger.

When called before the Warren Commission, the officer in charge of the autopsy at Bethesda, Commander James J. Humes, testified that the back wound was located near the base of the back of the neck. Yet on the face sheet diagram marked by the doctor assisting Humes, the wound is clearly spotted several inches below Kennedy's right shoulder, a location corroborated by FBI reports filed by agents in attendance at the autopsy and made public years later. In fact, in its summary report of the proceedings dated December 9, 1963, a report that came to light only after further research by critics two years after the commission's report, the FBI concluded that Kennedy's back wound had not traversed the body. If the autopsy doctors had found that the bullet causing this wound had exited the president's throat, critics asked, why did the subsequent FBI report not come to a similar conclusion?[8] After performing the autopsy on the night of the 22nd and approving the diagram's location of the wound, Humes spoke the following day to Dr. Malcolm Perry, one of the Dallas doctors, and only then learned that the opening at the front of the neck was a bullet wound and not just a tracheotomy incision. Humes now had to account for this wound without being able to reexamine the body. He did so by explaining that what the Dallas doctors had thought was a front entrance wound was, in his opinion, a wound of exit for the bullet that had caused the back wound. According to his testimony before the commission, Humes burned the original draft of his autopsy notes at home and submitted a revised second draft as his official report on Sunday the 24th. Commission critics seized upon the destruction of the original and the discrepancies between the Dallas and Bethesda observations of the neck wound. Humes, they suggested, had bungled the autopsy and had been forced to speculate on a bullet path he had never seen but which was now required because of the information supplied by the Dallas doctors and because freshly published reports had stated that the shots had come from the rear of the limousine.

The issue was further complicated by the schematic drawings Humes used to supplement his testimony about the wound, drawings that were made not at the time of the autopsy but three months later on the basis of his memory and notes. These drawings, published in the commission's Volume 16 of exhibits show a bullet's path traversing Kennedy's neck. However, none of the Secret Service or FBI accounts made during the autopsy reports any of the doctors finding such a path on the night of the 22nd. Indeed, critics pointed out that, according to the FBI report cited above, Humes had concluded the night of the autopsy that "one bullet had entered the President's back and had worked its way out of the body during cardiac massage."[9] Furthermore, critics argued that bullet holes in the shirt and suit coat worn by Kennedy did not match up with a wound located at the base of the neck, but rather with one that passed through the cloth four inches below the collar line.[10]

It is important to keep in mind that the crisis surrounding the autopsy emerged over the course of the next two decades as government documents became public. At first, assassination critics followed the medical evidence through newspaper accounts of leaked information, details that presented a fragmentary picture of the body. When the official autopsy was made public ten months after the assassination, critics worked with what few images were present in the commission's exhibits and thus had to imagine the body as a composite of artist's drawings and verbal descriptions. Various questions surrounding the autopsy could not be pursued until the appearance of FBI documents — again in the form of words rather than images — in early 1966. The autopsy evidence — photos, x rays, tissue sections of the body, and the president's brain — had been held by the Department of Justice until 1966 before being entrusted to the National Archives. It was stipulated that no one was to be allowed access to these materials for the next five years.

However, prior to the five-year expiration date, a new government panel was appointed by Attorney General Ramsey Clark to study the autopsy photos and x rays. In its report of January 16, 1969, the Clark Panel issued findings that it claimed corroborated the autopsy doctors' original conclusions and reasserted that the assassin's bullets had struck from the rear. However, critics identified discrepancies between the panel's observations and those recorded by the autopsy doctors. Harold Weisberg, for example, pointed out that, whereas in 1963 the head wound was located "slightly above" the occipital protuberance, the bump along the back of the head, the Clark Panel located this wound four inches above that point. Whereas the autopsy doctors had taken the hole in the front of the president's neck to be that caused by a tracheotomy, the Clark Panel claimed that the bullet wound could still be identified despite the incision made by the Dallas doctors. Whereas Humes had told the Warren Commission that "no metallic fragments were detectable by x-ray examination" of the throat wound, the Clark Panel reported that "several small metallic fragments are present in this region."[11] Critics thus perceived the Clark Panel as a further confusion of the body and yet another government report in which conclusions were at odds with content.

Interpretive struggle around the body continued to be a central, somewhat sinister aspect of the general debate, as critics highlighted discrepancies between the statements of the Dallas doctors and the Washington doctors, and lobbied for access to the photographs. But assassination buffs consistently came up against reports that materials stored in government archives confirmed the Warren Commission's conclusions. Dr. John Lattimer became the first private citizen to examine the evidence, and although his observations did not always agree with the commission's data or procedures, he argued that the photographs and x rays confirmed two shots from the rear.[12] The House assassinations committee not only weighed in on the side of the original findings but, taking seriously some critics' charges that autopsy imagery had been tampered with, sought to authenticate the photos and x rays as well. Most of the Dallas doctors ultimately came around to endorsing the Bethesda findings, reinforcing the consensus that had been constructed by the Clark and House committee reports.

Critics continued to note that at least one Dallas doctor contradicted his colleagues, insisting that he had observed a large wound in the back of Kennedy's head.[13] Not content with how the HSCA had read the autopsy images, some critics maintained that either these materials had been altered to obscure the facts of the body or that the corpse itself had been surgically altered so that, although the autopsy photographs were authentic, they were in fact records of a prior forgery. Researchers Robert Groden and Harrison Livingstone charged that the x rays of JFK were fakes because they indicated that the right eye and right forehead had been damaged by a bullet while the autopsy photographs showed the president's face fully intact.[14] In his book *Best Evidence*, David Lifton argued that the body could be viewed from at least three perspectives: the corpse as viewed by Dallas doctors, the perspective of Dr. Humes at Bethesda, and the body as recorded by the autopsy photographs and x rays. All three, he claimed, described the body differently. In his account of the discrepancies, Lifton outlined one of the debates' more fantastic theories — that Kennedy's body had been operated on by a clandestine medical team sometime between its examinations at Parkland and Bethesda.

From the day of the assassination and the press conference held by the Dallas doctors, any single narrative account of the body as evidence would eventually, and sometimes quite quickly, fall prey to what appeared to be contradictory knowledge. This narrative instability did not always undermine the critics' faith in the body as best evidence. Not unlike the faith in camera vision's potential to reveal truths, many still believed the body to be a site for irrefutable conclusions. And yet the body was also a site of such devastating illegibility that the narratives attempting to account for it grew to include even more macabre contradictions. Researchers detailed major discrepancies in the descriptions of the president's coffin as it left Dallas and as it arrived in Washington; so, too, with the ways the body was wrapped and the kind of bag in which it was transported. Suspicions were raised about how many caskets were taken from the plane from Dallas or were delivered to Bethesda. Confusion persisted over how many photographs and x rays were taken at the autopsy. Most sinister perhaps was the revelation that, when the Kennedy family donated the forensic evidence to the National Archives, it was subsequently discovered that two items were missing from that deposit: either lost or never returned to the Archives were slides of tissue sections of the wounds and, more mysteriously, the president's brain.

Over a thirty year period the assassinated president's body seemed to change in death, resembling one of those 3-D postcards on which images move, come, and go as the viewer's perspective shifts left or right. Wounds seemed to move, and their trajectories appeared to shift, their origins apparently relocated. Indeed, the confounding nature of the Kennedy assassination springs not just from allegedly mob-silenced witnesses or from government duplicity but from the inability of representation to speak the truth about the case. The opacity of representation is not the only problem. The status of these texts as evidence or counterevidence, their relative clarity or opacity, was conditioned by the discursive formations in which they operated and by the institutional demands placed on them. I am not suggesting that these assassination signifiers eventually came to mean anything, though their constant juxtaposition makes this a tempting conclusion. Rather, I am interested in situating their provisional meanings to see how the various discourses or formations of knowledge interacted.

Soft-Core Visibility

Perhaps nowhere is this interaction better exemplified than in the meeting of the assassination debates and pornography, a mutually enhancing combination centered on the body and resonating, as we will see, in the Hollywood cinema of assassination. It was in fact Abraham Zapruder who first foresaw the connection. In his account of *Life*'s acquisition of the film, editor Richard Stolley wrote: "Time and again he [Zapruder] described what he feared most—the film's being shown in sleazy Times Square movie houses, while men hawked it on the sidewalk."[15] Earl Warren's decision to make the autopsy materials and the president's clothing unavailable to the public expressed a similar concern, motivated by his fear that "scavengers" were intent on establishing "a museum which they proposed to show around the country at County Fairs, etc. in a highly emotional manner."[16] As the autopsy photographs remained hidden and the Zapruder film available only through back channels, the assassination debates migrated to the site of the illicit, discussed in the pages of soft core and assuming the formal tropes of pornography. Rather than fashion a new definition of the pornographic, I want to speculate about why assassination literature found its way into soft-core magazines and how this phenomenon articulated questions about the legitimacy of authorship and the politics of looking.[17]

The presence of assassination literature in soft-core magazines was consistent with the public ebb and flow of the debate, surfacing first in the pages of *Playboy* in November 1965 and then, roughly coincident with the publication of the Thompson and Meagher books, twice during 1967. These latter issues played host to extensive interviews with Mark Lane and New Orleans District Attorney Jim Garrison, both of whom used the opportunity to attack the Warren Report. By the mid-seventies, articles on the assassination and such related topics as the activities of the CIA and organized crime would become staple feature articles in men's soft core. But muckraking of this sort was not the rule at *Playboy* in the mid-sixties, and although its attention to Lane and Garrison anticipated the subsequent alliance between subject matter and medium, these interviews functioned as much to legitimize the critics' discourse as to ghettoize it. Indeed, the cultural status of *Playboy,* especially in the sixties, in what might be termed the illicit mainstream, suggests the same kind of dual social standing as that of the assassination critics around 1967. For the magazine the illicit mainstream was a product of juxtaposing photographs of half-naked women with prose by some of the nation's most acclaimed authors. Critics of the Warren Commission, while still under attack from a range of sources within the journalism community, would perhaps never again enjoy the degree of social validity or national attention accorded their dissent during 1967 and 1968. In this sense, *Playboy,* far from venturing into risky journalistic waters, was in step with various mainstream periodicals and publishers in recognizing the assassination as a subject with historical significance which also helped sell magazines. (It is in fact difficult to determine to what extent history or commerce maintained the assassination in a top spot on the country's journalistic agenda.) Whether *Playboy*'s readers were as sophisticated as it advertised, the space accorded Lane and Garrison was significant; although other magazines had called for a new investigation — most notably at this point, *Life* and the *Saturday Evening Post* — such calls generally accompanied articles penned by staff writers. Here two of the most flamboyant critics, their flamboyance undoubtedly attracting this attention in the first place, were allowed to outline their cases in their own words. Garrison's was the longest interview *Playboy* had printed up to that time.

Compared to the reemergence of the assassination debate in soft-core magazines of the mid-seventies, the attention it garnered in the previous decade seems demure and far from scandalous. Whereas the interviews were printed without any accompanying photographic evidence, the pieces from the mid-seventies were frequently structured around visuals. The slow release of classified materials, the infringement case victory of Thompson concerning publication of the Zapruder frames, and the nationwide telecasting of the enhanced Groden print were major factors in the widespread surfacing of Dealey Plaza imagery in such magazines as *Playboy* and *Gallery.* Also at work, however, was the fluctuating status of the assassination discourse, in particular its social illegitimacy after the Garrison debacle. Sources from all sectors of the debate, pro– and anti–Warren Commission, criticized the New Orleans conspiracy trial, and after many critics had worked in relative silence in the early seventies, their work resurfaced in more marginal publications. After the Garrison trial, the critics' case was tinged with the perception of fraud, and hard news periodicals rarely served as advocates for continuing the investigation up until roughly 1975.

By this time the soft-core trade, which targeted the economic and social class approximating *Playboy*'s sixties' readership, had expanded and moved toward more explicit imagery. This increased explicitness in the representation of the model's body (and in published prose as well), especially in magazines such as *Penthouse* or *Gallery,* had its corollary in assassination imagery. Two overriding and related factors facilitated the shared exhibition of assassination and soft-core photographs. First, the status of the critics' work constituted dangerous or illicit knowledge; what, according to Walter Kendrick, promoted the corruption of youth in the nineteenth century, and was thus deemed pornographic, now promoted practices that could endanger the authority of the state.[18] Dangerous knowledge — theories of clandestine government operations, secret teams of assassins, coverup concerning the president's autopsy — censored by the dominant cultural mechanisms thus found expression in illicit publications, magazines often sold in paper wrappers. The two sets of knowledge — porn and Dallas — also came to share sites of distribution and exchange: memorabilia collectors' shows, mail order catalogues catering to the bizarre and the scandalous.[19] For the mainstream media the most widely circulated and acceptable equivalent of this illicit knowledge were stories linking Marilyn Monroe to the late president, its very soft-core imagery highlighted by a provocatively dressed Marilyn singing "Happy Birthday, Mr. President" at Madison Square Garden in 1962.

Pornographic and illicit knowledge, the issue of censorship and a critique of mainstream journalistic authorship, came together in May of 1967 with the most notorious parodic text yet issued from the underground press. Paul Krassner's *The Realist* offered as its cover story for that month a bogus article titled "The Parts That Were Left out of the Kennedy Book." For the first time anywhere, it claimed, *The Realist* was making public an episode deleted from all published editions of William Manchester's account of the assassination, *The Death of a President*. The fraudulent excerpt had Jacqueline Kennedy confiding to Manchester, the family-approved author, that on the *Air Force One* flight back to Washington, D.C., she found President Johnson "crouching over the corpse" and "moving his body rhythmically." The article continued with Mrs. Kennedy admitting:

"And then I realized—there is only one way to say this—he was literally fucking my husband in the throat. In the bullet wound in the front of his throat. He reached a climax and dismounted. I froze. The next thing I remember, he was being sworn in as the new President."

The article continued:

[Handwritten marginal notes: 1. Check with Rankin—did secret autopsy show semen in throat wound? 2. Is this simply necrophilia or was LBJ trying to change entry wound into exit wound by enlarging?][20]

Krassner's lampoon mocked the controversy stirred up at the time concerning the Kennedys' censorship of Manchester's book. But more importantly, it underscored the connection between conspiracy theories (hence the note to Rankin) and the pornographic. Its perverse encounter between the dead president and LBJ carries the necrophilic aspect of the case to its most bizarre but perhaps logical conclusion. Most of the article is devoted to expanding playfully on the gossip about Kennedy's infidelities, his trysts with Marilyn and various models, the illicit anecdotes to which the journalism community had been confined up until then. But in Krassner's piece, how JFK used his body in life carries over to its role in death, as the slain president's final tryst is with his successor, his final act to deep-throat LBJ.[21] In Krassner's article, then, the discourses intersected: knowledge that could not be made public, representations of illicit sex, images of the corpse. But it is the combination of the three that makes the article so suggestive, pushing a definition of assassination porn beyond the concept of dangerous knowledge.

Indeed, what accounts for the presence of the assassination debates within soft core, the base that cements their cohabitation, is what film theorists have termed the *ideology of the visible*. In his essay "Machines of the Visible," Jean-Louis Comolli articulates the historically conditioned linkage between truth and visibility, tracing it to the development of codes of perspective and the eye's position at the center of representational systems.[22] But for the topic being considered here, it may be more accurate to localize the dramatic impact of this linkage somewhere toward the end of the nineteenth century. For Comolli, the ideology of the visible, though dating back to the Renaissance, enters a period of "frenzy" by the middle of the 1800s: "It is, of course, the effect of the social multiplication of images: ever wider distribution of illustrated papers, waves of prints, caricatures, etc."[23] Coupled with the effects of industrialism, the dominance of the visible is reinforced.

Thanks to the same principles of mechanical repetition, movements of men and animals become in some sort more visible than they had been: movement becomes a visible mechanics. The mechanical opens out and multiplies the visible and between them is established a complicity all the stronger in that the codes of analogical figuration slip irresistibly from painting to photography and then from the latter to cinematography.[24]

This "complicity" between knowledge and optics, Comolli points out, is obtained at the cost of the eye; camera vision asserts its superiority over the power of the human organ. The photographic image, despite its differences from the world it represents — its lack of real depth, the limits of the frame or of color — has been taken as a faithful representation, its differences disavowed. And it in turn has reasserted the dominance of the visible, an improvement on and guarantor of human vision. The camera, and by extension the cinema, then, did not establish the dominance of the visible so much as enhance it, functioning to fix the bonds between knowledge and vision. This reinforces, in the words of Serge Daney, "a world where 'I see' is readily used for 'I understand.'"[25]

In her book *Hard Core,* Linda Williams enlists Comolli's argument about the ideology of the visible for her study of cinematic pornography.[26] She traces one of the genre's defining impulses back to Eadweard Muybridge's well-known motion studies, in order to establish the historical connection between cinema and the power-knowledge axis defined by Foucault as the *scientia sexualis.* Williams's discussion of these experiments is immediately relevant to my point about how the cinema was epistemologically implicated in the search for truths about the body. Indeed, the Muybridge imagery has a striking similarity in both motive and method to the deployment of assassination imagery. As a subsequent chapter will explore, the gridlike format of motion studies conducted in the late 1870s find their formal parallel in the layouts of magazines devoted to the assassination as well as in the designs of Andy Warhol's silkscreen portraits. For now, the important point is the one Williams makes concerning the optical machine's capacity to construct bodies that are ideal for scientific examination, the way that photographic technology created a new body of and for knowledge. Freud understood the fetishization of the female body as resulting from the encounter with castration, and various theorists have regarded the cinema as enhancing this fetishization. Williams, however, suggests that the Muybridge experiments (or the apparatus they put into effect) created, rather than reenacted, the operations of the subject so often discussed by psychoanalytic film theory.

The fetishization enacted in this originally scientific exploration of movement is historically quite new and inseparable from the unprecedented hallucinatory impression of reality encoded in the image of bodies produced by the machines. In this case the cinematic magnification and projection of human bodies would not simply restage the original scenario of castration (and the male "solutions" or escapes of fetishization and voyeurism) at the sight of female difference. Rather, it would produce a new kind of body, which viewers experience through this optical machine. The new, larger-than-life, projected film body is ideally visible; although on display for the viewer, it goes about its business as if unaware of being watched.[27]

This new body, "ideally visible," is the product of an optical machine that has supplanted the eye and in the process has renewed its power. The new film body, which is projected as a larger image, a moving image, an image that can be slowed, stopped, and reversed, inaugurates a subject for whom knowledge, truth, and the visible are as synched together as the four legs of a horse lifted off the ground in the middle of its gallop. And it is this film body that is constantly exposed or projected by pornography, enabling it to insist that its imagery renders sexual truths. This revelation, Williams notes, is most thoroughly inscribed by hard-core porn and its presentation of the "truths" of the unfaked and involuntary orgasm. The moving image can make this "involuntary convulsion" visible and by doing so can certify itself as transmitter of knowledge.[28] Borrowing from Gertrude Koch, Williams identifies pornography as a "drive for knowledge" which functions on the basis of providing "maximum visibility."[29]

The principle of maximum visibility operates in the hard core film as though Muybridge's measurement grid were still in place, trying to gauge with increasing exactitude the genital equivalent of "at which point in a leap the female breast is highest."[30]

Maximum visibility in turn would seem to rely on a faith in the image, a Bazinian ontology that understands the photograph or film as a tracing of the real. What for Bazin were the unique properties of the image, the organic character of its coming into being and its apparent ontological bond with the phenomenal world, has been thoroughly critiqued by contemporary film theory. Cinema's "realism" is understood as a historically conditioned aesthetic, the result of ideological rather than ontological factors. Nonetheless, the culturally encoded or, to use the term Williams borrows from Foucault, "implanted" discourse of visible knowledge continue to exert considerable power over the social deployment and function of images. Porn not only taps into these discourses in the display of bodies, inviting the scrutiny of the gaze, but implies that the bodies it offers are ideal for interrogation and ultimately for pleasure.

Pornography thus provided an ideal forum for the assassination debates precisely because they, too, insisted on the principle of maximum visibility as the cornerstone for the "drive for knowledge." The epistemology that Williams claims for hard-core film also applies, I would argue, to the power of soft-core static imagery, even if the latter lacks the nonperformed signifier of bodily truth: the orgasm. Undoubtedly the temporal and spatial dimensions of hard-core film embody the "frenzy of the visible" to a far greater degree than soft-core photography, but the allure of the latter is still underwritten by a similar principle. The Zapruder footage, the autopsy photograph, and the pornographic image each offered up the film-body for interrogation, circulating in a context that insisted that to look was to learn. Frequently this context was the pages of the same magazine. Thus, during the mid-seventies, the epistemological conditions for the prolonged scrutiny of one set of imaged naked bodies facilitated the displacement of the gaze onto another set of bodies: those belonging to Kennedy and Lee Harvey Oswald.

Beyond this displacement, the nesting of Dallas imagery in porn publications often functioned as soft core's hard-core insert, with the Zapruder imagery operating as the equivalent of the snuff film. The 1975 appearance of the Zapruder film on national television and in soft-core magazines coincided with public discussion and concern over the production of snuff films. In her book, Williams argues that snuff films rested at the intersection of hard core and the slasher genre, carrying porn's ideology of the visible to its horrific extreme. Not content with the contours of the woman's body, snuff films imaged its dismemberment, extending the penetration of intercourse into the "penetrating violation of the body's very flesh."[31] Hard core's attempt to document the unperformed orgasm thus literalizes the climax as a "little death."

'Going all the way' in hard core could now encompass the possibility, already imagined by Bazin but not widely contemplated in the American popular filmic imagination, of the perverse pleasure of witnessing the involuntary spasm of death.[32]

What seems particularly disturbing about such visions, in the case not merely of Snuff but of violent aggression within pornography proper, is the sense in which a new form of the 'frenzy of the visible'—here, an involuntary spasm of pain culminating in death—becomes imaginable as a perverse substitute for the invisible involuntary spasm of orgasm that is so hard to see in the body of the woman. We see, then, how snuff seemed a perversely logical extension of hard core pornography's quest to see pleasure displaced onto pain.[33]

Zapruder's film could thus serve as a compensatory representation for the pleasure spasm which soft core could never quite image. It registered the violent spasm of Kennedy's body after the throat wound and, more importantly, after the fatal head shot. Indeed, the head snap in frames 313 through 315 became the site of an investigatory fetish, not only because they fixed a vision of the wound, but because interpretations differed as to the causes and meaning of the "involuntary spasm." Was Kennedy's body driven backwards by the force of a bullet fired from the front, or was its motion determined by a neuromuscular reaction to a blow to the brain area? The underground circulation and subsequent publication of JFK autopsy photos can be read as an extension of the same principle, the visual penetration of a body which on the surface cannot supply the necessary knowledge. But the Zapruder film stills, or sketches based on its most graphic frames, were the most widely reproduced images. The veracity of its pro-filmic event meant that despite the limitations of its being a still photograph, it achieved some status as a snuff equivalent.[34]

The fact remains, however, that whereas the Zapruder imagery may function in the snuff role, the mutilated body it represents is that of a man. My use of Williams's terms should not therefore be seen as a dismissal of the important argument she makes concerning the content of pornographic representations: the violence inflicted on the female body in either snuff or slasher films. We will see in subsequent chapters how Andy Warhol transferred the look from JFK to Jackie in his silkscreens drawn from images of the motorcade and how, in several Hollywood films, investigation into an assassination results in violence being done to a female character. However, both sets of representations — the assassination photos and the pornographic (but not snuff) imagery — display similar effects. In their respective searches for truth through "maximum visibility," both fall prey to repetition and delay. This is characterized in porn through the repetition of poses, camera angles, and scenarios of fantasy, a chain of arrangements that situates the body in increasingly familiar ways. The specificity of any particular body is surmounted by the dominance of any given trope. Thus, the look is displaced from one body to another with each monthly issue or new film, each body promising a new opportunity to look and seek knowledge. Assassination imagery was similarly subjected to repetitions, a rotation of surfaces picturing an ever-familiar set of bodies moving through a seemingly endless array of duplicated motions. Here, however, the bodies remain for the most part the same, so the repetitions seem intensified, more inescapable than the recurring poses of pornography.

As if revisiting the impact of the fatal bullets, the inquiries into the Zapruder film and the autopsy images penetrated clothing and flesh, stripping away layers of protective covering to search the body and learn the causes of death. As the contest over who would write the history of the assassination waged on, the body was repeatedly concealed and exposed, covered and uncovered, in gestures that came to approximate and feed off of the spirit of pornography. One dead body would surely have been enough to sustain this process, but as would be true throughout the debate, a doubling existed. For there was a second body to consider, one that also fell victim to a killer's bullet that weekend and subsequently also fell victim to a crisis of representation. This was, of course, a more mysterious body — the frequently doubled and decidedly uncanny figure of Lee Harvey Oswald.

Chapter 3 **Images of Oswald**

O
n June 3, 1960, FBI Director J. Edgar Hoover sent a memo to the State Department: "Since there is the possibility that an impostor is using Oswald's birth certificate, any current information the Department of State may have concerning subject will be appreciated."[1] Hoover's request may be the first hard copy suggesting possible confusion over the alleged assassin's identity, but that confusion would multiply throughout the next twenty years, culminating in October 1981 with the exhumation of the body buried in Oswald's grave.[2] Indeed, the shifting status of Lee Harvey Oswald in images and narratives again exemplifies the plight of representation in the assassination debates, marking a point at which its instability reached its uncanny limits.

The Backyard Photos

Narrative accounts of Oswald's activities and minibiographies of him were compiled and circulated immediately after the assassination. But none of the photographs that accompanied these texts implicated him directly or could be categorized as evidence proving Oswald was responsible for the shooting.[3] However, more incriminating photographic evidence would make its way into the public domain by February of the following year. On the day after the assassination, Dallas police allegedly discovered two photographs while searching the house of Mrs. Ruth Paine, the boarding house where Marina Oswald lived at the time of the assassination. Each allegedly showed Oswald standing in the back yard, a pistol holstered to his hip, holding the murder weapon, the Mannlicher-Carcano rifle, and two left-wing publications, *The Worker* and *The Militant*. When confronted with these photographs later that day, Oswald told his accusers that the pictures were forgeries, that his face had been superimposed onto someone else's body. News of the existence of the photographs made the papers of Sunday, November 24, but the photos were not published until the following year, when one of them ran on the front page of the *Detroit Free Press* on February 17, 1964. According to a *Newsweek* magazine article from March 2, a set of photographs, including one of Oswald holding the alleged murder weapon, had been offered anonymously to a *Life* photographer. After initially refusing the offer, *Life* purchased the photo from Marina Oswald's business advisor

71

for $5,000. However, other sets of Oswald photos were also in circulation, one of which was purchased by a *Detroit Free Press* reporter for $200. Before *Life* could run the Oswald-with-rifle picture on the cover of its February 21 issue, the Detroit paper featured it on page 1 on the 17th. Obtaining the photo from the *Detroit Free Press,* the Associated Press supplied copies to interested buyers so that the *New York Journal American* of February 18 and the *New York Times* of the 19th, were also able to scoop *Life*'s cover story.[4]

Regardless of where the photo ran first, by the end of February 1964 it had been prominently featured on newsstands across the country. The cover of *Life* read: "Lee Oswald with the weapons he used to kill President Kennedy and Officer Tippit." Inside that week's issue, *Life* ran the photograph uncropped and told its readers: "Dallas police have confirmed that this is the rifle found in the Texas School Book Depository." Oswald's posthumous prosecution was sustained by such journalistic reports, many of which neglected to include words such as *alleged* or *accused* before Oswald's name. Though the mainstream press had almost unanimously declared his guilt since November 22, visual evidence linking Oswald to the murder had not been presented to the public until the distribution of this photograph a full seven months before the Warren Commission concluded its investigation and published its findings.

Yet this imagery, like so much other imagery, operated within its own discursive formats, which were in turn regulated by various institutional demands. Thus it was not just a case of various publications printing the same photograph and accepting it as a reliable representation of the truth. The reliability of the photograph was not simply reflected by these publications — it was manufactured by them. The competition of the journalistic marketplace and the sensational nature of the photograph may well have compelled *Life,* the *New York Times,* and others to run the photograph without much attention to its authenticity, without probing the very circumstances of its production which were so essential to its status as evidence. Exactly how the journalism community deployed such imagery came under the Warren Commission's scrutiny, and it was through the commission's investigation that the demands of layout and publication were revealed to play a crucial role in the construction of truth.

In response to speculations about the backyard photos' inauthenticity, the Warren Commission asked FBI Special Agent Lyndal Shaneyfelt to examine them. He testified before the commission that the image that appeared on the cover of *Life* had in fact been retouched, and the commission gave the magazine an opportunity to respond to Shaneyfelt's testimony. In a telegram to the commission's general counsel dated June 25, 1964, and then in a letter dated June 29, *Life* editor Edward Thompson informed the commission that the "picture appeared in Europe with the telescopie [sic] sight retouched out" and that the photo had been cropped on the left to fit the shape of the magazine's cover. He further noted: "The retouching, as you can tell from comparing with the cover as published, was simply to bring the figure out a little more clearly."[5] Commission counsel also asked *Life* for a copy of the retouched print on which its cover reproduction was based. After the magazine's first response, commission counsel asked for the original print on which the retouching was done, and on providing this, *Life* editor Thompson wrote: "I note, on close examination, that the retoucher was a little careless in making the rifle stock straight instead of with a slight dip. There is a little more retouching around the bolt but a comparison with the original will convince you, I'm sure, that nothing essential has been changed."[6]

Commission counsel made similar inquiries of *Newsweek* and the *New York Times*. In a letter dated June 17, 1964, a *New York Times* assistant managing editor told the commission that, although the paper had retouched the Oswald photo, its adjustments did not "change the facts of the photograph — that is to say, it did not alter any essential feature of the photograph." His letter continues: "the only retouching that has been done is to outline Lee Harvey Oswald's head and right shoulder, to highlight the stock of the gun he is holding, to put a crease in his trousers and tone down somewhat the shadow cast by his figure." What the newspaper deemed unessential — especially the shadows behind the body — was in fact crucially important to commission critics. *Newsweek* responded a week later, informing the commission that during retouching "the technician inadvertently brushed out the telescopic sight."[7] The negotiating status of the photographic evidence was thus a result of different institutional practices, shifting definitions of what constituted essential facts of representation. Independent researchers who based their pre–Warren Report studies on evidence available through mainstream publications worked with imagery that had been altered but which they may have taken to be relatively unmediated forms of evidence. Indeed, depending on the source, a critic could be studying an image (in this case an image of a rifle) that differed considerably from what was being taken as an identical piece of evidence by another critic or by the government. Only perhaps through close readings of the Warren Commission volumes devoted to testimony and exhibits could such methodological pitfalls be avoided.

The commission recognized the backyard photographs as credible evidence against Oswald, but as early as March of 1964, assassination critics were already suggesting that the photos were not what they appeared to be; that in fact Oswald was telling the truth when he complained that the images had been forged in order to frame him for the murder.[8] Since that time, these two photographs[9] of Oswald have been the site of intense visual analysis, invoked either as evidence against him or as proof of a conspiracy to frame him.

Critics pointed out that, although the angle of the shadow cast along the ground by Oswald's body differs from one photo to another (presumably the pictures were taken moments apart), the angle of the shadow on his face cast by his nose (with his head cocked slightly to the left) remains the same. Marina Oswald testified that the pictures were taken on March 31, 1963, yet critics claimed that this date poses two problems: (1) the bushes behind Oswald appear in bloom, yet typically these plants are not even in bud at the end of March; and (2) although it appears a clear day with the sun casting a strong shadow behind Oswald, weather bureau records indicate that on March 31 the skies were cloudy and overcast. Like the still frames from the Zapruder film, the backyard photos were subjected to a series of optical inquiries. Independent analysts argued that a faintly discernible "grafting line" was detectable running just above Oswald's chin and that, whereas the portion above that line was from an image of Oswald, the portion below was not. The backyard pictures, it was argued, show Oswald with a square chin while other photos of him, most notably those taken while he was in police custody, show his chin to be pointed and cleft.[10]

The Uncanny at Work

The problems of representation articulated by the images of Oswald allow this discussion to open out slightly, to move away from the textual analysis of specific photographs to more general, albeit speculative, considerations. Perhaps more than the other imagery in question, the debate around Oswald and his representation addresses the uncanny intricacies of the assassination debates. I want to turn specifically to Sigmund Freud's essay "The Uncanny" in an attempt to further theorize the status of representation, employing his admittedly provisional conclusions on the subject less as a comprehensive explanatory model than as a useful vehicle for mapping the historiographic and interpretive process.[11]

In "The Uncanny," Freud is concerned with the causes of what he takes to be a fairly familiar form of psychic stress: feelings which, following the work of others, he links to a sense of terror and dread. He separates his discussion into two procedures: (1) an inquiry into the term *uncanny* (*unheimlich*) and its various meanings; and (2) a consideration of those events, objects, or experiences, aesthetic or outside the aesthetic, that produce feelings of the uncanny. He begins along the first path by citing the work of E. Jentsch and the latter's ascription of uncanniness to "intellectual uncertainty," a sense of not knowing where one is. But in his etymological research, Freud finds that the definition of *heimlich* has taken on a dual character, meaning both that which is familiar and that which is withheld from knowledge. He writes:

What interests us most in this long extract is to find that among its different shades of meaning the word heimlich exhibits one which is identical with its opposite, unheimlich. What is heimlich comes to be unheimlich. . . . In general we are reminded that the word heimlich is not unambiguous, but belongs to two sets of ideas, which without being contradictory are yet very different: on the one hand, it means that which is familiar and congenial and on the other, that which is concealed and kept out of sight.[12]

Etymologically, then, the uncanny has shifted between divergent meanings, between what is comfortable due to familiarity with one's environment (Jentsch's intellectual certainty) and what is on the side of anxiety, leading to dread due to concealment. What is crucially important with respect to dread is Freud's connection between uncanniness and questions of vision, the way that the psychic stress caused by the *unheimlich* is motivated by that which is "kept out of sight." Keeping to Jentsch's tentative formulation for the moment, epistemological certainty or uncertainty is thus less bound up with spatial orientation, of having a sense of where one is, than with having or being prevented from having visual access to objects or information.

This anxiety over the powers of sight and the potential for its loss is precisely what Freud takes up in the second half of his essay. He turns his interpretive skills to E. T. A. Hoffmann's short story "The Sand-Man," a tale into which Freud reads a number of uncanny elements. Most central is the dread experienced by the story's main character, Nathaniel, the fear of losing his eyes to the mysterious and ultimately evil Sand-Man. Seizing on this image, Freud discounts Jentsch's theory and locates uncanny dread in the fear of losing the organs of sight: "the feeling of something uncanny is directly attached to the figure of the Sand-Man, that is, to the idea of being robbed of one's eyes; and [that] Jentsch's point of an intellectual uncertainty has nothing to do with this effect."[13]

From here it is a quick step to associating fear over the loss of the eyes to castration anxiety. Freud, as one would perhaps expect, reads the former as a substitution for the latter, assigning priority to the more deeply rooted anxieties of the castration complex.[14] Indeed, much of the rest of the essay becomes devoted to locating elements of the uncanny within the more fundamental psychoanalytic categories Freud had developed up to that time: ego identification, primitive psychic beliefs about the omnipotence of thoughts, repetition compulsion.

For Freud, uncanny dread was related to the anxieties of repetition compulsion. In fact, one of the traits he assigns to it "is that class of the terrifying which leads back to something long known to us, once very familiar."[15] That familiar, terrifying, yet long-repressed knowledge is, of course, the encounter with castration. It is the deep-rooted and formative aspect of this experience that accounts for the extreme level of dread or anxiety reproduced by the uncanny object or situation. I would suggest, however, that the uncanny can be maintained as a category referring to extreme anxiety, still productive of a range of social/psychological phenomena (which I will discuss below) without relying on the repressed fear of castration. I suggest that the uncanny dread motivated by the Sand-Man and his threat to the eyes be explored without recourse to the castration complex and furthermore that Freud was mistaken when he saw no connection between Jentsch's notion of "intellectual uncertainty" and those definitions of *unheimlich* associated with concealment or loss of sight. The form of epistemological certainty threatened by the uncanny, with which I am interested here, may well be as formative as the knowledge acquired by way of the castration complex but is founded on the cultural discourses discussed earlier with respect to the writings of Comolli, those discourses that have, certainly since Freud's own time, linked truth with the visible.

It is precisely this relationship between knowledge and the visible, constructed along that path from perspective painting to photography to cinema and as much an aspect of the viewing subject as it is an effect of technology, that is put into crisis by the instability of representation running through the assassination debates. Whereas for Freud uncanny terror is manifested through fear of blindness, the Sand-Man's pleasure in stealing young boys' eyes, the assault on vision occasioned by the assassination inquiries was of a somewhat different order. Apart from various classified materials, the visual evidence was not totally concealed from the gaze of the public or of critics. Rather, the problem of visibility arose from the inability to make a wealth of images cohere in a stable explanatory scene. The uncanny anxieties of the case are in fact accentuated by this dilemma because the bodies represented in the motorcade film or the photographs of Oswald were not kept from sight but were available for close analysis. The result, though, was still a form of "intellectual uncertainty" which was continually buttressed by the discovery or reinterpretation of new evidence. It was not just that new evidence overrode old evidence — that the Zapruder film, for example, nullified the other footage shot in Dealey Plaza because of its superior perspective, or that film evidence superseded still photographs — but that individual pieces — the Zapruder film, an autopsy sketch — had to have their own status reevaluated as either new methods of analysis, new methods of looking, or other evidence became available.

Haunted by Doubles

Despite my interest in shifting Freud's emphasis from castration to an anxiety over the visible, the uncanny elements he identifies in his essay are clearly applicable to the assassination case. Paramount among these is the figure of the double. Although he is ultimately unable to account for the severe feelings of uncanniness resulting from encounters with the double, Freud, borrowing from the work of Otto Rank, claims that this mirroring figure performed a self-saving function for the ego. The double with which the self can identify "was originally an insurance against destruction of the ego, an 'energetic denial of the power of death', as Rank says; and probably the 'immortal' soul was the first 'double' of the body."[16]

The motif of the double haunts the assassination investigation, but not as an ego-saving mechanism for the critics. The bizarre splittings of identity that run throughout the inquiries are the result of a combination of factors: the illegibility of representation, the already-constituted force of the double as a narrative trope, and the eyewitness testimony and evidence pertaining to the case. Most relevant to the present discussion are the theories of doubling that became attached to Lee Harvey Oswald. The identity of the alleged assassin was characterized by ever-increasing mutations as critics juxtaposed images of Oswald and found in them serious discrepancies. On the basis of photographs alone, and without the corroborating stories built around them, several Oswalds are identified. Images of Oswald with Marina in Minsk appear to show a man of softer features than images of him recorded in New Orleans or Dallas a year or two later. As already discussed, the authenticity of the well-known backyard photos was questioned in part because they appear to depict Oswald with a different facial structure than other images of him. Indeed, to work closely and continuously with this literature is to see a multifaced synthesis of imagery attached to the signifier "Oswald," a synthesis that, depending on the context — his years in Russia, in New Orleans, in the Dallas jail — seems to slide smoothly through a series of Zeliglike transformations.

In 1966, Richard Popkin consolidated the various eyewitness accounts of multiple Oswalds into a theory that an impostor had been used to frame Lee Harvey Oswald for the murder.[17] He and subsequent writers pursued a trail of Oswalds during the three months leading up to the assassination. In September of 1963, a man resembling Oswald appeared at the Selective Service office in Austin, Texas, seeking alterations in his military discharge. The Warren Commission, however, locates Oswald in Mexico City at this time. In November of 1963, a man identifying himself as Lee Harvey Oswald test-drives a car at a Lincoln-Mercury dealership in downtown Dallas, frightening the salesman along the way by driving 70 miles per hour on the highway. And yet other sources have Oswald at home in Irving, Texas, on this day. Furthermore, critics claimed Oswald did not know how to drive. Among the many multiple and contradictory sightings of Oswald, was one on September 26, 1963, when a Mrs. Sylvia Odio was allegedly visited by three men; she would later identify Lee Harvey Oswald as the one introduced as Leon Oswald. She testified that the men inquired whether she, a leader in Cuban refugee activities, would contribute to violent anti-Castro activities and that when one of the men called on the following day, he (not Oswald) made references to presidential assassination. The Warren Commission ultimately disregarded the Odio story, concluding that Oswald was in transit to Mexico at the time, but the unresolved details of her story were repeatedly cited by critics as a major episode among many involving the Oswald double.[18]

As with the evidence surrounding Kennedy's body, Oswald's medical documents also contributed to theories of multiple identity. A 1956 Marine Corps medical exam listed Oswald as 5'8" with hazel eyes. His Marine Corps exam from three years later had him at 5'11" tall with gray eyes. Records for a job physical from July 1962, however, listed his height as 5'9". The arrest bulletin issued by Dallas police as well as FBI files referred to him as 5'10", while Oswald's autopsy put him back at 5'9" with gray-blue eyes.[19]

If there was a solitary Oswald, he no doubt contributed to the process of his own doubling, producing aliases throughout his adult life. Variations on his name, such as O. H. Lee, appear on letters and official documents. Even more popular was some variation of the name Hidell: Oswald gave Robert Hidell as a reference; Dr. A. J. Hideel was found on a vaccination form; A. J. Hidell was the name on identification cards found on Oswald when he was arrested the day of the assassination, including a Selective Service card bearing his photo; Alec Hidell was listed as the only other member of the Fair Play for Cuba Committee (FPCC), an organization in which Oswald was the only local member.[20] Although the Warren Commission wrote off Hidell as a fictitious identity invented for the FPCC, the name is far from trivial in the case, serving as the link between Oswald and the alleged murder weapons. The Mannlicher-Carcano and the revolver allegedly used to kill Dallas Police Officer Tippit were purchased in Hidell's name.

The presence of the double throughout the case, especially as it involved questions of Oswald's identity, can be explained in part by the possibility of conspiracy, a situation in which aliases or multiple identities would be expected. But the diversity and character of doubling patterns here must also be linked to the constantly shifting status of representation. The double as it appeared in the assassination investigations embodied a crisis of vision precisely because it was so often a product of the investment in and expectations associated with the epistemology of the visible. That is, doubles appear as a result of a faith in camera-enhanced looking, the trust that additional pieces of image-based evidence might compensate for the inadequacies of other forms of representation. Thus, the inadequacy of the Zapruder film is counterbalanced by the filmed reenactment produced for the Warren Commission. In the reenactment, stand-ins and doubles abound — for Kennedy, for Zapruder, and most importantly for Oswald. The recreation of the assassin's proposed lines of sight, a double for his vision, is constructed to compensate for the visible limits of the Zapruder film. As with the Muybridge experiments Williams discusses, new visible bodies are presented. This motorcade and these bodies are for representation, but the stand-in for Oswald is there not to provide the sight of a body previously unseen, but rather to record in somewhat more ideal fashion his alleged view of bodies we already know quite well.

Similarly, when confronted with the questions concerning the authenticity of the backyard photos, the FBI sought to compensate by recreating the photograph. FBI agent Shaneyfelt simulated one of the backyard pictures by photographing another agent holding the Mannlicher-Carcano in roughly the same pose as that struck by the original figure. But there seems to have been almost no reason for this photographic simulation other than the sheer accumulation of additional compensatory representation. In his testimony before the Warren Commission, Shaneyfelt was asked if his simulated backyard photo helped the FBI deduce whether the rifle pictured in it (and thus, one assumes, the rifle in the original) is the same rifle found on the sixth floor of the School Book Depository. The question borders on the ridiculous, because the rifle Shaneyfelt used for the simulation *was* the one found on the sixth floor and was given to him for the purposes of the simulation.

Far more to the point would have been queries about the nature of the shadows cast behind and on the face of the agent posing with the rifle, especially since Shaneyfelt apparently sought in his simulation to match up the angle of the sun as it fell on the original figure in the back yard. And yet the face in the simulation is blocked out, the agent appearing as a gunman without a head. This image, essentially worthless as evidence, rather absurdly comes to redouble the intrigue about the identity of the backyard figure and calls into question its very purpose. The headless FBI agent in the photographed simulation suggests with rare uncanniness the very point it was meant to disprove: the possibility that the "real" face has been removed from the backyard photo so that Oswald's might be matted in. As I have stated and as this photograph testifies, the instability of assassination imagery was not solely a result of post–Warren Report attacks on government procedures (although they served in large part as catalyst) but was a process already initiated by the state's faith in and deployment of representation.

Whereas the identity of Lee Harvey Oswald was explicitly linked to various doubles through the course of the debate, a far subtler double for him was implied immediately after the murder, during the period leading up to the release of the Warren Report. That double was the president himself.[21]

Here the double is not so much a figure in likeness as a mirrored inversion. Both Oswald and Kennedy were married with two children, but whereas the president was a genuine leader, a figure in history, his double was understood as a self-deluded leader whose illegitimate claims to greatness and absence from history are posed as the motivation behind his lethal actions. Where Kennedy is glamorous, Oswald is plain; where Kennedy represents sexual prowess, Oswald, it is reported, suffers from sexual malfunction.[22]

For all their talk of Oswald's loneliness and isolation and of the madness of his crime, most commentators needed to picture him, like his noble victim, as a representative man. Oswald represented—such was the official consensus—the worst in American life, just as Kennedy represented the best and the brightest.[23]

Oswald is thus constructed as a double so that his identity might be imbued with guilt. Motive is written into his portrait as an aspect of character such that whatever limits may be posed by the evidence, especially the visual evidence, they cannot ultimately obstruct the prosecution. The construct of the double here also serves its function, as outlined by Freud and Rank, with respect to preservation. In juxtaposition with Oswald, Kennedy's image, as it was understood in 1964, remains intact, and his identity can continue to turn around issues of style. The shooting itself can be written as an encounter of personalities.

Yet other, seemingly stranger examples of doubling do appear in response to the crisis of the visible. Some critics sought bizarre comparisons between Kennedy and Abraham Lincoln: both had a "lazy muscle" affecting one eye; both had relatives who became U.S. attorney general; before elected president each had a sister die; both were succeeded by vice presidents named Johnson; Kennedy was shot riding in a Ford Lincoln whereas Lincoln was shot sitting in Ford's Theater. At least one book-length study brought the medical and ballistics evidence of their assassinations together in one volume.[24] Juxtaposing images and narratives pertaining to Lincoln's assassination, while not advancing the JFK investigation, served merely to add representation to a debate in which the visible evidence continuously faltered in its support of specific claims.

A further uncanny component of these debates has to do with the double as an effect of representation. In his essay, Freud offers as a first example of the uncanny encounters in which it is difficult to tell whether a specific object or figure is alive. Citing Jentsch again, in an extremely suggestive remark, he writes:

Jentsch has taken as a very good instance "doubts whether an apparently animate being is really alive; or conversely, whether a lifeless object might not in fact be animated"; and he refers in this connection to the impression

made by wax-work figures, artificial dolls and automatons. He adds to this class the uncanny effect of epileptic seizures and the manifestations of insanity, because these excite in the spectator the feeling that automatic, mechanical processes are at work, concealed beneath the ordinary appearance of animation.[25]

In the uncanny feeling of dread experienced when one sees an epileptic seizure, in witnessing what Freud calls "automatic, mechanical processes," echoes the impression of watching the uncontrolled reflex of the president's head snap as it is struck by the bullet in Zapruder frame 313. It is the fright engendered by encounters with what appears to be unmediated, unperformed, unfaked. It speaks, so one thinks, to some truth of the body. Thus, frame 313 functions here not unlike the visible male orgasm in Williams's discussion of hard core. It records the president's "involuntary convulsion" and, as will be noted later, will function as the "money shot" for Oliver Stone's *JFK*. A similar though far less uncanny impression might be associated with the images of Oswald's death, but here the cleanliness of the wound and the almost theatrical way in which the victim doubled over (in some way suggesting the performed) seem to mitigate the terror of the spectacle. There is, however, something more frightening in the audio recording of this shooting, in Oswald's cries of pain, which seem more in line with the "automatic, mechanical processes" to which Freud refers.

Also operating in certain assassination texts is the uncanny effect caused by confusion over whether an object is animate or not, the dread aroused by "wax-work figures, artificial dolls and automatons." Autopsy imagery may always suggest this confusion, but the effect is accentuated in the assassination literature by the seemingly continuous alterations ascribed to the president's dead body. The slow process of public revelation — verbal descriptions and postautopsy sketches from the doctors in 1963 and 1964, the questions raised about these descriptions in light of other physical evidence, the report of the Clark Panel, then the release of x rays and the autopsy photos — imaged a body that seemed to change in death, to be reanimated with each new piece of forensic evidence. Kennedy was dead but his corpse kept changing, wounds appeared and disappeared, parts of the cranium were intact according to one study, absent in another. Some critics even claimed there had been surgery on the head prior to the official autopsy, suggesting that the president's forehead had been reconstructed at some point. Images of the corpse on the autopsy table, its eyes and mouth open, only enhanced the "artificial doll" effect, the limits of this uncanny confusion being the scandal sheet declarations that, in fact, Kennedy was not dead, that he had survived the shooting. Recall that, for Foucault, the autopsy revealed "the space of the organism and the time of the disease," that which belonged to the body and that to the infiltration of death. But the mapping and remapping of Kennedy's body kept shifting the apparent details of the causes of death. The uncanny effect is sustained not because there is genuine doubt as to whether Kennedy is dead, but because the causes of death, ostensibly verifiable by the voluminous representation used to document it, cannot be satisfactorily articulated.

A somewhat different, though still related effect characterized the mutability of Oswald's body. Here it is not so much a question of the body in death as much as an uncertainty over its defining features. Yet this uncertainty carries the sanction of death in that there is no living body against which to verify the fluctuating representation of the last thirty years. Oswald comes to appear as a man of many faces, somewhat freakish in that regard, more suitable for the circus or fairground, in line with the genre of spectacle one might associate with the wax museum. For some he can be constructed in terms of the Manchurian candidate, an individual whose humanity has been removed in order to program a guilt-free assassin.[26] Even without such a hyperbolic characterization, the bulk of assassination literature succeeds at creating a Zeliglike portrait. Oswald is linked, often convincingly, with FBI or CIA operatives and had contact with the KGB while in the Soviet Union. Theories stressing his multiple connections to these organizations have the cumulative effect of constructing Oswald as easily manipulated, a patsy or fall guy devoid of human will or agency. In this sense he can appear similar to Freud's automaton, a figure whose uncanniness is in constant negotiation with its representation.

Narrative as Confession

Oswald as changing man or the president's reversed double stemmed not only from the complexities of the visual evidence but from the absence of an official confession. As a result, the accumulated imagery became linked with an ever-widening pattern of narrativization. It should be clear by now that the process of narrating the events surrounding the assassination was set in motion when Kennedy arrived at Parkland Memorial Hospital in Dallas.[27] Despite my emphasis on the degree to which images negotiated between legibility and an epistemological anxiety, I want to stress that this crisis was thoroughly bound up with a destabilizing of narrative. Indeed, writing the history of the assassination was never understood by anyone — even the editors at *Life,* where pictures often overwhelmed the words that framed them — as solely a process of juxtaposing the right images. The Warren Report is structured largely as a series of interlocking stories. The opening section, titled "Narrative of Events," works according to a strict chronology and is followed by biographies of the major players. Subsequent investigators also frequently, and not surprisingly, relied on the organizing function of narrative. In fact, many of the early critics devoted their energies to piecing together in storylike form the evidence they felt the commission had treated fragmentarily. As perhaps the outstanding example of this, commission critics decried the fact that the government's twenty-six volumes of testimony and exhibits were unindexed, that to read the commission's report in detail was a narrative nightmare.

Over the next thirty years the nightmare would become recurrent. My analysis of the image-based texts has already hinted at, if not directly addressed, the crisis spiraling out of the multiple scenarios manufactured around the assassination. What I want to discuss briefly here are the most salient examples of narrative compensation resulting from this crisis, the way that the multilayered narratives about Dealey Plaza and its surrounding episodes were displaced onto or written in tandem with various meta- or supernarratives. It is important to keep in mind, however, that these forms of text became almost immediately inseparable from the analyses of photographic and film imagery and the problems of its fluctuating legibility or the issue of the double.

It should not be surprising that the Warren Report suggests a discursive strategy that characterized much of the subsequent literature on the case — especially those studies supporting the government's conclusions. That strategy juxtaposed biography and material evidence, largely because there was no confession on which to found a set of conclusions. In *The History of Sexuality,* Foucault stresses the cultural connections between confession and truth, a relationship not relevant only to his study of the *scientia sexualis* but to most contemporary conceptions of self-knowledge: "In any case, next to the testing rituals, next to the testimony of witnesses, and the learned methods of observation and demonstration, the confession became one of the West's most highly valued techniques for producing truth. We have since become a singularly confessing society."[28]

Working with a set of visual representations that were periodically thrown into states of interpretive flux and lacking an admission of guilt from Oswald, the investigation produced narratives that could function as a substitute confession. Thus the psychological studies that mapped out a litany of minor emotional or psychic disturbances to tell the truth in Oswald's absence, drawing motive from a posthumous portrait.[29] Most significant among these was Priscilla Johnson McMillan's *Marina and Lee,* a detailed biography of the couple based in large part on extensive interviews with Marina Oswald.[30] Accepting that the Warren Commission had fully explained the logistics of the shooting, McMillan sought to answer questions of motive. She argued that, having been relegated to the margins of history, Oswald acted out of a mixture of resentment and delusions of grandeur.

McMillan's book gave volume to an old thesis. As early as 1964 and *Life*'s publication of Oswald's "Russian Diary," the mainstream press had effectively substituted questions of why for questions of how.[31] But note how McMillan's book was reviewed, the terms in which its reception was framed in 1977. In the *New York Times Book Review,* Thomas Powers performs the investigative sleight of hand, arguing that the facts of the shooting must be made to conform to the biography of the alleged assassin.

If skeptics are to preserve their conspiracies, they will have to squeeze them into the corners of Oswald's life. McMillan achieves with art what the Warren Commission failed to do with its Report and 26 volumes of lawyerly analysis, testimony and supporting evidence. She makes us see. [italics his][32]

Recognizing the crisis of vision which by 1977 had thoroughly saturated the case, Powers finds in McMillan's biographical confession the "truth" that apparently cannot be elicited from images. He also finds in it a rebuttal to whatever has been deduced from the visual evidence, implying that to make Oswald "come alive," as McMillan has done, is to make gunmen on the grassy knoll disappear. But the sense in which Oswald "comes alive" in these studies creates a curiously paradoxical subject. On the one hand, the circumstances of Oswald's life — the absence of his father, his domineering mother, his slight physical stature — helped produce a resentful loner whose alienation prompted the violence of the assassination. According to this profile, Oswald, though constantly frustrated in his endeavors, remains a determined individual, able to move to the Soviet Union and then back to the United States and able to assassinate the president. On the other hand, it is suggested that at some point in his personal history, Oswald's agency, his determined responses to the frustrations he encountered, gives way to some larger force. Oswald is no longer himself but a figure out of a Proppian character typology, his actions overdetermined by an archetypal narrative.

There is a dimension of human existence in which it seems that the individual who acts is not the true agent directing his action. He acts, he is the one who presses the trigger, but it is as though something beyond him is doing it. . . . Something that is more than personal, causes the event to happen. Thus the continuity of events within the life of Lee Harvey Oswald, his questing and his repeated frustration, all the inner continuity of his life which is what comprises the <u>psychology</u> of the person, drew him to the time and place at which the shooting occurred.[33]

Language like this nearly returns us to Freud's uncanny automaton. And just as the photographic imagery of Oswald suggested the changing man so, too, do the confessional biographies and psychological studies: Oswald as Oedipus, as Sir Modred killing King Arthur, as the youngest and most pampered child, as the figure who knew emotional deprivation throughout childhood. Set within the terms of child psychology or the history of literature, the Oswald biographical texts fell into various narrative economies, the primary function of which was to displace the evidence connecting Oswald to the crime onto various psychological and sociological questions. The messy and morbid details of the case were left to the "buffs" while other authors, their status affirmed by the cultural legitimacy of their discourse, shifted the national agenda to less threatening and ultimately unanswerable questions.

In the liberal and in the national news media as a whole, speculation about the assassination thus came to hinge not on the question of whether Oswald murdered Kennedy unassisted—a question left for the most part, in the Sixties, to "cranks" and "conspiracy-mongers"—but on the seemingly much larger, momentous question of what his action revealed about the national psyche.[34]

Oswald, then, was no longer a player in the assassination of JFK as much as a symptom in a larger and, for some, more troubling national story. In the ensuing literature, Oswald becomes both a central and a marginal figure: he is positioned at the center of various psychological narratives, many of which are Oedipal, and is offered as a prime example of the assassin syndrome. In these reports, the affect is that of Oswald and his doubles. In the hope of constructing a psychological category through which Oswald's actions might be satisfactorily explained, clinicians describe psychiatric patients whose social positions and individual profiles are similar to his.[35]

But in the attempt to construct such interpretive categories, the psychological literature contributes to yet another tendency of the assassination debates: one that simultaneously marginalizes Oswald and shifts attention away from the specifics of Dallas. This tendency is the supernarrative, the way the multiple scenarios and the crisis of the image-based evidence resulted, by the end of the sixties, in the JFK case's being written as part of a larger narrative—either the history of assassination in the United States or the problem of social violence in contemporary America.[36] Both of these larger narratives are found in the various reports issued through the National Commission on the Causes and Prevention of Violence established in June of 1968 by President Johnson.

Although clearly a response to the deaths of Robert Kennedy and Martin Luther King, Jr., and the urban violence of the mid-sixties, the report by the commission's Task Force on Assassination and Political Violence also served as an extended sequel to the Warren Report.[37] Written and published amid the second wave of anti–Warren Commission literature—the Thompson and Meagher books, the Garrison trial—this new report functioned to seal the conclusions of 1964 into a master history of American political violence, seamlessly encoding the government's case against Oswald alongside the stories of presidential assassins Booth, Guiteau, and Czolgosz. In the report of the task force, the history of assassinations becomes, in turn, a set of episodes within a grander narrative: the tradition of violence in America. The causes of political murder are considered not in terms of individual cases but within a discussion of the traditions of vigilantism and political extremism that are said to be part of American culture. As with the psychological Oswald biographies, the result is a form of deflection in which the specifics of the Dallas shooting are partially obscured by the historical survey. In the early seventies, with many commission critics on the retreat after the Garrison case, the point of focus was frequently deflected even further as these narratives explored not only the psychology of the assassin and the society, but the psychology of the conspiracy theorist as well.

Like Oswald, critics of the Warren Report were put on the couch and found to be suffering from their own anxieties within the family drama. Constructing conspiracy theories was, according to some accounts, the reaction of those unable to face the idea of parricide or the fragility of everyday life.

If we must suffer parricide, if our father is to be taken from us, he must be taken by a most powerful, if malignant, counterforce. We cannot lose him to a casual crank. To do so is to stand shivering and unprotected, not only bereft of our father but exposed within ourselves to our own vulnerability. Far better to be convinced of a manichean diabolism than a trivial mechanical doll as the instrument of our destruction.

. . . We cannot hope to convince those whose own psychic needs require a belief in such conspiracies. We can, however, comfort the many who accept the overwhelming evidence of the lone, mentally ill assassin, but who still feel disturbed and uneasy about that evidence. This uneasiness is a product of the primal anxieties created by the archetypal crime of parricide—not the inadequacy of the lone assassin.[38]

Two crucial substitutions characterize these suggestive paragraphs. First, the president is replaced by the reader as bereavement gives way to "our own" exposure. The common citizen now feels "unprotected." Second, Oswald, again in uncanny fashion, is replaced by "a trivial mechanical doll." The result is the negation of historical specificity, for the political identities of JFK and Oswald are obscured, and the ahistorical narrative about primal anxieties is mapped onto their figures. The intended effect, as the authors explicitly state, is to "comfort" the uneasy, the implication being that the curious or the unconvinced need therapy. Indeed, critics of the Warren Report were frequently characterized as suffering some medical condition. They represented malignancies on the body politic, they had "conspiracy fever."[39] More often, the skeptics were diagnosed as needing to find order in chaos.

The total senselessness of the attacks has led them to construct theories to "make sense" of the seemingly unexplainable. Despite the lack of evidence, they have constructed theories of political conspiracy that make the assertion a "logical" outcome of its irrational assumption.[40]

The Struggle over Authorship

The broad historical survey and the displaced confession of the psychological biography were two forms of compensation for the narrative instability surrounding the assassination. Both succeeded at drawing attention away from the political implications of the work being done by commission critics, undermining the challenge they posed to the government's role as author of history. But it would be inaccurate to say that these narrative displacements resulted strictly from a crisis of the visible. Although the unstable status of assassination imagery was a contributing factor, the various narrative forms that developed around the case were clearly mobilized by existing social discourses. The terms of popular psychology had been thoroughly internalized, and the institutional structures of sociologists, demographers, and opinion pollsters were in place more than during any previous time or any comparable event.[41] These structures carried with them a social legitimacy upon which both the government and its critics could draw in the battle for historical authorship. But whereas the sociological community accumulated a wealth of data purporting to reflect mass opinion — the public's emotional reaction to the death, the percentages of those who felt Oswald acted alone — the publication of these data was generally found in volumes that tacitly endorsed the government's conclusions.

Indeed, the struggle between the government and its critics continued to amount to a contest over the legitimacy of discourse. The images of illness that were used to characterize the Commission's critics can also be read as attacks on the cultural space from which the critics worked.[42] They were painted as small town muckrakers or a network of housewives. They were self-appointed experts or part-time historians. Throughout the debate the boundaries of legitimate authorship shifted, seemingly along with the status of the photographic evidence. During the period 1966–1967, with the reevaluation of the Zapruder film in several mainstream periodicals and the increasingly widespread challenge to the government's position on Vietnam, assassination critics achieved a tenuous legitimacy. The outcome of the Garrison trial eroded that legitimacy, however, driving critics away from officially sanctioned forums for the discussion of their work. But by the midseventies, a further reexamination of the visual evidence (the nationwide airing of the enhanced Zapruder film) combined with another challenge to government legitimacy (the congressional probes first into CIA and FBI activities and then the HSCA) re-elevated the critics' status until roughly 1980.

Throughout that time, the critics' work succeeded at exposing crucial questions of historical authorship. Without recourse to or knowledge of Foucault's language, the collective effect of the critics' varied approaches and arguments was to articulate the concluding questions from "What Is an Author?"[43] The critics traced the channels through which the evidence flowed, sought to determine who controlled those channels, articulated the links between assassination theories and their institutional sources, and critiqued each other's work. The critics' own form of deconstruction mirrored the multilevel struggle for authorship that their investigative work exposed and enacted.

The government's historiographic efforts necessarily relied on a network of authors. The Warren Report, its writing assigned to various subgroups, was based on the reports filed by the FBI and Secret Service as well on investigations carried out by the commission itself.[44] Yet despite the ways the report foregrounded its multiple authorship through references to testimony or tests conducted by the FBI, the commission ultimately appeared to speak in a unified voice, a voice further solidified by its support in the mainstream press. Commission critics splintered this voice, highlighting contradictions or discrepancies between the accounts offered by federal agencies. They characterized the Warren Report itself as a place where various forms of authorship clashed and theory struggled with evidence. As critics and conspiracy theorists collaborated or debated among themselves for the next three decades, this struggle became the defining feature of the assassination debates. As much as new investigations attempted to engage with that evidence most relevant to their points of inquiry — the shooting, Oswald's ties to organized crime, the autopsy — each had to take part in the ever-increasing metadiscussion concerning historiographic issues. As such, individual texts often devoted less space to investigating some aspect of the assassination than to critiquing the existing surface of its representation. Undoubtedly, the early critical works were analyses of representation, but the later works came to enact a kind of analysis once removed. One unavoidable consequence was that assassination literature became increasingly difficult to comprehend for those who had not kept diligently up to date with developments, with new studies which often found their way into the forum through somewhat obscure channels. The debate thus became an ever more private dialogue, circulating by way of limited-edition, privately printed books or buff newsletters. This limited the general public's access to the topic but increased bibliographic demands on the buff. It also meant greater alienation between the buffs and mainstream institutions, which were perceived as increasingly uninformed about the case.

The shifts in the legitimacy of authorship can be gauged by a crucial difference between the Warren Commission and the House Select Committee on Assassinations. In the case of the select committee, the government clearly granted provisional validity to critics and buffs, recognizing that the case had grown so complex that "official" agents of investigation may not have been fully or satisfactorily qualified to author a second inquiry. Thus the House committee not only drew on the vast literature of dissent but actually called upon various critics to assist in the new investigation.[45] This extremely mild form of inclusion came after some fifteen years of confrontation. Throughout the sixties and mid-seventies, at various times and places, in a climate characterized by widespread attacks on government policies, the authors of the official version were challenged to defend their conclusions in person, debating assassination critics at forums held across the country. When not directly confronted, supporters of the commission's account were assailed in abstentia as critics toured the college lecture circuit criticizing the Warren Report.

Two other responses to narrative instability and the problems of authorship deserve brief mention. One was the fictionalizing of the assassination. This will be a central issue in the chapter devoted to the commercial cinema and its deployment of assassination issues. But it is worth noting here that the fictionalizing of the characters and events surrounding the case *could* take part in a process that delegitimated the commission's critics. The novelistic borrowing of images or ideas from the inquests could have the reciprocal effect of making those inquests appear fantastic. As a result, questions of the legitimacy of discourse shift from authorship issues to those of genre: the more that assassination studies resembled fiction or that fiction resembled assassination research, the less commission critics seemed to be the proper source for historical revision.

I am not insisting on the impermeable boundaries between fiction and history here, nor am I going to recount the blurred distinctions between these categories. But I do want to note that the struggle over discursive legitimacy and the status of authorship was so central to the assassination debates that the novelizing of various theories could make truth appear the exclusive domain of "official sectors." Fiction begins to appear the last refuge of the conspiracy theorist, whose identity slides from historian to novelist or from historian to fictional character. The latter transposition is exemplified by Edmund Aubrey's *The Case of the Missing President*.[46] This work concludes that Lee Harvey Oswald served, perhaps unwittingly, as part of a conspiracy and presents the critic in the form of Sherlock Holmes. At book's end, the British crime sleuth offers his findings to a roomful of U.S. government officials and dignitaries. The narrative content of such works did not necessarily undermine the efforts of more "serious" writers, nor did such texts seriously sidetrack the investigation. Still, these fictions could serve to classify the work of assassination critics as outside the boundaries of historical investigation.

Much depended, however, on the status of the author in question, on the way his or her reputation was founded on critical endorsement, or on the other subjects about which he or she wrote. Indeed, well before Don De-Lillo's *Libra* brought literary respectability to the subject, novelists and literary critics were being suggested as the proper candidates to author a new investigation. In 1966 Norman Mailer proposed that a new inquiry be organized under the leadership of Dwight Macdonald and Edmund Wilson.[47] The implication was that the critical powers of such writers could muster the disparate and confusing evidence into a plausible and coherent account. These would be men and women whose credentials as cultural critics certified their understanding of character, who had insight into motive, and who had mastered the trade of fashioning narrative. It was also implied that those who had toiled in the realm of the aesthetic could bring to their work a moral clarity unfettered by politics. And so, poet Allen Ginsberg wrote:

Norman Mailer's style of personal critique, for instance, carries more information than the inferior prose style of the Warren Commission report. . . . Mailer's proposal for a commission of literary persons whose goodness of temperament is more trustworthy than that of politicians makes simple common sense. The nation's in a mess. Dwight Macdonald's as trustworthy to straighten it out as LeRoi Jones or President Johnson.[48]

To commission critics there often seemed a sharp disparity between who was best able to clean up the mess and who could officially declare that the mess was gone. In a way that ultimately limited their critique's potential, assassination critics consistently looked to the government for an official sanctioning of their efforts. By repeatedly calling upon the state to reopen the investigation and by insisting that previous wrongs could only be righted through a federal acknowledgment of the Warren Commission's mistaken conclusions, the critics reinforced the government's status as legitimator of discourse. Various buffs and assassination public interest groups saw a new congressional investigation as the goal to which their work inevitably pointed.[49] Many who had called into serious question the procedures, if not the motives, of the Warren Commission and the various federal agencies that conducted the investigation still needed institutional endorsement. In part, this clinging to state authority fed off of what now appears as a naive faith in the ultimate righteousness of those who held public office, or in the moral force of constitutional law above and beyond those invested with power.

In fact, there is a hyperpatriotic tone to much of the literature of dissent, an insistence that truth has a will of its own which the American system, perhaps slowly but inevitably, will allow to emerge. This faith in or reliance on institutions that are simultaneously being critiqued is accompanied by a simultaneous acknowledgment of social change and a fear of collapse. The literature interprets Kennedy's death as no doubt tragic and irretrievably the catalyst for deep changes in society. But these works' apocalyptic tone is based not just on the assassination but on the fear that the killers have gone unpunished. In this sense, the critics made an important intervention in insisting that the problem lay not in the national psyche but in the institutional procedures of government. And it was their investigative efforts, rather than the so-called end of Camelot, that made the assassination part of the era's wider culture of contestation. But the perceived failure of justice also gave rise to rhetorical flourishes by assassination critics who warned of the collapse of the social structure, as if only this event would determine the future course of American institutions.

I believe deeply that our society is not safe when a murdered President can be dishonored with a palpably inadequate and entirely unsatisfactory official investigation by the government that succeeded him, by a dubious inquest that is not unfairly designated a "whitewash." No president and the institution of the presidency are ever safe when this can happen, and it did happen. All of the basic institutions of our society are thus in jeopardy.[50]

And most Americans know that the tragic and almost sacred moment that unites so many people in this country has been profaned by a government that has, now for almost twelve years, suppressed the evidence and hidden the truth. Zola wrote, "if you shut up truth and bury it under the ground, it will grow and gather to itself such explosive power that the day it bursts through, it will blow up everything in its way."[51]

Cooperating with this faith in a new congressional investigation was the idealization of JFK. A government-sponsored inquiry that revealed the truth of conspiracy would not only honor the slain president but also restore an institutional integrity which critics believed had been lost along with him. The mourning of Kennedy's promise, no matter how substantive that promise may really have been, sought solace not only in the apprehension of the guilty parties but implicitly in a mythical vision of America redeemed. In the process, the assassination literature took part in the wider social dialogue concerning Kennedy's politics and contributed over the years to a reevaluation of his tenure in the White House. For some, this meant constructing Kennedy the liberal, target of the far right, whose death forever changed the course of foreign and domestic policy. What went wrong throughout the rest of the decade was read in terms of Kennedy's absence, and critics in search of either motive or post-mortems struggled to find in "the thousand days" signs of a never-realized future for civil rights and Vietnam.[52] For some investigators, JFK as icon of a more innocent America inspired a search not only for killers but for a restoration of the self. The rhetoric of nostalgia for a pre-Dallas identity, ultimately unobtainable, gave the continuing inquiries as much a personal as a political challenge, each critic seeing in its resolution a debt owed to him or herself.

For the extreme left, Dallas does not matter. Kennedy, they say, was no different from his successors. Only we know he was, and that, because of him, we were as well. In that sense, his assassination killed a bit of all of us.[53]

Assassination critics often framed their work in such terms: a search for truth as much as a critique of government practices, personal vindication alongside a search for assassins. Within this context it is important to underscore the parallel between the status of representation and the status of the state in authoring history. Just as assassination critics had faith in the knowledge-bearing powers of the image and yet had this faith repeatedly called into question, so, too, was their critique of the government persistently accompanied by a dependence on, if not exactly a faith in, the government to bring the case to "legitimate" closure. This appeal for the government's imprimatur and the frequent reluctance to see JFK in any way other than the mythic often circumscribed the efficacy and scope of their political critique.

Yet the assault on various dominant institutions survived the strategic and rhetorical limitations of assassination critics, for independent researchers and historians often succeeded at eroding the power of these institutions to control public debate. Throughout this period both the government and its supports within the journalism community were forced to defend their historiographic legitimacy. Furthermore, the issues and questions generated by assassination critics contributed to the critique of the national security state, the secret foreign and domestic operations of government intelligence agencies. That these operations have continued to grow since 1980 is a reflection of both their entrenchment within standard government activities and a failure on the part of critics, media institutions, and the public to investigate and demand an accounting for the abuses of state power. However, because such demands and protests were among the defining features of sixties' culture in the United States, then any chronicle of that period must include a portrait of Kennedy's assassination and the debate over its encoding into history.

That process of portraiture, that debate over the writing of history extended well beyond the authorial efforts of the government and the assassination critics. Here was a historic event and a controversy with images at its core, emerging alongside the maturation of television news and at a time when the production methods and aesthetic strategies of certain pop artists and underground filmmakers had turned to the commercial image. As the culture of the sixties and early seventies witnessed this exceedingly public challenge to official versions of events, this complicated telling and retelling of a national tragedy which could not be made to cohere within a stable and traditional form, artists worked to compose their own response. Their films, silkscreens, paintings, and sculptures reassembled the assassination debates into some of the most provocative pieces of contemporary American art.

I n 1964 California artist Wallace Berman created the last issue of his mail art magazine, *Semina*. First sent to friends and acquaintances in 1955, *Semina* consisted of a large envelope containing poetry, photographs, verifax images — an assemblage of paper documents, sometimes wrapped in twine. As a collaged communiqué, *Semina* embodied the aesthetic and attitude of the painters, poets, assemblagists, sculptors, and filmmakers who made up Berman's West Coast community of beat and funk artists. It featured found objects, personal photographs, and an unslick, handcrafted production style which resulted, in the words of one of its correspondents, in "an act of soul-building."[1] As a prism for the cultural scene in which it was created, the assemblage magazine reflected some of the most provocative strategies of underground art: circumvention of commercial-industrial modes of production and distribution, a challenge to dominant tendencies of institutional art and criticism, a personal debt to the spirit of surrealism, and circulation among a community of artists who shared a sensibility of cultural rebellion and aesthetic experimentation.

In this last issue from the summer of 1964, Berman sent out a manila envelope on the cover of which was a slightly altered version of the well-known photograph in which Lee Harvey Oswald is being escorted by Dallas police and Jack Ruby is crossing in front of them, his gun pointed at the left side of Oswald's abdomen. Composed with the help of the verifax machine Berman used so often, this image presents the photo with a slight modification: the sheriff's deputy to Oswald's right is doubled so that his right arm and head appear twice. It is a subtle but significant change, eliciting a double take from a first-time viewer and then perhaps a second search of the image for other doctored details. Inside *Semina* number 9 was just one artifact, a poem by Michael McClure entitled "November Texas Song for L.H.O. and J.F.K."[2]

DOUBLE MURDER! VAHROOOOOOOOHR!
Varshnohteeembreth nahrooohr PAIN STAR.
CLOUDS ROLL INTO MARIGOLDS
nrah paws blayge bullets eem air.
BANG! BANG! BANG! BANG! BANG!
BANG! BANG! BANG! BANG!
BANG! BANG! BANG! BANG! BANG!

BANG! BANG! BANG! BANG! BANG!
BANG! BANG! BANG!
Yahh oon FLAME held prisoner
DALLAS!

The random collisions that would have taken place between the enclosures of earlier *Semina* envelopes are acted out here in the language of McClure's poem. As the unfamiliar words are sounded out, their materiality is foregrounded, and the violence implied by the repetition of "BANG!" echoes in the collision of sounds within McClure's structure. The poet plays with the violence, hammering out "BANG!" twenty-two times, to its comic extreme, as in a child's game or the patter of a gangster movie's soundtrack. And yet the apocalyptic resounds as well, in the clouds that roll into marigolds and in the flame that toward the end also suggests the one burning at JFK's grave.

But I really want to focus on Berman's verifax here because it points toward the visual and thematic concerns of the artwork discussed in the following chapters. His appropriation of the photograph taken by Jack Beers for the *Dallas Morning News*, circulated by the AP, and featured prominently in *Life* magazine a week after the assassination, rehearses a strategy employed by several artists who worked with assassination imagery. Just as elements of pop and assemblage art would juxtapose found objects with national colors or emblems, Berman's mail art becomes (accidentally) montaged with the postmark and the patriotic postage stamp. Suddenly, Lee Harvey Oswald and the American flag adorn the envelope together, underscoring the discrepancy between political symbol and substance. Here the artist's signature literally comes between the two, as Berman has of course hand-addressed *Semina* to his friends and penned his initials above the photograph. As with collage in general, authorship becomes implicated in the space between found objects, in the intervention and reorganization of familiar imagery.

Berman's verifax suggests the degree to which image appropriation and collage would characterize artistic involvement in the assassination discourses. These artistic strategies paralleled the efforts of assassination critics who worked with the government's texts and reinterpreted the amateur films and photography. Although Berman's image speaks implicitly to the doubling of Oswald's image throughout the case, it is of course the figure of the sheriff's deputy that is repeated. Berman's target is thus the official image of authority, appearing here as a clone, doubled as if to reinscribe the deputy's failure to protect Oswald from Ruby's assault. Berman's image also offers a correction to the same photo as published by *Life*. In its best-selling issue of November 29, 1963, *Life* chose to crop the picture just to the left of Oswald, almost eliminating the deputy to Oswald's right. Berman challenges the mass-produced perspective, subtly and humorously drawing our attention away from the prisoner and to the fact that something is wrong with the Dallas police.

In some ways the Oswald verifax seems anomalous within Wallace Berman's work. The photographs he used rarely depicted such an immediately familiar personality or incident, and there seems little to suggest that he was interested in the subject beyond this cover for *Semina*. Yet Berman's work does intersect with that of two artists who are central to the following chapters: Bruce Conner and Andy Warhol. Conner was part of the same California community of artists that nurtured Berman, and their collage work occasionally shares subject matter if not always form. On the other hand, the common ground between Berman and Warhol was certainly confined to the space within the frame, the two possessing different temperaments and occupying radically different production environments. In his verifax collages, Berman's work shares with Warhol's an interest in seriality, repetition, and the role of the machine in the process of production.

As suggestive as Berman's Oswald verifax can be, it only serves to introduce the forms more fully explored by the practitioners of sixties' pop art. When these artists turned to JFK's assassination, they often encoded in paint or film the same dual impulses of faith and crisis that ran throughout the investigation literature. They borrowed from the mainstream media and reauthored its imagery. They questioned long-held conceptions of art and its universality by building works composed of the disposable and the everyday. They rehearsed the gestures of assassination critics by producing work on the margins, succeeding on occasion at forcing their perspective to the center. Finally, as we will see beginning with the work of Andy Warhol, they challenged the solemnity, even the sacredness, that had developed around the murder, its image, and the ensuing years of inquiry.

Chapter 4 **The Warhol Silkscreens**

As I was coming down from my operation, I heard a television going some-where and the words "Kennedy" and "assassin" and "shot" over and over again. Robert Kennedy had been shot, but what was so weird was that I had no understanding that this was a second Kennedy assassination—I just thought that maybe after you die, they rerun things for you, like President Kennedy's assassination.[1]

These remarks by Andy Warhol aptly characterize one of the domi-nant features of the long debate over the death of JFK. In recollect-ing his near-death dream, the pop artist suggests the degree to which the images of Dallas had become deeply inscribed in popu-lar memory: November 22, 1963, as colossal rerun. Ironically, however, it was Warhol's own work that had contributed considerably to this phenome-non, this sense of a set of moments frozen and recurring, and the sense, too, that news from the present — in this case the death of Robert Kennedy — as well as future similar events, would always rebound off the screen or the page that imaged the Dallas motorcade or the subsequent funeral.

In a series of important pop art works created between 1963 and 1968, Warhol gave shape to many of the assassination discourses outlined in Part One. In *Jackie (The Week That Was)* (1963); *Sixteen Jackies* (1964); *Nine Jackies* (1964); *Three Jackies* (1964); *Gold Jackie* (1964); two versions of *Round Jackie* (1964); three pieces titled *Jackie* (1965), one with eight panels, another with thirty-five blue panels, the third with sixteen panels; *Jacqueline Kennedy No. 3* (1965); *Silver Jackie* (1966); *Two Jackies* (1966); and *Flash — November 22, 1963* (1968), the shifting status of imagery, its fluctuation be-tween and simultaneous consolidation of the poles of affirmation and cri-tique, is richly inscribed.[2] The formal strategies and critical tropes of the as-sassination debates are traced through these silkscreen portrait grids. They figure either individually or as a series, the processes and effects mobilized around the investigation.

By the time of his first one-man show at the Ferus Gallery in Los Angeles in 1962, Warhol had demonstrated an interest in the iconography of popular culture, choosing as his content such objects as the Del Monte can and the Coca-Cola bottle cap. His works from the early sixties combined this pop imagery with traces of the modernist gesture, such as dripping paint or the incomplete composition. Also present in his work circa 1962, in the paintings of dollar bills or of S&H Green Stamps, is a growing interest in seriality and repetition. By 1964 Warhol combined pop content and serial imagery with various photographic processes, most importantly for this discussion bringing silkscreening techniques to bear on his portraiture of Hollywood celebrities and the documenting of social violence. In these categories his best-known works remain the multiple Marilyns and Elvises, and the series of race riot and electric chair pieces from 1963–1964. The issues traced through these works, violent death and morbidity, celebrity and banality, are also at work in the various pieces devoted to the assassination.

In the Jackie silkscreens, however, the structural tensions that have been ascribed to Warhol's early work — the juxtaposition of indifference and emotion, authorial signature and its effacement, uniqueness and the replication of consumer culture — became enfolded with similar tensions in the investigative dialogue surrounding the death in Dallas. These works contributed to a shift in aesthetic values within the art world by incorporating imagery from a political debate (the assassination) which was itself assaulting dominant structures in the sphere of discourse. The Jackie silkscreens both critiqued this debate from outside its main corridors and registered, through astoundingly precise formal compositions, the transformations being undergone by the status of photographic imagery.

Warhol's work from this period, primarily the portraits of Marilyn and the disaster imagery of the electric chair and car crash series, has been read in terms that apply directly to the Jackie silkscreens. Recent discussions of this work have stressed its compound qualities in an attempt to resist what by the mid-sixties had become the conventional wisdom on Warhol's pop imagery. Early commentators on Warhol's art, perhaps merely following the artist's lead of self-styled dispassion and his proclamations of passivity, understood these works as acute indifference, a seemingly casual approach to tragic events.

In general, Warhol's subject-matter choices have been regarded as essentially indiscriminate. Most commentators have displayed little interest in them, other to observe that, in their totality, they represent the random play of a consciousness at the mercy of the commonly available commercial culture.[5]

It is not that qualities of the everyday and the indifferent are not operating in the silkscreens from the early sixties, but that critical readings of them have tended to stress the effects of such formal features as repetition and image reversal to the point of omitting entirely their emotionally saturated content. Shortly I will address how their grid formats in fact mitigate against a reading that overvalues the effects of repetition, but the point here is that the predominant formal attribute of these works, a reliance on the multiplication of images, succeeded at obscuring whatever more socially specific messages were embedded in their photographic content. Critics have generally failed to locate the Jackie portraits within the social debate over the assassination, noting little beyond how the death of JFK, registered in Warhol's choice of subject matter, fundamentally altered the course of American history or shattered some spirit of national idealism. Critics have, however, argued for a dialectical reading that assigns each piece a more complex attitude than mere indifference.[4]

I want to extend this dialectical approach to Warhol's silkscreens by arguing that within the various Jackies is a rehearsal of the same approach to images deployed by the pro– and anti–Warren Commission forces. Remembering Foucault's definition of the event — "the appropriation of a vocabulary turned against those who had once used it" — Warhol's grids must be understood as a confrontation with a set of discursive events as much as a commemoration of the death in Dallas. At work within these grids is a similar negotiation between a faith in the truth-bearing powers of the image and the epistemological anxiety resulting from prolonged scrutiny and juxtaposition of the photographic evidence. I refer to the first as the axis of insistence (a term borrowed from Gertrude Stein), to the other as the axis of crisis.

The Axis of Insistence

In her essay "Portraits and Repetition," Stein suggests that the essence of an individual can be rendered through a compositional process that resembles repetition but is in fact a form of multiple and refined insistence.

Each time that I said the somebody whose portrait I was writing was something that something was just that much different from what I had just said that somebody was and little by little in this way a whole portrait came into being, a portrait that was not description and that was made by each time, and I did a great many times, say it, that somebody was something, each time there was a difference just a difference enough so that it could go on and be a present something.[5]

As if offering Stein's "difference just a difference enough" with each insistence, with each image of Jackie within a multiple-panel portrait, Warhol teases the spectator into the role of examiner, into an alliance with the assassination buff's optical obsessions. The alliance is implicitly one of investigatory faith as well. Indeed, the term *insistence* labels an attitude toward the image that can be variously translated into notions of authenticity or modernist originality. To search for minute or subtle differences between the multiple Jackies is to entrust the image with an authenticity of expression and with the capacity to render an immediate (or less mediated) experience of the original event. Whereas the credibility of the Zapruder film rested in part on its amateur status, its aura a result of its mode of production, the Warhol texts register a similar credibility within their own epistemological sphere through use of wire service photographs. The gesture of insistence here coincides with the documentarist tendency of Warhol's pop. Again the Race Riot silkscreens are the best example of this tendency which is even more acute in the Jackie portraits than in the silkscreens of Marilyn or Elizabeth Taylor. On the other hand, the hyperbolization of the glamour pose, the smile and the stare, accent the artifice and mass production in the Marilyn portraits, as does the exaggerated application of color to hair and lips. The point is underscored even better by comparing the assassination silkscreens with the single portrait *Red Jackie* from 1964. *Red Jackie* makes use of a posed photograph, Jackie looking relaxed with a half smile, her lips red, her gaze fixed directly at the camera. Unlike the precise narrative coding of the assassination portraits, the documentary element is absent here, and *Red Jackie* seems to stand to the side of history. Its image could be from either before or after Dallas, and were it set into a multiple-panel grid of the same photograph, it would not resonate with the axis of insistence characterizing the assassination Jackies.[6]

Jackie (The Week That Was) from 1963 was the first of the assassination portraits, within which Warhol presented all the images used in the subsequent Jackie silkscreens. The insistent use of these images — Jackie in the motorcade, at the reception at Love Field, at the swearing in of LBJ aboard *Air Force One,* at the funeral — across the series of silkscreens suggests the constant and recurrent investigation of the same photographic materials performed by the Dallas inquiries. The decidedly cinematic effect of the thirty-five-panel blue version of *Jackie* (1965) echoes the fragmentation of the film evidence, the frame-by-frame analysis of motorcade footage. In *Jackie (The Week That Was)* and *Sixteen Jackies,* Warhol multiplies and reverses images as if searching for some essence, as if the right arrangement might yield an as-yet-unnoticed insight or perspective. In *Jackie (The Week That Was),* six of the images are repeated only once, but the duplicated photograph has been reversed. Each image thus has a double, each view a variation. The seventh image appears four times, but two of them are slightly magnified so that one has the impression that the two reversed pairs derive from different photos. Moreover, in three cases the doubled images differ in color, tinted in combinations of either amber-blue or amber-white, suggesting in the latter perhaps some light of revelation, as if some skin of amber tint had been removed, the photo cleaned or dusted. Mobilized in concert with the multiple imagery, the subtle variations between individual panels in fact works against their status as mere repetition.

Because of the oblique time-element that Warhol introduces into the paintings, each repetition of the same image seems to be unique rather than a duplicate of the others. Thus the internal variations and the slippage that arise as consequences of the printing techniques give life to what was originally a static image, in particular by making the viewer think that time is moving.[7]

In using as his source material images taken from the news wire services, Warhol mimed the strategy imposed on assassination researchers. The struggle over authorship waged by Warren Commission critics, at least in its earliest stages, was fought over a terrain dominated by the official institutions of information. At the center of this struggle was a set of imagery whose meanings had to be wrested from its original contexts: the government and major news media. Significantly, six of the seven images used in the Warhol portraits appeared in *Life* within two weeks of the assassination, one of them on its cover for the December 6 issue.[8] In prying these images away from the interpretive frame supplied by *Life* and the explicit lone assassin theory that informed it, Warhol engaged in a similar struggle for authorial control. His reordering of these same images thus took part in a rejection of history as constructed by the government and its advocates in the mainstream press and dislodged the narrative procedures by which this history was transmitted.

Assassination critics brought the case out of the commission chambers and the secret classifications of federal agencies and into the buff networks, the kitchens of housewives, and the college lecture circuit. Warhol delivered this same set of imagery to a new social location: the art gallery and eventually the museum. In so doing, Warhol argued that these images, captured by wire service photographers and amateur filmmakers, although admittedly subjected to his own formal recompositions, be classified among the central works of his time. In this spatial transformation, from the pages of the Warren Report and *Life* to the subject matter of pop art and its exhibitions, Warhol implicitly made the case for the inclusion and rearrangement of this imagery within the popular domain. The egalitarianism of pop between 1963 and 1966 thereby worked in consonance with the claims of assassination critics who called for a democratization of the research and ridiculed the power of the state's secretive methods.

Pop arose out of problematizing the question of taste itself, and, in its more purist forms, was addressed directly to the media processes through which cultural taste is defined and communicated. Not only did it deny the imposition, from above, of seemingly arbitrary boundaries of taste, but it also questioned the distanced contemplation, interpretive expertise, and categories of aesthetic judgment which accompanied that imposition.[9]

In the case of the Jackie silkscreens, this attack on taste translates into not only an assault on the imposition of "interpretive expertise" by the various media giants, but also a critique of the elitism of the Warren Commission and the privatization of the case by federal investigative agencies. Apparently, and characteristically for Warhol, these impositions were posed in terms of feelings rather than politics:

I'd been thrilled having Kennedy as president; he was handsome, young, smart—but it didn't bother me that much that he was dead. What bothered me was the way the television and radio were programming everybody to feel so sad.[10]

These and similar remarks by Warhol no doubt played a role in the ascription of indifference to his brand of pop art. Into its rejection of traditional standards of taste was read a total divestment of sincerity, the depletion of feeling from emotionally charged imagery.[11] This reading, of course, springs not only from pop's use of everyday images, but from its dominant formal characteristics as well. As I will discuss with reference to the axis of crisis, the strategies of seriality and repetition and the compositional idiosyncrasies of silkscreening can be seen to transform tragic content into banal reproduction. But despite these visual re-formations, pop's assault on elitist conventions or, in the case of the assassination silkscreens, its critique of image deployment need not be seen solely as a stance of indifference.[12]

In his discussion of Warhol's Marilyn silkscreens, Thomas Crow argues for an interpretation that admits, even emphasizes, the emotional saturation of the portraits. Beginning these works within two weeks of Marilyn's death, Warhol necessarily infused them with commemorative aspirations. For Crow the memorial function is best served in the single-image silkscreens of Marilyn against a gold background, a mise-en-scène that signifies "an eternal other world."[13] With the Jackies, the memorial is inscribed less through coloration than through choice of imagery. Images from the funeral or the swearing in of LBJ dominate most of the portraits.

The Kennedy assassination pictures are often seen as an exception in the artist's output, unusual in their open emotion and sincerity, but the continuity they represent with the best of his previous work seems just as apparent. As with the Marilyn images, it is a death that galvanizes Warhol into a sustained act of remembrance.[14]

Amid the predominance of funereal images, the presence of photographs taken *before* the shooting—at Love Field, during the motorcade—works to increase the overall commemorative function. Their juxtaposition with the postassassination imagery imbues *Jackie (The Week That Was)*, *Sixteen Jackies*, *Jacqueline Kennedy No. 3*, and *Jackie* (1965 eight panels) with a temporal or historical component which resists freezing the moment and forces the spectator to mentally reenact the narrative sequence each time the portraits are encountered. Crow's argument against an interpretation fixed on indifference extends also to the issue of referentiality. Such works as *Tunafish Disaster* (1963) and *Saturday Disaster* (1964), contrary to readings that see in them commentaries on the breakdown of meaning, are still able to communicate the drama of private tragedy and inspire authentic responses of sympathy.

In this case, the repetition of the crude images does draw attention to the awful banality of the accident and to the tawdry exploitation by which we come to know the misfortunes of others. But the pictures do not mock our potential feelings of empathy, however inadequate they may be. Nor do they direct our attention to some peculiarly 20th-century estrangement between an event and its representation.[15]

Thus the Warhol imagery, too, shares the debates' tendency to trust film and photography to render a faithful, perhaps even redeemable, account of the traumatic events with all their details of space, time, and emotion. Adhering in these portraits, then, is more than some self-conscious statement on the various levels of filmic mediation or the autotelic function of mass-produced imagery within the postmodern. Nor is it only the highly charged nature of the subject matter that sustains these works along the axis of insistence. For their silkscreen processes are a perfectly appropriate form for the theme of remembrance. Function and technique become enfolded.

The screened image, reproduced whole, has the character of an involuntary trace: it is memorial in the sense of resembling memory, which is sometimes vividly present, sometimes elusive, and always open to embellishment as well as loss.[16]

Buttressed by a formal technique appropriate to its extremely familiar and emotionally rich content, Warhol's silkscreens, according to Crow, maintained for a short time something of a pop threat, "a pulp-derived, bleakly monochrome vision that held, however tenuous the grip, to an all-but-buried tradition of truth-telling in American commercial culture."[17] As this pop threat, with its stark presentation of various renditions of the American nightmare, its assault on the proper forms of imagery within the modernist tradition and on elitist impositions of taste, and its problematizing of the role and function of the author/artist, Warhol's Jackie silkscreens enjoyed a kinship, no matter how culturally distant, with the assassination inquests. Within the context of these inquests, "truth-telling in American commercial culture" took the form of distrust and then critique, as consumers of real soup cans proved unwilling to consume the state's portrait of history.

107 *The Warhol Silkscreens*

The Axis of Crisis

The axis of insistence, however, addresses only one of the epistemological vectors at work in the Warhol portraits and in the wider assassination debates. Pop's documentary impulse and commemorative function are in fact forced to negotiate with the axis of crisis, the vector leading to the illegibility of the photograph and the temporal contradictions of the film evidence. Indeed, Warhol's formal choices, his use of silkscreen, but moreover his use of the grid, precisely articulate the tensions that would characterize the shifting status of representation throughout the next several decades.

In her essay "Grids," Rosalind Krauss lays the pivotal groundwork for my reading of the Jackie silkscreens.[18] Borrowing from the structuralist work of Claude Lévi-Strauss, Krauss suggests that grids be understood in mythic terms; that is, as the modernist form that has served to spatialize a fundamental historical contradiction. Dating back to the fifteenth and sixteenth centuries, a distant ancestor of the modern grid was used to construct perspective, as a guide for the rendering of paintings with spatial depth. However, the modernist employment of the grid has not been geared toward mapping the real onto a surface and has been rather decidedly "antinatural, antimimetic, antireal."

Unlike perspective, the grid does not map the space of a room or a landscape or a group of figures onto the surface of a painting. Indeed, if it maps anything, it maps the surface of the painting itself. It is a transfer in which nothing changes place. . . . Considered in this way, the bottom line of the grid is a naked and determined materialism.[19]

Krauss turns to the works and writings of the modernists who pioneered various uses of the grid for confirmation of this materialist approach to form. She finds, however, that such artists as Mondrian and Malevich spoke not of some interest in their respective materials but in terms of spirituality, finding in the grid access to universal conceptions of thought and being. Here, then, is the cultural contradiction encoded into the rise of the grid in the early part of the twentieth century: the wider social dialogue and dilemma being waged around the secular versus the spiritual, the materialism of science versus the sacred faith in creation. It is the equivalent of Lévi-Strauss's mapping of the various myths concerning the origins of humanity, the autochthonous versus the biological. Perhaps the most pronounced formal sign of this contradiction is located in the grid's opposing spatial potential, its competing centrifugal and centripetal axes. The former suggests that the grid is circumscribed by rather arbitrary boundaries, the extension of its coordinates theoretically endless. The latter holds to the opposite: that the grid points not toward an infinite expansion out to the world, but from "the outer limits of the aesthetic object inward."

The grid is, in relation to this reading a re-presentation of everything that separates the work of art from the world, from ambient space and from other objects. The grid is an introjection of the boundaries of the world into the interior of the work; it is a mapping of the space inside the frame onto itself. It is a mode of repetition, the content of which is the conventional nature of art itself.[20]

Whereas the early twentieth-century grid gave form to the struggle and contradictions between the secular and the sacred, Warhol's grids of the early sixties spatialize one of the central contradictions of their time, one that lies at the core of the assassination debates. This contradiction is of course the investment of epistemological certainty in the visible, through camera vision in negotiation with and frequently undermined by a crisis of representation, the inability of imaging technologies to render a reliable, useful, and legible transcription of the original event. If the grid persisted as "emblematic of the modernist ambition," it continued to function, under Warhol's direction, as uniquely suited to the issues of the postmodern as well. Cohering in its form are what David James had identified as the dual and often interpenetrating impulses characteristic of alternative cinema in the United States during the sixties: the utopia of authenticity and the anti-dote of fabrication.[21] More specific to the project at hand, the grid structure of the Jackie portraits gives formal expression to the fundamental tensions at work in the assassination critics' approach to images: the insistence on legibility amid and despite the interpretive crisis arising out of the various photographic enhancement processes applied to the evidence. The grid, furthermore, expresses the contradiction in temporality that characterized analysis of the Zapruder film, the demand that it simultaneously exist as film and as still frame.

The contradiction of film and still frame is most pronounced in *35 Jackies, 16 Jackies,* and *Jackie (The Week That Was)*. The filmic effect is equated here with repetition, with the endless looping of the evidence as short film fragments are projected again and again. The still frame, while destroying temporal flow, allows for the shock and information in the image to be analyzed closely. For Peter Gidal, the Jackie portraits reference both tendencies while disallowing neither. "Thus, we are neither wholly presented with a statement about 'repetition ruins effect' nor are we made to feel that repetition enhances effect."[22]

Still, I want to elaborate fully the axis of crisis, expressed largely by repetition. In *Jackie (The Week That Was)* Warhol anticipated the uncanny doubling that would quickly become a recurring theme in the case. The use of repetition throughout the series, especially in *35 Jackies,* also foreshadows the interpretive crisis that would slowly emerge in the investigation. The insistence of the assassination buff gives way to the sheer replication of images, as photographs from the motorcade or the funeral are presented as a series of spaces or moments without order or hierarchy. One look now seems little different from any other, and no image seems discernible as the original. The repetition hints at an encroaching banality in the investigation, the recurrent study of the same visual evidence which results more in exhaustion than in discovery. The shocking imagery is looped to the point at which the public, on whose behalf the private researcher is ostensibly working, grows increasingly alienated (if not amused) by the obsessive industry of the assassination buff. Referencing a precise and well-known narrative, repetition permits the silkscreens to retain an antinarrative effect, throwing into crisis the crucial issue of sequentiality and frustrating the gaze that might seek temporal reconstruction. As the eye moves down or across each row of photographs in *16 Jackies* and *Jackie (The Week That Was)*, their order is clearly out of synch with the historical sequence of events. Any return to the arrival at Love Field or the happier moments of the motorcade must pass over (or through) images of the funeral or the traumatic postassassination moments on *Air Force One*. From 1963 to 1966, across the series of silkscreens, Warhol figured the work of assassination critics as he sought new combinations — three Jackies, sixteen Jackies, thirty-five Jackies — which result in new, yet nondefinitive narrative sequences.

Out of this crisis of sequentiality springs the familiar sense of a moment frozen, the perpetually present quality of the images which has functioned as both cause and symptom of an apparent compulsion to repeat the tragedy of Dallas. Warhol's use of the grid articulates the temporal component of the mass dissemination of assassination imagery, the serial effect of magazine covers and contents displayed across the country. The effect is enhanced in the Jackie portraits by an apparent crisis of motion, of movement stunted and stopped. In stopping motion, the grids speak to the inadequacy of cinema, its unreadability at eighteen frames per second, the need to slow or stretch the flow of visual information. But this notion of a perpetual present must coexist with a sense of historical distance, of passing time marked by layers of mediation. The rectangles comprising the multipanel silkscreens suggest, despite their reversed aspect ratios, the frame lines on a strip of film or the edges of a screen. As such they imply that, however close to the present the event may still seem, its very presence results from a reframed set of viewings that stand as testimony to increasing historical remoteness. What is prescient about Warhol's assassination work is his recognition as early as December 1963 that, despite media claims to the contrary, the superabundant imaging of these events could have a distinctly alienating effect. The Jackie silkscreens both anticipated and contributed to this media-accelerated passage of history. Operating in these portraits, then, is not just a sense of the events repeated, but of the spectator's return, willingly or unwillingly, to the scene of the crime. The time shifts from November 1963 to the space and action of the viewer, and with each return to assassination imagery, the spectator reexperiences his or her own distance from the event. The dominant temporal dimension for each silkscreen becomes not so much that of the Dallas narrative as that of the spectator's reencounter. Addressing Warhol's use of the silkscreen technique, Gidal makes a similar point about a shift in temporality:

The differences of image within one painting (35 Jackies, 1964, Marilyn, 1962) are due not to a movement forward in their (Marilyn's, Jackie's, etc.) real time, narrative time. The changes are due to Warhol's real time (the change in hand-pressure while screening; mood; unconscious posture; movement of the wrist, etc.) when reprinting the same image at (by necessity) successive moments in time.[23]

Throughout the period in question, it was not the case that assassination images circulated autonomously through the culture in various books and magazines. It is perhaps easy to speak of the Dallas imagery as a presence that would not go away, as if its own cultural importance or traumatic resonance kept it surfacing on the national agenda, in whatever form, for nearly three decades. It should go without saying (but often does not) that the recurring presence of this imagery was the result of individual or institutional efforts, of discursive and technological determinants. As Gidal suggests, Warhol's silkscreen technique inscribes not so much the return of the image as that of the investigator. It is possible, therefore, to read in the Jackie portraits further traces of the conditions of inquiry that confronted assassination critics.

Most significant in this regard is the way silkscreening implies a simultaneous presence and absence of the image. Portions of each panel are less distinct than others, again as a result of the pressure applied during the time of production. The play between presence and absence — which can be read either as the image coming into being yet not fully formed or as the image in decay and being worn away — is best exemplified in *Jackie* (1965, eight panels) and *Silver Jackie* (1966). Of *Silver Jackie* Gidal notes:

In the Silver Jackie this is emphasized because the image changes from positive to negative depending on the light (silver on white is the equivalent of a negative image plate). We see a constant flicker from positive to negative, a change of visage, literally.[24]

This flicker from positive to negative and the varying degrees of distinctness in the silkscreened image echo the elusiveness of assassination imagery for critics throughout the sixties, the lack of access to the Zapruder film as well as to the secret material evidence. The tonal idiosyncrasies of the Warhol panels also suggest the inconsistencies of image quality encountered by critics as they worked with bootleg or last-generation copies of the photographic evidence. The minute discrepancies in film grain, which could be crucial points of issue (and often sources of paralysis) for the critic's work, become the determining factors of difference for portraits that are otherwise nearly identical. This is especially the case if one compares *Gold Jackie* and *Round Jackie*, both from 1964, in which the only differences are a grainier chin area and a quarter-inch diminution in diameter for *Round Jackie*. (Indeed, studying the two portraits side by side and concentrating on the chin, one is reminded of a similar interrogation of the Oswald backyard photos).

It is significant that *Silver Jackie* was produced in 1966, well after *Jackie (The Week That Was)* and well into the interrogation of the Warren Report. Its ghostly play of presence and absence suggests the gap between the event and efforts at its reconstruction. Moreover, its reversed tonalities hint at the instability of meaning. Jackie's light pink suit and matching pillbox hat are represented with darker tones, while the black trim around the neck of her jacket and her dark hair appear in shades of white. All of the silkscreens challenge the epistemology of the visible in some way. The grid composition, especially in *35 Jackies,* denies access to spatial depth, a vital factor in the analysis of bullet trajectories and the arrangement of bodies. As Krauss suggests, the grid succeeds at mapping not the real but the area of representation. The transparency of the photograph or film, as it was often naively postulated by assassination critics, is thoroughly refuted by Warhol's strategies. His compositions block any visual analysis that seeks to probe beyond the surface plane of the image. As mentioned in Part One, by the time the debate entered its third generation of critical studies, its texts took on increasing self-consciousness, their contents necessarily devoted to a kind of private dialogue among themselves which often succeeded at plotting not the event but the contours of the investigation. The multipanel Jackies thus anticipated the kind of textual self-reference that would come to characterize the assassination debates.

If the look is deflected across the surface in the multiple-panel portraits, it is more fixed when encountering *Gold Jackie* and the two versions of *Round Jackie*. The temporality of these works is the moment made still, a single nonmourning image abstracted from the narrative (as much as this is possible) and stood alone. Yet these portraits are still inscribed with great tension, the spectator knowing that Jackie's smile will soon be obliterated. Their circular framing allows their emotional status to move between several positions. It presents them as medallions, keepsake images, contents for a commemorative locket. They also have the look of oversized campaign buttons, advertisements for a political visit, the motorcade. But more ominously, their circularity suggests the image of the first lady as seen through a rifle scope, the potential vantage point of a grassy knoll gunman.

However, the varying emotional or interpretive readings in the silk-screens can still be seen as fairly restricted given the possibilities available through the collage strategies of Warhol's most important pop predecessor and colleague, Robert Rauschenberg. In his essay for the Museum of Modern Art's 1989 retrospective of Warhol's work, Benjamin Buchloh cites the crucial distinctions between the Warhol silkscreens and Rauschenberg's collages from the early sixties:

First of all, and most obviously, Warhol deprived his paintings of the infinite wealth of associative play and simultaneous multiple references, which Rauschenberg's traditional collage aesthetic had still offered to the viewer. By contrast, Warhol's image design (whether in its emblematic single unit structure or in its repetition of a single unit) extinguishes all poetic resources and prohibits the viewer's free association of the pictorial elements, replacing the latter with the experience of a confrontational restriction. In a very literal manner Warhol's singularized images become hermetic: secluded from other images or stifled by their own repetition, they can no longer generate "meaning" and "narration" in the manner of Rauschenberg's larger syntactic assemblages.[25]

Buchloh's reading of the restrictive aspects of Warhol's compositions, their obstacles to the generation of "meaning" and "narration," aligns them with the axis of crisis, with the epistemological ruptures that came increasingly to characterize scrutiny of the visual evidence. Yet Buchloh's reading may itself be restrictive in scope, failing to fully address the spectatorial associations of the Jackie silkscreens. He is certainly correct in finding in the Rauschenberg collages a diversity of images and design and thus a greater potential for associative play between signs within the frame. But it is this very diversity of materials that may allow the Rauschenberg collages to remain ultimately more hermetic than the Warhol portraits, the loose and seemingly arbitrary arrangements of the former providing the spectator with a *surplus* of representations. The viewer is perhaps less compelled to move beyond the surface of the work, allowing its own textual multiplicity to provide sufficient interpretive clues. Conversely, the Warhol silkscreens, their singularity or repetition arguably making them less "social," demand through their restrictiveness a more urgent dialogue with representations operating outside the frame or the museum. With less to go on, the spectator is forced to bring an array of cultural meanings, identities, and narratives to confrontation with the work. The "seclusion from other images" thus both guarantees and compromises their hermeticism, insisting, perhaps in true pop style, that the viewer discover connections between the portraits and the more general textual practices from which their contents are derived.

This amendment to Buchloh's thesis notwithstanding, his contrasting of the two pop styles offers an angle on the effects of Warhol's methods which conforms nicely to the analytic frustrations inscribed across the assassination literature.

Paradoxically, the restriction and hermeticism of the semantically isolated image was at first generally experienced as the effect of absolute banality, or as an attitude of divine indifference, or, worse yet, as an affirmation of consumer culture. In fact it operated, first of all, as the rejection of conventional demands upon the artistic object to provide the plenitude of iconic representation. Warhol negates those demands for a pictorial narrative with the same degree of asceticism with which Duchamp had negated them in his Readymades.[26]

In their rejection of the demands of plenitude, Warhol's silkscreens speak to the impossibilities of the visual evidence, the confrontation between the critics' funereal and investigative seriousness and the resulting crisis of camera vision. Alongside this rejection is pop's assault on traditional concepts of the proper content or subject matter for art. Warhol's contribution on this front, his silkscreens of Coke bottles and soup cans being the best examples, not only helped sully the issue of aesthetic legibility, of telling art from nonart, but made explicit the crucial connections between art and the marketplace. It is hard to say whether any of Warhol's work, especially from the early sixties, can escape this connection, even when the subject matter is not explicitly about consumer goods. The authorial signature attached (however ironically) to the Campbell's soup cans shadows his subsequent work, bringing with it the residue of pop's engagement with commercial culture. The Jackie portraits, with their shared strategies of silkscreened repetition, cannot help but transport these issues to assassination imagery. In the multi-panel grids especially, Warhol underscores the role of the marketplace in the selling of the assassination, the powerful links between the commercial giants of journalism and the privileged authorial voice. Indeed, the assassination as a consumer good, mass produced and sold on newsstands not far from the soup cans in grocery stores, is one of the inevitable messages of the Jackie portraits. Certain images of Dallas 1963 were not only retailed nationwide but became themselves recognized as outstanding points of promotion. Severed from the context of political struggle surrounding their interpretation, images of the assassination, like the allure of celebrity or of the illicit, became agents in the sale of newsprint, air time, and the advertising these exhibited.

The negotiable status of assassination imagery, its shifting meanings within the Warren Commission/anti–Warren Commission debate, is also inscribed in the Jackie grids when these are set next to Warhol's other most famous silkscreens: his images of money and trading stamps. In *Front and Back Dollar Bills, Eighty Two-Dollar Bills, 192 One Dollar Bills, S&H Green Stamps* and *Seventy S&H Green Stamps,* all from 1962, Warhol takes as his subject matter that which is intrinsically worthless but is assigned value as a medium for exchange. Money, of course, acquires its currency through negotiability, where Green Stamps, redeemed through exchange, lack autonomous meaning within the economy of the brand name. Here, then, is another element in Warhol's rather prophetic encoding of assassination imagery—pop's interest not so much in the disposable (the assassination would never be that) but in the transferable aspects of representation, Green Stamps one day, the Zapruder film the next, all within the increasingly mobile contours of aesthetic convention.

The formal similarities between Warhol's dollar bill silkscreens and the assassination grids should not obscure the significant differences in their multiple images. Warhol's focus during these years on Jackie and not on the murdered president suggests the divergent spheres of interest for pop and for the investigation proper. The gaze of the assassination critic sought out the concealed image, seeking to analyze and make public the autopsy, the Zapruder film, and classified documents. Its attention thus fell on the concealed body. But pop's engagement with the commercial gaze, with that which is accessible to the everyday, necessarily turned to the public body. Those who were cued to study motorcade imagery for clues about the shooting would have their look frustrated by Warhol, perhaps not unlike their encounters with much of the reproduced images in the mainstream press.

If studied in conjunction with the portraits of Marilyn Monroe and Elizabeth Taylor, the various Jackies might be read in terms of Warhol's preoccupation with celebrity and death, and thus within the categories of camp which also accommodates the tales of Hollywood Babylon.[27] But again the point of intersection for these issues would seem to be the quite different silkscreen *Red Jackie.* As previously mentioned, *Red Jackie* presents a relaxed and mildly amused woman who appears posed for a single camera. In the assassination portraits Jackie may well be posed for a camera (undoubtedly multiple cameras) but her attention is elsewhere. The crucial difference turns around the look. In *Red Jackie,* the viewing spectator and posed object stare at one another, and any sense of off-frame space seems confined to the path between Jackie and viewer. In the assassination silkscreens there is an overwhelming sense of the importance of space outside the frame and Jackie serves not as returner but as mediator of the look. Encountering these images, the spectator sees through her, and she functions as go-between for mourning, surrogate witness to the out-of-frame body of the president. Though decidedly the focus, Jackie as spectacle and as pleasurable object for the gaze, is downplayed, especially in comparison to the face presented in *Red Jackie*. All of the grids negate her body below the neck, the deemphasis underscored by the radical cropping of the photographs. The repetition only increases the sense of fragmentation as the well-known pictures of the first lady at Love Field or standing beside LBJ aboard *Air Force One* are reduced to choker closeups. The monochromatics of the silkscreens also deeroticize her features, whereas the red lips and blue-touched eyes in *Red Jackie* display her clearly as object rather than as mediator of the look.

The centrality of Jackie's image throughout the assassination silkscreens echoes her social role, fixing her as the body of mourning and focus of the public gaze. But by 1966 her centrality, at least for Warhol's application of assassination imagery, seems to have waned with the variations of presence and absence radiating from *Silver Jackie*. In 1968, when Warhol returned to the subject with a project titled *Flash — November 22, 1963*, the focus shifted back onto the image of the slain president, and as Jackie's image became minimized, so, too, did the traces of commemoration that were present in the earlier silkscreens.

Flash — November 22, 1963 was presented in the form of a portfolio of eleven silkscreened prints and a two-sided cover. Produced simultaneous with and assigned the same title as this portfolio were three additional serigraph portraits of JFK. In 1968 Warhol produced two hundred such portfolios. When exhibited, they were enclosed in Plexiglas and accompanied by a blown-up copy of what appears to be the original newswire bulletins describing the shooting. Of the eleven prints, six contain images of the president drawn from various sources — the television screen, campaign posters, mass-circulated photographs. Three prints refer explicitly to Lee Harvey Oswald: one reproduces the magazine advertisement for the Mannlicher-Carcano rifle, another a previously published photograph of the School Book Depository's sixth-floor window, the third an image of Oswald taken while under arrest in the Dallas police station. One of the remaining prints depicts a faint reproduction of the presidential seal, while the other presents three clippings apparently drawn from newspapers, the most prominent of which is an image of Jackie during the motorcade.

Flash — November 22, 1963 presents a number of significant contrasts to the Jackie portrait grids. First, Warhol maintained a mild form of repetition but not through seriality. Rather, he abandoned the wholesale replication of images in favor of a rare use of superimposition which produces repetition within rather than between individual panels. While it shares with the Jackie portraits the silkscreen technique and thereby rehearses a process akin to the Hollywood mode of mass production, its diverse imagery presents a more visually complex articulation of assassination themes. If the various Jackies can be understood as celebrity excerpts from a movie of JFK's death (and here their relationship to the portraits of Marilyn, Natalie Wood, or Warren Beatty might be stressed), the portfolio format of *Flash* advertises that movie as a kind of press book for local exhibitors. Included are representations of the major players with hints as to narrative incident and motif: the rifle, the campaign trip, the Depository window. Then, as the portfolio is freed from its cover and the eleven prints are displayed through Plexiglas alongside the script of newswire bulletins, its quasi-storyboard composition and image contents refer to levels of filmic mediation in far more specific terms than the Jackie portraits.

The assassination as representation is underscored most definitively through two prints, one in which a sound film clapboard is superimposed over multiple images of JFK and the presidential seal, the other in which the same clapboard is superimposed over Oswald's face. The web of associations spiraling out from the clapboard, the only signifier that does not somehow belong within or pertain to the work's overall diegesis, address both Warhol's mode of production within The Factory and the cinematic construction of the event as history. It references the function of editing and the artifice of synchronization which were both effaced and foregrounded by the assassination literature. And it isolates the president and the alleged assassin as generic constructions rather than as political entities. It anticipates Hollywood's appropriation of the story and cites Kennedy's affection for and connection to the star system. The clapboard replaces serial imagery as a signifier of repetition, hinting at the implications of takes and retakes, much as they were executed throughout the investigation. There is ultimately something conspiratorial if not sinister about the clapboard, inserted as it is into the frame by the hands of unknown producers who lurk beyond the gaze. The effect is more haunting in the panel of Oswald, which becomes a screen test for the killer or the patsy. The way that the clapstick melds with Oswald's face, its diagonal lines forming his eyebrows, hints at the media-made persona, if not physiognomy, of the accused.

The formal manipulations of Kennedy's image suggest a similar reading. His body, essentially absent from the earlier silkscreens, reemerges in the portfolio as the filmic body, constituted by and for representation. The documentary impulse of the news bulletin, which is implied by the title *Flash,* is corroded in each print by the thorough saturation of bright color and the ghostly presence of photographic negative. *Flash* refers less to urgency than to the light of the visible which in its various technological forms has rendered both the evidence and the event indistinct. The surface of the body which had been mined for clues is for the most part denuded of detail or specific contour here. The assault it suffers comes not from bullets but from photographic processes, its legibility more a question of representation than of forensics. Warhol places the presidential seal in two of the prints and all three of the additional serigraph portraits. Like the Green Stamp or the dollar bill, the seal is independent of specific identity, infinitely transferable to whomever stands behind it. Through superimposition *Flash* renders as equals the seal and images of Kennedy's face, a face subject to untold reproductions, which is itself infinitely transferable. The mobility of its meaning is in large measure due to the textual practices of the assassination debate.

Thus, by the time he had endured an attempt on his own life, Warhol had applied his signature style to the assassination, enacting visual strategies that despite his radically different social location, ran parallel to and offered a critique of those strategies being executed in the investigation. *Flash* broke with the Jackie silkscreens by abandoning their concentration on a single figure to incorporate the ever-expanding array of assassination signifiers being exposed and circulated by the critics. As its impersonal title suggested, *Flash — November 22, 1963* was not a portrait. Warhol's use of newswire text acknowledged the position of this imagery within a wider social dialogue, a fact not always admitted by the partial hermeticism of the earlier Jackies. It also created an explicit exchange between competing discourses: the words of the mainstream press set against the visual experiments of pop art. By 1968 even Warhol's fascination with the individual celebrity, his characteristic distillation of a narrative down to its star, had shifted to register the widespread dispersion of controversial images which rebounded throughout the debate. In its attention to the assassination, Warhol's work would be the most prolific and pronounced, but it would not stand alone. Indeed, the pop aesthetic, especially as it was inscribed by the work of Ed Paschke and Edward Kienholz, was engineered to challenge the frames of reference around the images of JFK's death.

Chapter 5 **The Pop Camp**

Andy Warhol's cover for *Flash — November 22, 1963* was a characteristically pop deformation of news imagery. A newspaper headline declaring "President Shot Dead" is overlaid with a pattern of flower-shaped decals. The documentary impulse is thus undermined, its visual contents literally obscured by the decorative gesture. The decals, emblems of the cheap and mass produced, lowbrow forms of embellishment, become the very medium through or around which one must view news of the president's death. They mount a seemingly benign assault on legitimized forms of discourse by forcing the headlines to struggle for legibility. As such they underscore the newspaper itself as mass produced and cheap, concerned with pattern and layout. The front page as enduring record of the event and the day, its potential as a collector's piece, is presented here as a decorative cover, hinting at the disposability of historical accounts. In the cover for *Flash,* Warhol's *Daily News* painting (1962) meets his silkscreen *Flowers* (1966–1967), and the funereal function of the Jackie portraits appears to be replaced by a more explicit acknowledgment of the image as ornamentation.

Warhol's assassination art was but one instance of pop's encounter with American political and nationalist iconography.[1] Rearticulations of the flag in Claes Oldenburg's constructions, Jasper Johns's paintings or George Herms's assemblages were perhaps the most common experiments. As both a player in and a product of the image culture, JFK was ideal for pop's appropriation of national symbols and can be found in the paintings of Robert Rauschenberg and Larry Rivers. In James Rosenquist's *President Elect* (1960–1961), two female hands appear to emerge from Kennedy's face, each offering a piece of cake with frosting, while behind them sits a new car. Kennedy as the first media-made president is thus compared with other great American commodities, his image no less a product of the ad man's sales pitch. Pop's fascination with the art of advertising and corporate journalism, from television to comic strip heroes, forced it into direct confrontations with the imagery of consumer culture. The supermarket bag held the contents for a perfect still life. Thus, pop was well prepared to comment on the selling of the Warren Report and the government's posthumous manufacture of Kennedy's identity.

119

JFK as Found Art

Indeed, in its incorporation of the assassination, pop's interest in the everyday and the obsolescent could be read as an increasingly critical stance. For within weeks of the shooting the public sphere turned quickly to memorializing the slain president by naming and renaming various structures in his honor. Schools, airports, and bridges were given Kennedy's name in a process that both involved and concerned Washington lawmakers. Three weeks after the assassination, a joint congressional session of the House and Senate Committees on Public Works convened to consider naming the nascent national center for the performing arts in honor of the late president. Each witness before the committee articulated essentially the same point: the need to erect an homage to JFK which would symbolize permanence by showcasing works of enduring cultural value. The idea of a memorial worthy of its name was underscored by expressions of concern about the expanding list of structures or institutions being named in Kennedy's honor.

All Americans hope that his personal example of devoted duty and the boldness of his goals for the country will never be forgotten. Yet in this moment of sorrow and mourning we must be careful not to debase our grief by attaching the Kennedy name to everything in sight. Surely, no one had a greater sense of the fitting and appropriate gesture than President Kennedy.[2]

Testimony before the committee was punctuated by attempts to identify the performing arts center with the late president's character. A living memorial, it was claimed, would capture Kennedy's youthful enthusiasm while standing simultaneously as a monument to the timeless values for which he had an astute appreciation. Kennedy's identity was not only transferred to the structure but was itself rewritten to conform with the center's function as home to the arts.

I think it is particularly an appropriate memorial to a President who had an immutable capacity for many of the arts. I consider he was a very great artist. His capacity to use the English language was unmatched, I think, by anyone, save perhaps President Lincoln, who only just about a hundred years ago suffered the same fate as President Kennedy. He had great sensitiveness to all the arts. He himself was an artist in the true sense of the word. He won a Pulitzer Prize for one of his books.[3]

Just as the uncanny double was created by photographic representation, by its scrutiny and epistemological crisis, so, too, did the double function within the memorializing discourse surrounding architectural representation. The monument as double gave way to images of Lincoln and then to the slain president's emerging multiple selves. Freud's source for the double, psychic efforts to stave off death, rebound not only in the concrete public structures, but in the attribution of great artistic powers to JFK. The dead became elevated to agent of universal language, unbounded by the temporal and spatial conditions of existence.

President Kennedy had a keen sense of history and of the lasting values of our society. His particular insight was that of a leader who envisioned and championed, not those things which resulted in advantage of a transitory nature, but, rather, one with the foresight to be concerned with that which would result in the establishment of values representative of this Nation with those virtues which would endure throughout man's history.[4]

Flying in the face of such rhetoric was pop's portrayal of JFK as media image rather than universal poet. Pop's use of found objects, everyday items culled from the cultural image bank or trash bin, staked out a position that questioned the virtues being attached to art in Kennedy's name. Its objects paid tribute, if they paid tribute to anything, to the antithesis of the lasting monument, to those structures of a more "transitory nature." In their resurrection of disposable objects and transitory images, pop artists took part in a process of recontextualization akin to the reidentifications being enacted on the late president himself. But rather than being monuments to a life, pop objects often were a reclaiming of the dead. If the memorial structure-as-double displaced the lost self onto other figures, pop returned attention to the dead body, transferring objects from the cultural graveyard to the museum.

Pre-pop artists, especially those associated with the California funk beat scene, had resurrected the disposable and the discarded in the fifties, producing art that challenged the tenets of abstract expressionism and offered explicit opposition to cold war consumerist values. One of its leading figures, Ed Kienholz, juxtaposed found objects and patriotic colors in *Untitled American President* (1962). Here Kienholz arranged an abstract sculpture out of common materials, the nameless chief executive embodied by a milk jug painted with the stars and stripes topped off by a bicycle seat. His *O'er the Ramparts We Watched Fascinated* (1959) also combined national symbol with discarded objects, but here old electronic parts and the severed body of a plastic doll trace a line from disposability to decomposition. The body is portrayed as unsalvageable, fragmented under exposed electrical wiring in front of a half-painted and seemingly corroded red-white-and-blue emblem. As such, these assemblages paid homage to the unenduring and the inconsistent, rearticulating dead objects into three-dimensional montages. In his best-known work, Kienholz assembled freestanding constructions in which these dead objects resembled or became parts of a body. Life-size sculptures such as *Back Seat Dodge* (1964) and *The Wait* (1964–1965) produced uncanny bodies, figures that border on the horrific, formed from disparate discarded materials which rest motionless in a space between the animate and the inanimate. Thus, while Congress proposed to attach a self to a structure by transferring Kennedy's lost body to a new building, Kienholz had been experimenting with this transposition for years, making the transfer eerily literal. Tables became torsos, clocks were used as faces, as Kienholz went beyond the living memorial to propose the body as building.

In 1964 Kienholz incorporated his assemblage strategies with images from the assassination in a piece titled *Instant On.* The assemblage is a mock television, the body of which is formed by an old gasoline can. From the rear of the top rises an antenna; along the front is an imitation TV screen, and next to the screen are two dials taken from the controls of an electric blanket. Dominating the screen are two images: on the left, a still drawn from the Warren Commission reenactment, a look at the limousine from Oswald's alleged sixth-floor perch; on the right, a photograph of the School Book Depository Building through which Oswald's face can be seen when a lightbulb inside the assemblage is turned on. Unlike Kienholz's earlier work cited above, *Instant On* is not a composition of separate objects operating in juxtaposition. Rather, it fuses its various components into a unified piece, melding its parts just as television's flow melds a wealth of disparate communications. *Instant On* suggests not only the reclaiming of abandoned structures but their full transformation into new objects and uses. While the slain president is eulogized in the chambers of the nation's Capitol with a celebration of transhistorical values, Kienholz's work presents trash as the literal substratum of television, the defining contours of the culture's primary source for news and history.

This use of junk both undercuts art's pretense to beauty and monetary worth and devalues the role that television had come to assume in American life. The discarded materials also denote material impermanence and human mortality which go against the grain of America's emphasis on the new, the youthful, and the immortal.[5]

Kienholz's work suggests the degree to which conceptions of art were becoming problematic in the age of television, despite senatorial claims about the universality of poets and painters. In *Instant On,* the status of assassination imagery is quite literally implicated within the frame of these changes. Kienholz's insertion of these photographs in his junkyard TV marks them for subsequent reclamation and renaming. The artist's choice of imagery underscores the interpretive flux suggested by this composition. On the screen Kienholz juxtaposes photographs denoting radically opposed lines of sight: Oswald's alleged view through the scope of his rifle and the view of a bystander on the ground in Dealey Plaza. He forces the two perspectives to negotiate within a single frame, a depiction of the very struggle that would characterize the use of assassination imagery throughout the years of investigation.

Pop Images of Oswald

As Kienholz's *Instant On* and Berman's *Untitled* verifax suggest, photographs of Lee Harvey Oswald were almost as prominent a feature of the assassination imagescape as those of the widowed first lady. Ed Paschke incorporated the most notorious and widely debated image of Oswald into his painting *Purple Ritual* (1967). Paschke was a Chicago pop artist whose work during the sixties clearly displayed a formal debt to the early Warhol.[6] Like Warhol, Paschke had worked as a commercial artist and would, over the course of the decade, develop an increasing fascination with the emblems of popular culture. Warhol's favorite subjects tended to be the glamorous products of the media age, but Paschke focused more on the marginal, even the freakish individuals. Side show attractions and tattooed wrestlers made up Paschke's star system. In Chicago and later in New York, Paschke was also introduced to the American avant-garde cinema and, influenced by the aesthetics of Bruce Conner, experimented during the decade's middle years with collage filmmaking. Like Conner, Paschke cut Hollywood imagery and military and newsreel footage into rapid montages.

First shown at a 1968 exhibition at Chicago's Museum of Contemporary Art entitled "Violence in Recent American Art" — a show that also included Warhol's *Race Riot* (1963) — Paschke's *Purple Ritual* uses as its model one of the backyard photographs of Oswald, the one that appeared on the February 21, 1964, cover of *Life*. The photo-realist Oswald and the surrounding space are tinted a light purple and framed by four eagles, each clutching a stars-and-stripes shield and appearing to rest over billowing American flags. Paschke's focus on the assassination came during the crucial year of 1967, the year in which the Thompson and Meagher books issued from the buffs, Manchester's *The Death of a President* was gaining national attention, and New Orleans District Attorney Jim Garrison announced his plans for a conspiracy trial. Furthermore, the Chicago exhibition that first showcased *Purple Ritual* was devoted to violence in art and was clearly intended as a response to that city's summer riots. As discussed in Chapter 3, Oswald's identity had acquired an extremely mobile status by 1967, surfacing, depending on its context, in the form of a foreign or domestic agent, a programmed automaton, a lonely psychopath, a framed patsy. Paschke's painting reflects this situation in its own rewriting of the Oswald identity: "Rifle in hand, revolver in pocket, Oswald is the newest member of the American pantheon of gunslingers, the latest image in a national gallery that bestows undifferentiated attention on its heroes and its criminals."[7] Inclusion within the gallery of Paschke subjects further suggests the cumulative effect of Oswald's multiple identities and parallels the literature that assigned Oswald to sordid subcultural spaces.

Government-sponsored reports on violence in America had written the Kennedy assassination into the tradition of vigilantism, abstracting Oswald from the historical specificity of his alleged actions. In refuting those critics who had linked Oswald with various New Orleans and Dallas personalities (whether members of organized crime, the federal government, or a foreign power), these official histories situated him alongside such personalities as Booth and Guiteau. *Purple Ritual* comments on this process by eliminating the background found in the Oswald photograph. Gone are the details of location and time, the backyard with its tall fence and infamous shadows. Also dissolved in Paschke's painted reproduction is the name on the newspaper (*The Militant*) allegedly being held by Oswald, another trace indicator of political and historical specificity.

Indeed, the transfer from photograph to painting allows Paschke to render aspects of Oswald's image — the contours of his body, the details of the alleged murder rifle — somewhat less distinctly than the photograph does. Thus *Purple Ritual* figures the various makeovers allegedly perpetrated on the photographic evidence of Oswald. By painting rather than appropriating a photograph, through either collage or silkscreening, Paschke tests the spectator's scrutiny by presenting an uncannily similar image which is also not a faithful record. Recall that Oswald himself allegedly set up the backyard pictures and instructed Marina in how and when to take them. They thus became forms of self-presentation which were used against their maker, either by a conspiracy which framed Oswald or by the Warren Commission and the press which used them as evidence of his guilt. In *Purple Ritual*, Oswald's identity seems to be similarly lost or taken up within the textures of representation, his image not so much used against him as receding into the materials of the medium. The well-known photograph is made strange through its rendering in paint, its substance and bodily shape oddly present in outline yet imprecise in its presentation in oils. These elements of portraiture struggle against the contemporary meaning of the infamous photos and further the tension of Oswald's identity, the dual time frames into which he was being inserted in the sixties' assassination literature.

In *Purple Ritual*, Oswald's significant relationship is not with the space behind him but with that which frames him: the gaudy and hyperpatriotic stars and stripes. Like them, he has been elevated to the realm of emblem. Commenting on this, Paschke has noted:

I intended it to be a symbol of the American way of life. That is why I set Oswald down against the flag and seals. The only literal thing I did in the painting was to color him purple—the color associated with death and official mourning.

But whose death? Oswald's or Kennedy's? Both in a sense. My main concern was not the death of either man but rather the relationship between both incidents and their place in the fabric of our heritage.[8]

Like the Warhol silkscreens, then, *Purple Ritual* can be understood as commemorative gesture. Given Paschke's rather vague characterization, Lee Harvey Oswald can be mourned alongside JFK. In the painting he stands framed within, if not victimized by, nationalist discourses which are cloaked by the patriotic appearance of seals and flags. But in Paschke's painting even the flags are not immune to the decay resulting from the assassination. Into the red, white, and blue surrounding the painting now flows the purple death in which Oswald stands. Paschke has it seeping beyond the frame, encircling the eagles, so that it runs, as the artist states, into "the fabric of our heritage."

The Pop Challenge

Throughout the early to mid-sixties, pop's confrontation of aesthetic standards, its inquiries into the "proper" materials and subject matter of art, its enlistment of contemporary images and photographic processes, kept it nicely poised to anticipate the formal critiques and imagery of the assassination debates. It seems unwise to suggest that the presentation of Warhol's silkscreens in galleries and then museums played any role in the formation of the anti–Warren Report network, because their social location for the most part isolated them from those sectors in which the critique began. However, it is also clear that the formal concerns raised by various pop texts ran synchronously with the questions that assassination researchers were increasingly articulating. The task at hand seems less a matter of identifying how one sphere of activity influenced the other than of underscoring how the practices of assassination critics and pop artists drew upon or responded to various historical circumstances. The historian Johan Huizinga has noted: "History creates comprehensibility primarily by arranging facts meaningfully and only in a very limited sense by establishing strict causal connections."[9] The issue here may not be so much "arranging facts" as comparing discursive procedures and the situations that gave rise to them. But these two social settings shared a set of responses to the plethora of Dallas-related imagery and the efforts of the dominant press and the state to consolidate representation. Those responses — challenges aimed at the issue of authorship, the singularity of image interpretation, and the legitimacy of those who framed the discourse — were part of a joint process, the textual effects of which accelerated the shifting status of visual representation.

Certainly it was not a matter of these political or aesthetic challenges being "in the air" during the early part of the decade, a common but worthless explanation for the confluence of discursive activities. Rather, the availability of the assassination for representation — the cameras at work in Dealey Plaza, the analytic powers of the apparatus, the slowly increasing public scrutiny of the autopsy materials, and the crucial reinforcing power behind the ideology of the visible (itself renewed throughout the case) — established the base for these challenges.

Pop's engagement with the current event, its use of photography, and its foregrounding of the art/commodity/news alliance strengthened its role in the assassination debates. But there is a certain distortion in the above discussion of pop's presence, or more specifically, of the function of Warhol's assassination texts. That is, when read in some consolidated fashion, the axes of insistence and crisis in these works come into relief in a way they could not through the typical modes of display in the art world. I know of no show in which Warhol's assassination silkscreens were the sole or primary works on exhibit. As a result, because their formal concerns would have been in juxtaposition with other Warhol pieces or perhaps other works from the period, the application of these forms to assassination discourses were diluted and minimized. In isolation, each silkscreen can appear to refer more to an event than to a process, fossilizing the assassination in a way that counters the active quality of the artwork as I have been reading it here. This is not to say that their mode of display thoroughly undermined the associations I have outlined, but the edge carried by early pop was largely absorbed by the social and critical spaces of its fine arts environment. Its interest in the disposable and the transitory, its antimonument stance, could be undercut by the museum space itself. In addition, the Warhol silkscreens have been understood within the terms of art history rather than, say, political science or the history of the assassination. Although the buff's literature does mention the presence or impact of novels or commercial films centering on the event, their citations never include the Warhol portraits. Within the art history discourse, on the other hand, the challenge these works pose to the status of authorship is generally subsumed by discussions of the postmodern effacement of boundaries between individual imprint and public sign. Whereas the buff's discourse has no conceptual room for dialogue with the forms of pop art, the art history literature, though frequently referencing the proliferation of imagery in a television-made culture, generally tethers meaning back to some aspect of the characteristic Warhol signature.[10]

Dallas Camp

The mass duplication of assassination imagery, especially as in the Warhol silkscreens, also functioned to create an array of products around which a specific subculture slowly developed, one that was quite alien to the network of buffs and researchers. Kennedy artifacts—salt and pepper shakers of JFK and his rocker, dinnerware displaying the first family—would eventually become staples of camp merchandise. Indeed, the aesthetics of camp came to include Vaughn Meador (First Family) records and pink pillbox hats, and though the assassination may not have assumed the camp status of other sixties' idols or events, themselves Warholian subject matter, it is worth considering the important points of contact between camp and the wider assassination debate.

The migration of Kennedy artifacts into the category of camp is based less in the image of Camelot than that image's graphic collapse with the shooting in Dallas. The tragic and horrific nature of the event fulfilled certain camp requirements: "all of the necrophilic trappings that embellish its initiates' 'sick' fascination with the link between glamour and death."[11] Just as the spectrum of canonized camp stretched from the popular to the private, from Elvis on velvet to Jack Smith's version of the star system, so, too, did assassination artifacts. Dealey Plaza postcards identifying Oswald's alleged window or the trajectories of bullets were readily available, while more serious enthusiasts could obtain Oswald autopsy photos from assassination mail order companies.[12] Undoubtedly one of the rarest pieces to acquire camp value was a 1964 metal relief model of the assassination site $7\frac{1}{2}$ by $5\frac{1}{2}$ inches, complete with open sixth-floor window and the Hertz Rent-A-Car sign clock atop a 2-inch-tall School Book Depository building. By the nineties, replica magic bullets, imitation Jack Ruby business cards, and Fair Play for Oswald T-shirts could be obtained at assassination symposia. One-time signifiers of tragedy had their solemn meanings undermined. Emblems of homage or mourning were transformed into pieces for underground collecting and home display. In his essay "Uses of Camp," Andrew Ross writes:

The camp effect, then, is created not simply by a change in the mode of cultural production, but rather when the products (stars, in this case) of a much earlier mode of production, which has lost its power to dominate cultural meanings, become available, in the present, for redefinition according to contemporary codes of taste.[13]

With respect to the assassination debates, the relevant mode of production can be seen as the production of history as constructed by the joint efforts of the government and the mainstream press. The buffs and researchers who critiqued this mode not only challenged the official findings but broke down, often unintentionally, the attitudes of taste and the aura of solemnity that had originally enveloped the event and its representation. By attacking the structures of authorial legitimacy, the critics stripped away a set of cultural codes for decency and investigative seriousness to which they themselves often subscribed. As a result, the assassination debates became subject to at least two, often competing yet mutually enabling, discursive frameworks or modes of production: the investigative mode represented by the type of inquiries discussed throughout Part One and what might be termed the camp or pop mode exemplified by such commodities as post-cards and collectibles.[14] These modes are not distinct categories; however, their separation seems important as a way to register the divergent meanings that grew over time from a shared set of imagery. Nor is it the case that the investigative mode historically preceded the camp mode by much time. Warhol's portraits of Jackie suggest that the debate always existed within a period in which cultural meanings were somewhat unstable. Indeed, no challenge to dominant institutions operates totally apart from discursive struggles in what often seem to be quite separate social realms. Thus the destabilizations enacted by pop with respect to image making or image criticism must be read in kinship with those enacted by the assassination literature. If a range of institutional practices was contested during the six-ties to mid-seventies, it was only in combination, though admittedly com-binations often difficult to trace, that various practices succeeded in shifting the modes of production of cultural meanings.

That such shifts could produce camp values around the assassination also suggests that meanings were pried loose of their original context by factors beyond the individual practices of artists or Dallas buffs. For assassination critics, the destabilization of meanings surrounding JFK imagery actually exceeded their intentions or interests, and they could not avoid being iden-tified with the subculture of high weirdness. Even Ross, in his essay on camp, identifies Dallas conspiracy theorists as prime examples of "bad taste vanguardism," conflating both modes (the investigative and the camp) in which the debate had operated and assigning them to "a loosely defined nexus of cultish interests."[15] Thus it was not strictly the case that the inves-tigative mode of production had died off, thereby freeing its cultural prod-ucts to be assigned new meanings within the camp mode; such transfor-mations are rarely that neat. Rather, the representations that suffered an epistemological crisis did not merely subsist as culturally meaningless, but were appropriated and assigned various values within the assassination mar-ketplace. The legitimacy of the critics' discourse was continually forced to contend with these values, a task that after the House Select Committee's investigation was increasingly difficult.

If the investigative mode (as characterized by the critics' work) sought coherence — the contextualizing of diverse pieces of evidence into a stable form — the pop mode rearticulated assassination evidence in ways that ap-pear indifferent to coherence. Ross argues that camp "was an important break with the style and legitimacy of the old intelligentsia," a group that still courted the modernist values of originality and timelessness.[16] The integration of the assassination into the camp aesthetic, then, can be seen as a direct assault on the liberal intelligentsia's finest hour: the Kennedy White House and its showcasing of modernist artists. Warren Commission critics, many of whom identified with this aspect of the Kennedy aura and were perhaps motivated by the will to preserve or honor its glorious liberalism, became unwitting victims of the camp mode. Ross suggests, in fact, that camp reintroduces the question of taste in creating a new sensibility, one that is capable of recognizing the humor or other camp values in objects abandoned by the taste merchants of a previous era. As such it functions as an antidote to pop's egalitarianism and nonjudgmental approach to the artifacts it appropriates. In this case, however, the camp mode was essentially indifferent to the investigative efforts of those who toiled with the same images and identities. The pleasures of the camp aesthetic hinge upon a sensibility of threat, of an audience, however marginal, sharing a pose that is perceived as dangerous to traditional tastes. Those whose aesthetic rules are being mocked disapprove of camp values and the campist finds pleasure, perhaps self-esteem in this disapproval. (Those involved in the investigative mode did not.) While paralleling the critics' work of questioning traditional categories of expertise and authorship, camp could not avoid challenging the seriousness of the conspiracy theorists. To assassination critics, questions about who killed JFK and the government's performance of its historiographic function stil mattered, even if their quest for answers bordered on obsession. In the camp sensibility, such questions appeared to matter little if at all; the images and bizarre narrative speculations attached to them simply provided the raw materials for semiotic rhapsody.[17]

Within the framework of assassination buffs, distinctions between these two modes remained intact. Critics rarely demonstrated an adequate self-consciousness about their use of representation or an awareness of the status of such imagery within practices such as pop art or alternative film and video. The buffs could afford to be ignorant of the pop or camp subculture, but they could not really escape the values or rearticulations emanating from them. Pop artists, on the other hand, while not rigorously schooled in the details of assassination research, were attuned to the devices and effects of the conspiracy theorists. The methods by which they worked — silkscreen, found object sculpture, collage — depended on a dialogue with the investigative mode, as well as its materials. One artist, Bruce Conner, appears to have shared the psychological intensity of the buffs. Confessing to one interviewer that he was "obsessed" with the memorializing of JFK in all its solemnity and exploitation, Conner decided that he would take advantage of living in Brookline, Massachusetts, just blocks from the slain President's birthplace.

I decided then that I would dedicate myself to recording what had happened and what would happen in Brookline because he was going to be buried there and I would live there for the next two or three years to work on that film and make a pilgrimage to the grave every day with my camera and show what had happened. Well, then they took him away from me. . . . On his birthday, which was about five months after his assassination, at the hour and the minute he was born, I stood in front of the house. . . . Everybody knew it was his birthday. Hundreds of people went to the grave. Hundreds of people appeared in Dallas and I was the only person standing in front of the house in Brookline, Massachusetts at that moment. That impressed on me that I had some responsibility there. It appeared that I was the only person who would relate to President Kennedy in this way.[16]

With JFK's real body now interred at Arlington, Conner began to make his record with the cinematic body, using a Ford Foundation grant to obtain archival footage for a collage film that would be entitled *Report*. For all their rich encounters with the contours of the case, the work of Warhol, Kienholz, and Paschke was confined by its stasis. Silkscreen, sculpture, and painting were somehow not elusive enough, unable to fully challenge perception and therefore rehearse the problems of camera vision. Cinema could offer not just the violence of assassination imagery, but of the light that pulsated from its projector. And this projection offered the artist a mobility and temporality that could speak directly to the status of the image as it ricocheted throughout the assassination debates.

Chapter 6 **Bruce Conner**

You collect these objects, make these films and then they are put back out into the world again. The history always changes even if the film is the same. . . . But we have to be careful of believing in these constructions. Any construction one makes can also be torn down and built again. That's what interests me.[1]

Along with Andy Warhol's silkscreens, Bruce Conner's work represents the most compelling formulation of assassination discourses to come from alternative art practices during the sixties. A sculptor, assemblage artist, and collagist who turned to filmmaking in 1958, Conner produced work richly inscribed in form and theme with the tropes of San Francisco funk and early pop. Informed by mass media iconography and the rearticulation of found objects, his sculpture and film fixate on images of violence — the threat of technology, natural disaster, state-sanctioned annihilation — through the radical juxtaposition of disparate materials. His works are further characterized by a sense of morbid humor, an ironic stance produced by a tension between the tragic or apocalyptic nature of his raw material and the formal manipulations to which he subjects it.

Conner's assemblage and collage pieces juxtaposed geometric forms with pop imagery and found objects in a manner suggesting the decay of high-modernist purity. Conner's two-sided collage *Untitled* (1954–1962) illustrates the point. On one side is an abstract design dominated by two circles and two squares within a wooden frame. But the arrangement lacks geometric or tonal precision. Built from discarded pieces of cardboard, wood, and tin, the formalism of its shapes yields to the irregularity of its materials. Its blemished surfaces are traced with past lives and prior contexts which underscore the material preconditions of any modernist claims to universality. Conner's comment that "All the films I have made are poverty films" resounds in his collage work as well. In *Untitled,* Conner is the artisan junkman for whom the wealth of the abstract symbol works in precarious balance with a poverty of means and method. The rough edges, the scratched and pockmarked surface, bespeak not the authorial gesture but the wear of history, scars received independent of the art-making process. The reverse side of *Untitled* bears the faint outlines of a modernist grid, but whatever re-

131

sidual order it maintains is overwhelmed by the collage's contents. A dense arrangement of photographs cut from the pages of pornography, images that anticipate the contents of Conner's films, are set in montage with images of classical paintings, an anatomy diagram, the artist's notice to appear for an armed services physical, and decals that declare "Warning" and "Fragile." On display in *Untitled,* then, is an array of subjects defining Conner's work: references to war and physical danger, often combined with references to (hetero)sexuality; the reclamation and collaging of discarded materials drawn from industrial and stag films, commercials, and newsreel footage; a foregrounding of the processes of construction; and related to this the insinuation that the material basis for the medium is often joined to, if not somehow ontologically connected with, presentation of the female body.[2]

Conner and Warhol

As a prelude to a discussion of Conner's encounter with the assassination, I want to consider briefly how his cultural interests and formal strategies are characterized by a series of significant convergences with, yet equally pronounced divergences from, the work of Andy Warhol. Their overlapping subject matter and shared strategies of repetition and appropriation are at once startling and misleading. It is in some ways hard to imagine two more contrasting personas: Warhol in the East, a publicity seeker and product of the New York art world; Conner, working primarily out of San Francisco, staying on the margins of any organized film community, driven to exhaustion and illness by his contact with the New York art scene.[3] Both, however, were drawn to representations of violence, capital punishment, the bomb, and the assassination, and both centered important works around the image or implied image of Marilyn Monroe.

The first thematic overlap, concerning capital punishment, can be seen in Conner's sculpture *Child* (1959–1960) and his assemblage *Homage to Chessman* (1960) juxtaposed with Warhol's silkscreens *Red Disaster, Orange Disaster, Silver Disaster,* and *Lavender Disaster* (1963). *Child* depicts a small wax body strapped into a chair with tattered nylon stockings. Whereas Warhol presents the electric chair unoccupied and very much depersonalized, Conner presents the apparatus in action, holding an undersized body, mutilated and burned, seated and frozen in suffering, its mouth drawn open in a silent scream of electrocution. The contrast in fact suggests divergent approaches to the human body.[4] In Warhol's work from the early sixties, the body appears an artificial surface, distanced through repetition and the poses of the publicity still. It is a replacement body, a bloodless copy. It can be severed into a closeup, as in the many Marilyn portraits, wherein its lips and smile can be detached without a sense of dismemberment or a feeling of pain. These bodies are detached, as if the artist had a strong aversion to the features of real flesh. Conner's relationship to the body (almost always female) appears less detached, a fascination founded on attraction and horror which results in representations of texture and a greater sense of corporeality. A body's grotesque postures and sensual potential are factors in many of Conner's collage works. Yet he also considers the body's generic qualities, the namelessness of the multiple torsos found in stag films and pulp porn. The repetition of poses, serialized into weekly supplements, is exposed in a work such as *Untitled,* the female body moving from allure to banality. Whereas Warhol often crops a photo to retain the face, Conner is more likely to frame the torso and discard or obscure the head. In the work of both artists, however, the body is often conceived within the scope of its disfigurement or association with death. For Warhol, imaging the tragic celebrity is only one such example. More closely related to Conner's *A Movie* (1958), with its cars careening out of control, are Warhol's *Saturday Disaster* (1964), *Ambulance Disaster* (1963), and *Suicide (Fallen Body)* (1963). The mutilated bodies in these prints, like the wax figure in *Child,* are twisted like the metal of the cars on which they rest — the body as mangled shell.

In *Homage to Chessman* (1960) Conner abandoned the body for an abstract representation whose title referred capital punishment back to a specific individual. Caryl Chessman, though convicted of violent sex crimes that did not carry the death penalty, was also charged with kidnapping, a capital offense, because he moved his victims from their automobiles to his own. Before finally being executed, Chessman endured twelve years of appeals and eight stays of execution, and his case became the most celebrated rallying point for groups opposed to capital punishment. Like Warhol's prints of the electric chair, Conner's assemblage depicts the lifeless workings of the apparatus. Wax relief, frayed wires and strings, and a telephone earpiece are attached to a wooden board. The materials could suggest the fried remains of a high tech death. A statement attached to the back of the piece explains, "the piece was begun on the day the execution occurred as a protest against the event."[5]

But the body is central to most of Conner's collage films made during the sixties. In *A Movie, Cosmic Ray* (1961), and especially *Marilyn Times Five* (1973), the female body is assigned an ontological filmic status, as if like the exposed sprocket holes, frame lines, and academy leader that surround it, the image of a naked woman is an essential material of both film and its history. For Conner's films can be understood as histories of cinema, recording its tropes — the chase, the sexual innuendo — and its ideological commitments — soldiers marching, the costumes of heroes — alongside its familiar spectacles. Implicated within the industrial footage — the documentary images of Teddy Roosevelt, the fifties' educational films that establish the cinema as a discourse of knowledge — are the fragments from stag films. The female body is exposed as a primary component in the history of film and in the epistemology of the visible that has underwritten it. But the spectacle is not just the female body but its naked display, devoid of specific identity in the manner of the underground or pulp image.

Nowhere is this better exemplified than in *Marilyn Times Five*. In this film, parts of a stag reel are subjected to slow motion and repetition as a mostly nude model rolls on the floor playing with an apple and a Coke bottle. Juxtaposed with these images, themselves intercut with frames of black leader which intensify the peep show effect, is a soundtrack of Marilyn Monroe singing "I'm Through with Love." As the song is repeated five times, with each refrain the lyrics grow exceedingly familiar and the supposedly alluring images increasingly banal. The title and the song would imply that we are watching images of the young film star, and Conner may have believed this to be the case. But the model is clearly not Marilyn, the implication being that the essential spectacle is the naked body rather than the celebrated persona. When asked in an interview, "Is that really Marilyn Monroe in *Marilyn Times Five*," Conner responded: "Well, I understand that it may not be. I tell people that while it may or may not have been Marilyn Monroe in the original footage, it's her now. Part of what that film is about is the roles people play, and I think it fits either way. It's her image and her persona."[6] Conner's statement misrecognizes Marilyn's screen image. Furthermore, the model in the film would seem to have little or no persona to compare to Marilyn's. Conner's remarks here skirt the point while underlining it: that the film suggests little about Marilyn but much about the interchangeability of female bodies. Whereas Warhol's Marilyn insists on the recognizable publicity shot which can then be reformulated with color and repetition, Conner's film plays upon misrecognition and a substitution of the body. Both, however, focus attention on the generic aspects of celebrity, on the paradoxical construction of the star as unique and yet mass produced. Marilyn is constructed as one of a kind, but in Conner's film she becomes identified with the generic stag film, whereas Warhol's portraits make clear that the value of her image is sustained through seemingly endless duplication.

Both artists also address how representation can transform the individual into spectacle and frequently replace the individual with images of violence. Disaster, accidental and planned, becomes the star. In *A Movie,* cars spin out of control, bridges collapse, the Hindenburg explodes — all of which seem suitable for Warhol's multiple printing. In Conner's film *Crossroads* (1976) and Warhol's silkscreen *Atomic Bomb* (1965), the intertextual relationship is most pronounced. *Crossroads,* a thirty-five-minute collage drawn from footage of the first underwater atomic explosion at Bikini Atoll on July 25, 1946, is a meditation on the bomb (and the atomic age) as theater, the mushroom cloud as colossal sculpture. Code-named Operation Crossroads, the explosion was photographed by the U.S. Air Force and the Atomic Energy Commission with some five hundred cameras located on ninety U.S. and Japanese ships. When the footage became declassified, Conner collaged some of it into a structural film essay on the atomic bomb as national performance, the ultimate spectacle for a culture of violence. *Crossroads* achieves a distended temporality through slow motion, and its use of repetition affirms its status as a film grid, uncannily resembling Warhol's grid composition for *Atomic Bomb.* In *Crossroads,* the sweep of atomic fallout moves slowly across the frame, activating, as in other structural films, the shifts in grain and light. While the image remains legible, attention is also drawn to its material substratum, destabilizing the representation as the fallout expands to encompass the entire frame. Similarly, in *Atomic Bomb,* the varying pressure with which the ink was applied to the canvas allows the individual panels within the grid to differ in legibility. The effect is one in which the surface of the image seems obscured by the density of the mushroom cloud. Both works, then, use the bomb's explosion to focus attention on the surface of the image, simultaneously suggesting how the image mediates and distances the devastating effects of the bomb.

Report and Other Works

But of all the violent events that Conner took as subject matter, perhaps the assassination most occupied his attention. *Report* is the central work, but two others also deserve attention. One is a sculpture entitled *November 22, 1963:* "a scorched, melted head with a few teeth biting out from it; nearby a bride from a wedding cake whose groom is laid out under glass nearby."[7] A reading based on this description is easily constructed. The celebrated political couple, often associated in the public mind with the formal wear of a wedding or a state dinner, is depicted here in the post-Dallas pose, the dead president under glass but on display. More important though, is the formal resemblance between this piece and Conner's earlier sculpture. Unlike the clean architectural lines of the Kennedy Center and testimony about the timeless ideals of art which accompanied the official memorial, Conner here registers the horrific qualities of Kennedy's death. The poverty of his materials also registers the artist/citizen's marginal status with respect to both the cultural rearticulations of Kennedy's identity and, of course, the investigation into his murder.

Closer to *Report* yet retaining aspects of pop sculpture is Conner's piece *Television Assassination.* Produced at roughly the same time as the first version of *Report, Television Assassination* is composed of images of Oswald's murder filmed off the television. Conner slows the images down so that they last for fifteen minutes through six loops projected on a white-painted television screen.[8] Here the disparate materials of collage are consolidated into a hermetic dialogue between two medias, in a process that suggests the overwhelming authority of television during the four days following the assassination. A film shot off the television is projected back onto its screen as if to complete a self-enclosed loop, implying the displacement or transformation of the spectator. With *Television Assassination* the projector assumes the position of the viewer seated in front of a TV set, a viewer who cannot intervene but can only project back whatever transmission is received. Human agency has been replaced by an exchange between two dominant visual apparatuses, both functioning in some reciprocal exchange of identity and history.[9] The repetition of imagery through looping reinscribes the insularity of the grid, making it seem increasingly difficult to interrupt the flow and control of information. The painted screen literalizes the notion of an investigative whitewash, television's window functioning in reality as a site of cover-up. Conner's use of repetition is undoubtedly meant to rehearse the constant replaying of Oswald's death on national television. But it also succeeds in suggesting how television can restrict analysis or would come to limit the subsequent investigation by fixating on a given dramatic image and locking up the airwaves with its persistent repetition.

The same point is made in *Report*, when Conner isolates the Oswald shooting with a freeze frame. Looping Oswald's death six times and distending the moment into fifteen minutes hints at the multiplicity that would surround Oswald's identity. *Television Assassination* also draws attention to one of the intriguing aspects of Oswald's death's being captured on TV: it left little doubt as to his killer, gave the Warren Commission its lone assassin, and yet eliminated any possibility that Oswald's identity could be established with certainty. At the moment of his death, Oswald's identity became dispersed across a field of representations, images, and documents which existed while he was alive but took on greater significance and authority once he was dead. The repetitions that structure *Television Assassination* figures this dispersion. As with *Crossroads*, the use of slow motion underscores the enfolded relationship between the image's iconic content—in this case, Oswald's body—and its material substratum—the grain of the film or the electronic dots of the screen. Thus the alleged assassin materializes and dematerializes slowly and repeatedly over the course of fifteen minutes, just as he would over the next thirty years in the assassination literature.

However, the formal manipulations Conner achieves with *Television Assassination* can also be read as a rearticulation of various strategies employed by the buffs. Painting the screen white blocks the flow of information emanating from the mainstream networks. Like the assassination critics, Conner extracts those images he needs and reformats them. He then reapproaches the apparatus to distribute his own history of the event, thereby reversing the source and direction of the image flow.

Report

"No one really laughed watching *Report* until around 1976," Conner has remarked in an interview.[10] As I discussed in Part One, the arguments of some assassination critics had achieved a certain legitimacy within mainstream discourse by the mid-seventies, with a momentum that would carry through to the House assassinations committee's investigation three years later. It is not surprising, then, that Conner began to notice his film producing amusement as well as anger around this time. As I have noted elsewhere, the buffs' work had slowly, often unwittingly, stripped away the solemnity that had surrounded the case. They had successfully questioned the authority of those who had managed the imagery and coordinated the official version of events. The assassination could be increasingly rendered humorous in part because the source of public outrage had shifted. If the story of JFK's death had somehow been turned into a travesty, it was now due to the perceived incompetence of official sectors of discourse: the Warren Commission and its defenders among the pillars of American journalism.

Conner's film work had always articulated the cultural negotiation between humor and tragedy, the comic made perverse through its juxtaposition with morbidity and disaster. Although *A Movie* or *Cosmic Ray* contain images of horror and destruction, the generic qualities of their war footage or car crashes mitigate their emotional impact. No such anonymity surrounds much of the imagery in *Report,* especially during the first half of the film. Indeed, the historical specificity and dramatic structure of the opening sequence make the tonal shifts in the subsequent collage sequences more extreme. The first half of *Report* includes the repeated images of the motorcade, of Jackie trying to open an ambulance door, and of the Dallas police displaying the alleged murder rifle. The end of this entire sequence can be marked by the introduction of bullfight footage. Although the first half of the film is the more formally opaque, it also offers the more complex and arresting inscription of assassination discourses.

In a manner closely resembling the Warhol silkscreens, the first half of *Report* mimes the strategies imposed on assassination critics. The film appropriates the official (and only available) evidence and destabilizes its authority while retaining the imagery for a new argument. Lacking access to network footage, Conner obtained images from a distributor's annual News

Parade compilation reel. He then organized the footage into a thirteen-minute film which is quite precisely inscribed by the negotiating status of representation, alternately registering epistemological faith and anxiety. As in the silkscreened Jackies, the crucial formal principle in *Report* is repetition, beginning with the multiple meanings of its title (media, the Warren Report, and the sound of a gun). Specifically, repetition structures the motorcade footage, which has been multiply printed and runs for one minute and twenty-five seconds. The sequence invokes what I have earlier called, with Gertrude Stein's terminology, the axis of insistence and suggests the kind of viewing and re-viewing that accompanied detailed analysis of the visual evidence. The rearticulations of temporality allowed by repetition simultaneously serve the buff's authorial struggle and the truth-rendering potential of camera vision. Operating the film at his or her own speed and frequency, the conspiracy theorist is freed from relying on the running time of a network broadcast or on the static, frame-by-frame reproductions in Volume 18 of the Warren Report. The sequence, however, is not structured according to an exact set of repetitions for, as the presidential limousine appears to pass by each time, several frames are omitted from the beginning and included toward the end; the president does eventually pass out of sight to the left of the screen. Stein's repetitions which are separated by "a difference just a difference enough" apply equally well to Conner's film. Each run-through insists on new visual information, no matter how small, justifying, if not demanding, the insistent reexamination of the film as it was practiced by assassination critics.

It is also the first half of *Report* that best serves the memorial function. Despite the presence of funeral imagery and shots of the Lincoln Memorial in the collage of the second half, the drama of death and the soundtrack's descriptions of grief maintain the emotional tone of shock and mourning throughout the first half of the film. Women have fainted, one voice reports, and grown men are crying. Another voice explains that Father Oscar Huber has just administered the last rites of the Catholic church. Notes on the film's production also suggest that it is this opening sequence that is inscribed by homage. In his chapter on Bruce Conner in *Film at Wit's End*, Stan Brakhage tells us that, in addition to the multiple 16mm versions Conner was to make over a four-year period, there was first an 8mm version composed of shots Conner took off the television during the weekend of the funeral. Brakhage suggests that the 8mm version is a sketch, a precursor, composed under the stress and pain of immediacy.[11] That stress is clearly transferred to the first half of the 16mm version, not only through the use of alternating black and clear leader (an element I will discuss below), but also in the way all the images for this sequence (with the exception of leader fragments that read "FINISH," "PICTURE," "HEAD") are derived from the days in Dallas, encapsulating the trauma and sadness of that weekend. The stunted motion of the motorcade resulting from the repetition even appears to defer Kennedy's inevitable encounter with the assassin's bullet, as if the filmmaker were struggling to prevent his passage through Dealey Plaza. Like Warhol with the Marilyn and Jackie portraits, Conner began work immediately after the deaths of Kennedy and Oswald, and despite the cynicism that can be read in *Report,* especially in its second-half collage sequence, the film is also saturated with commemorative emotion.

Three other sequences in the film are characterized by repetition — Jackie trying to open the ambulance door, the alleged murder weapon on display in the Dallas police station, and the academy leader frame numbers counting down in synch with the announcement of the president's death. But here notions of insistence are overwhelmed by the axis of crisis. This looping of the image track creates the sense of a moment frozen. Conner repeats the shot of the alleged murder weapon four times, citing the press's fixation on a single piece of evidence and, by association, on the single assassin. Jackie's attempt to open the ambulance door is repeated five times, each interrupted by eight frames of alternating dark and clear leader. This is followed immediately by the extended repetition and fragmented motion of the motorcade, a phrase stunted by ninety-one interruptions of continuity, a violent and persistent assault on the smooth flow of images. The jarring effect created during this passage, which accelerates as the presidential limousine becomes centered in the frame, simulates Kennedy's movements upon bullet impact. For he appears constantly thrown back to the right of the frame, the rear of the car. During this part of the film, Kennedy's body cannot be fixed, and its multiplications suggest the various doublings that have haunted the case. Ultimately this passage implies the limits of the amateur films shot during the motorcade.

Yet no matter how many times it is shown, how laboriously it is broken down, the footage cannot reveal the process of Kennedy's death. Like the Zapruder footage, the ostensible documentation may be subjected to an extended scrutiny, but it can never be made to give up the truth.[12]

The most pronounced use of repetition occurs after the extended motorcade imagery, when Conner loops academy leader frame numbers counting down twenty-three times. The countdown is accompanied by a reporter's voice explaining that the justice of the peace has just given official notice of the president's death; the numbers correspond to Kennedy's final heartbeats. They also lend a somber tone to the filmic pun made at the outset of *Report;* that is, the presence of the words *finish* and *head* on screen during the initial reports that something is wrong in the motorcade. The pun, of course, turns around the idea of an exposed leader. But, more importantly, deployment of the frame numbers underscores the linkage between writing the history of this event and the struggle over representation. Once again, Rosalind Krauss's remarks concerning the grid are useful—specifically her identification of the form with a materialism that maps the coordinates of the image surface. Conner's academy leader seems a distant relative of Jasper Johns's *Gray Numbers* from 1958, a grid composition that indexes the plane of representation. Not only do the intersecting lines of the leader resemble the cross hairs of a rifle scope, but they subdivide the frame into gridlike quadrants. As such, they draw attention to the surface of the image plane rather than to any representation in depth. This surface will be the location of struggle, the site of contests over access to and interpretation of the imagery. Furthermore, the film's mapping of the screen rehearses a similar tendency in the post–Warren Commission inquiries; that is, an attention less fixed on the event than on the textual practices carried out in its wake.

The repetitions that structure the first half of *Report* are preceded, however, by an explicit assault on the potential powers of camera vision. For two minutes and thirty-four seconds Conner alternates dark leader with clear, creating a stroboscopic effect that frequently forces viewers to look away from the screen. This is followed by an additional forty-three seconds of uninterrupted dark leader. Juxtaposed with this visual assault is the "authentic" audio broadcast describing the motorcade in trouble. "Something is wrong here, something is terribly wrong," exclaims one reporter's voice. Conner stitches together recordings from various mobile radio units, and we listen as reporters guess who has been struck in each car. As the screen is transformed into a pulsating flicker, linkages between knowledge acquisition and the gaze are imperiled, the look is neutralized, and the documenting capacity of film is arrested at just the moment when its recording function is most crucial. The presence of narration on the soundtrack and the absence of representations on the image track appear to balance the acknowledgment and disavowal of the president's wounds. As the screen flickers, the tension between description and negation resists the type of immediate closure facilitated by the wedding of image and narrative that was organized by the mainstream press. Here the inaccessibility of the image in the film mirrors its inaccessibility outside, just as ownership of the Zapruder film by *Life* and top secret government classification kept much of the visible evidence beyond public scrutiny. The epistemology of the visible, the motivating force behind the constant reexamination of the films, photographs, and autopsy materials and the basis for a faith in their revelatory potential, is thoroughly undermined during this passage. A sense of relief comes with the images' return, yet the repetitions that follow quickly undermine it.

The long motorcade repetition sequence similarly questions the power of camera vision. Here the images are accompanied by a precise eyewitness description of the shooting and an account of the president's reactions as the wounds were inflicted. But the optical desires of the critic (and the investigation) are checked once again, because the image cannot supply the corroborative information about the timing of shots. From the standpoint of inquiry, the viewer is forced to watch the looped motorcade, frustrated that its information is so limited and its formal deformations so paralyzing. Of course, Conner was not interested in using these images to advance the investigation; the film is structured as a critique of dominant groups and their organization and use of the assassination. But despite Conner's stated intentions, his film rather uncannily rehearses the formal tropes and effects of the case. This passage from *Report* also captures the innocence and ominousness of these specific images. The president is not only alive and smiling, but this particular film fragment has none of the bloody horror of the Dealey Plaza imagery. Its pictures seem benign. And yet, because the more graphic imagery was not viewed as film until years later, what Conner does supply is a fetishized loop, images that mask the wound but always carry its confirmation at the same time.[13]

This use of repetition contributes to an overall structure that frustrates linearity, disturbing the temporal coherence sought by the various camps of investigation. Specifically, Conner inverts the temporal sequence by collaging Kennedy's arrival in Dallas *after* representing the shooting. The second half of the film departs from the specificity of Dallas and disperses images of death across an array of generic material. The president is associated through image/sound juxtapositions with both the bullfighter and the slain bull, while in subsequent imagery the Kennedys are compared to circus lions in a ring. The idea of the assassination as spectator sport or commercial entertainment runs throughout the second half of the film. *Air Force One* is montaged with a refrigerator ad. The cries of trouble from radio reporters are made banal through juxtaposition with an S.O.S. soap pad commercial.

When I started the big problem was that I had to show what had happened: the exploitation of the man's death. That's what I had to show. That's what I wanted to show and I had to show it because nobody else was. There was tons of other information coming through the media—but this exploitation was the most obvious thing to me.[14]

These remarks by Conner suggest a solemnity of purpose not present in Warhol's rhetoric. The attitude expressed by Conner's comments about the making of *Report* imply a sense of intervention, a commitment to fighting exploitation, whereas Warhol appears more ambivalent, striking a pose that often revels in the commercialization of events. *Report* is explicit in linking economic motive to the transmission of knowledge as Kennedy's death is offered as goods for the marketplace.[15] As Warhol suggested through his silkscreens and Conner through his collage, the commodification of the assassination succeeded at effacing the specificity of the imagery. The point is not just that the slain president's image would come to be exploited over the years. Rather, the point is that the commercial use of assassination film and photographs would contribute to their negotiable status; that, like the cereal boxes with which they are juxtaposed in *Report,* these images would grow increasingly transferable and removed from the context of their production. That context, as Conner reconstructs it, is itself characterized as fractured between the ritualized banality of political spectacle and the sinister and mostly invisible underpinnings of the assassination. Conner mocks the officially cheerful tone and mundane platitudes that frame the description of Kennedy's trip to Dallas. The weather in Dallas "couldn't be better," we are told, and yet "the brilliant sun" is imaged as an atomic explosion. Local police keeping the crowd at bay are rendered through archival war footage, machine guns mowing down a swarm of onrushing soldiers. Estimations of police security are similarly undermined. "This is a split second–timed operation by the Secret Service," the reporter assures us as the screen is filled with the chaos of a ring in which a bull has succeeded in attacking a matador. Reportorial ignorance, however, then turns to conspiratorial overtone as the image and sound tracks coincide with ominous implications. An announcer prefaces his description of the motorcade route by saying, "for those of you who are waiting along the parade route," at which point Conner screens a brief shot of the School Book Depository building. As the voice continues, "just to make sure you find yourself in the proper location," Conner cuts to the image of Ruby shooting Oswald. As images accumulate, it becomes clear that a central theme in the film concerns the ideas of path and trajectory. The montage parallels the motorcade route with the funeral procession that would follow days later, and as the voice details the street names along which the limousine will travel, the corresponding image is a slow-motion rifle bullet traversing and shattering a lightbulb. This latter image, no doubt a reference to the bullet striking the president, might also be read as an assault on the visible. It is followed immediately by images of Dallas police exiting their cars and looking upward in a vain search for an assassin.

These images are then montaged with excerpts from *The Bride of Frankenstein.* The president in his casket is associated with the monster on the laboratory slab. The commodification of Kennedy's death now makes sense within a cultural tradition that commercializes horror. It is the Zapruder footage as low-budget horror film or, perhaps more accurately, assassination imagery as genre, a not-so-distant relative of the Hollywood product, complete with graphic head wounds, coffin tampering, and exhumed corpses. The body is presented as a reconstruction, either a literal (and clandestine) makeover, as some buffs have argued about Kennedy's skull, or in Conner's aesthetic as a photographic collage, as in the case of the Oswald evidence. The indictment is clearly pointed at elements of the press who trade in generic convention and who, in Conner's opinion, will trade on the body of JFK to market their own products. Moreover, the shadowy machinations of the scientist in his lab hint at some behind-the-scenes manipulation of the event and its representation. This hyperbolic view of conspiratorial menace is juxtaposed in *Report* with the images of an IBM secretary. This woman, surrounded by contemporary technology — a switchboard and headset — represents even greater forces of invisible control, rendered seemingly benign here through the generic identity of industrial footage.

This footage, privileged as the film's last, features a closeup of the secretary pushing the SELL button. It returns *Report* to the issue of authorship. The implication is that now the forces of the marketplace will assume the determining role in the writing of history, that the power behind the organization of images and their mass dissemination belong to the multinational corporation, be it a manufacturer of computers, of movies, or of the evening news. Read retrospectively, the film's assertion of IBM secretary as author would imply a consolidation of materials and references under a unified controller of discourse. As tempting as this reading may appear, I think that Conner's film ultimately resists that consolidation while being able to suggest the menacing invisibility of authorial processes. Unlike *A Movie,* in which Conner mocks the declaration of authorship by repeating his name and setting it alongside found footage and the most generic of titles, the filmmaker's name is conspicuously absent from *Report.* Effacing his own position as controller of discourse, Conner acknowledges, through the varied registers of his material, the built-in collaging devices of historical authorship, especially as it would be characterized in the assassination debates. His struggle to make and remake the film through eight versions between 1963 and 1967 parallels the persistent return of government authors and Dallas critics throughout the next two decades. *Report* as an ever-mutable history text can thus be seen as one among the many works-in-progress that assassination critics produced and amended over the years. Indeed, the yearly (often monthly) revisions of the various theories was one reason for the criticism leveled against Dallas buffs by the mainstream press, the format of the dominant media demanding a stability that the discursive practices of assassination critics could not accommodate. As the conspiracy texts mounted up, they produced a rather daunting narrative instability, if not incoherence, but the process did make visible to a frustrated public the methodological problems and textual uncertainties involved in the writing of history.

Finally, *Report* addresses the shifting status of assassination imagery

143 *Bruce Conner*

through contradictions embedded generally within the collage format. Collage is a somewhat paradoxical form, implying simultaneously the two trajectories of faith and crisis that I have characterized as running throughout the assassination debates. On the one hand, it employs archival imagery, newsreel or industrial footage in Conner's case, and demands that these fragments be granted documentary status. Yet at the same time, collage recasts the meaning of such imagery through the juxtaposition of materials torn from diverse contexts, which achieves various levels of irony, humor, or anxiety. The collage film thus possesses a structural tension that activates and then critiques the documenting capacity of its found footage. David James describes this as a "tension between abstraction and literality, between reference to the medium and reference to the world."[16] He suggests, in fact, that this tension became paradigmatic not only for underground film but for sixties' culture in general. That culture was informed by a persistent search for authentic experience, a search punctuated by utopian visions and an optimism about emerging technologies. And yet that same culture was characterized by opposite tendencies, a growing recognition of the mass-mediated aspects of life and the power of the economy to bend utopian visions to the service of corporate profits.[17]

In both the form and the thematic content of its images, then, *Report* articulated a tension that ran specifically through the JFK case and more generally throughout sixties' culture. James concludes, "If the alternative cinemas were typically powered by obsessions with authenticity, they were as often steered by the perspectives allowed by the rear-view mirror of irony."[18] James's images of the alternative cinema as a car puns nicely with an analysis of those concerned with the path of the presidential limousine crawling through Dealey Plaza. Throughout the sixties, Bruce Conner kept returning to film clips of that limousine, producing perhaps the single most evocative work on the assassination. A few years later, the Ant Farm / T. R. Uthco video group returned the limousine to Dealey Plaza and titled their taped assassination performance / reenactment *The Eternal Frame*. Their trip would be steered entirely through the rear-view mirror of irony.

T he public debate over Kennedy's assassination once again intensified when in 1975 the Ant Farm video collective collaborated
with the group T. R. Uthco to produce *The Eternal Frame.*[1] Invig-
orated by events that had challenged government policy and procedure — a decade of attacks over Vietnam, the Watergate hearings — the
questions posed by Warren Commission critics were regenerated. Attaching itself to the limited self-examination the government was conducting
regarding FBI and CIA activities, the assassination debate migrated back
into the chambers of "official" investigation, resulting in the formation of
the House Select Committee on Assassinations in September 1976.[2] This
migration was accompanied by the widespread appearance (and reappear-
ance) of assassination imagery in mainstream circles, most notably the first
nationwide television broadcast of the Zapruder film.

The Eternal Frame

Thus, as various sectors of the nation returned to the events of Dallas, so,
too, did Ant Farm/T. R. Uthco. The video makers, however, foregrounded
it as a return to representation. *The Eternal Frame* records the performance
group's visit to Dallas and its reconstruction of the motorcade and assassination. The video not only is structured around a reenactment of the shooting
but includes interviews with the actor-participants, episodes of the production crew rehearsing the motorcade, and scenes depicting the responses of
tourists and onlookers who happend to be in Dealey Plaza at the time of the
taping. This complex interweaving of stimulated motorcade time and supposedly "real" production/response time allows the *The Eternal Frame* to
underscore the return to Dallas as performance rather than as investigation.
Indeed, the video functions as a critique of the investigatory mode, questioning whatever residual faith in the image continues to motivate visits to
the visual evidence. Whereas previous reenactments, whether literal ones
like that of the Warren Commission or the photographic ones articulated by
the buffs, relied on the efficacy of camera vision, Ant Farm/T. R. Uthco's
reenactment stresses the way the filmic evidence does not render a clear view
into the past but fixes a perspective for the future. It does this by situating
the Zapruder film at the very beginning of *The Eternal Frame,* positioning it
(and film in general) on the side of history, as the medium identified with a

145

past from which the performance and its video representation will be radically severed. The Zapruder footage is presented once (it appears even before the title credit) and then abandoned. At that point *The Eternal Frame* separates itself from the collage aesthetic that informs Conner's film and the textual appropriations that characterize the Warhol silkscreens. But while refusing to appropriate photographic materials, it does appropriate the point of view established by Zapruder's images, reinscribing the fixity of Zapruder's perspective in order to suggest its central role.

That role now asserts the Zapruder film as model. Subsequent representations, such as Ant Farm/T. R. Uthco's video reenactment, are thus representations of events as already imaged. Here the Zapruder film could be understood as a shooting script, its still frames as storyboards. The model from which the Ant Farm/T. R. Uthco reenactment is derived is thus an image, an already-focused and conventional piece of film, the perspective of which has become dominant. Thus Patricia Mellencamp notes in her analysis of the *The Eternal Frame* that "the real players simulated an image, turning a film into a live performance which is measured by historical audiences against the famous footage as reality or later in the tape against standards of 'art.'"[3] Caught up in this transference of ontological status are the spectators who stand in the plaza and photograph the reenactment/performance. In a sense, they have gotten what they came for: a glimpse of the murder. Apparently believing that they have witnessed an event staged regularly for tourists, they are moved to tears and glad not to have missed it. Both reactions rely on the disavowal of the differences between the assassination and its reenactment, a disavowal that reaffirms the video's central thesis: the power of the image to construct perspective and to assume the epistemological authority of the "real" or originating event in history. That authority then plays a significant part in the constitution/reconstitution of memory such that the chronological moorings of imagery are loosened. Implying that she remembers watching the event back in 1963 (an impossibility since images of the shooting were not broadcast for many years), one of the spectators to the reenactment comments, "I saw it on television after it happened."

By including bystanders' responses, the video extends its distanciation effects beyond that already created by shots of the crew and motorcade in rehearsal. That is, beyond revealing the signs of its own construction, *The Eternal Frame* creates a tension between its spectators and their on-screen surrogates. In the process, the video makers succeed at mocking the emotional responses of their on-the-scene audience, ridiculing the reception of the reenactment as so "real" and the enthusiasm with which bystanders want photographic souvenirs of the imitation motorcade. Absent from the video, then, are the overtones of mourning or commemoration traced

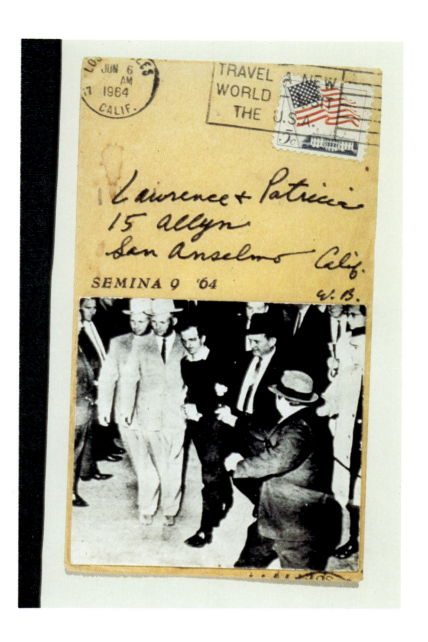

Cover of Semina 9 (verifax of Lee Harvey Oswald), 1964, by Wallace Berman

Above: Purple Ritual by Ed Paschke. Courtesy of
the Phyllis Kind Gallery, Chicago/NYC

Right: From The Eternal Frame by Ant Farm and
T. R. Uthco. Photos by Diane Andrews Hall

Untitled, 1954 – 1962, by Bruce Conner,
reverse, 60″ × 48″, paper,
paint, wood, etc. Collection
of Walker Art Center, Minneapolis,
Minnesota. Photo by Violet Ray

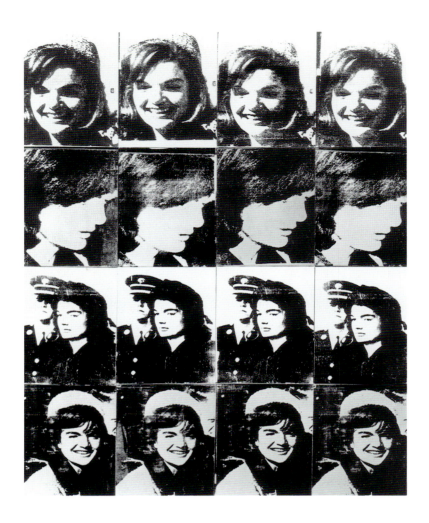

Above: Andy Warhol, 16 Jackies, 1964, synthetic
polymer paint and silkscreen ink on canvas, 16
panels, each 20″ × 16″. © 1995 The Andy Warhol
Foundation, Inc.

Right: Andy Warhol, Jackie (The Week That Was),
1963, synthetic polymer paint and silkscreen
ink on canvas, 16 panels, each 20″ × 16″.
© 1995 The Andy Warhol Foundation, Inc.

Instant On by Ed Kienholz, 1964, fiberglass
and flock, electric blanket control,
photographs, and antenna, 11″ × 6″ × 6″

through the Warhol silkscreens. Gone are the Warholian gestures of excess paint or pressure applied in the silkscreen process which signified emotional saturation. One of the women tourists watching from the street does in fact start crying, as memories of Kennedy's death return with the reenactment. But her emotion is hardly shared by the video makers. Her tears are made to appear ridiculous within the context of the motorcade as performance. Being commemorated here is not the slain president or whatever values he was believed to embody, but the 8mm film image that recorded his death. This transposition is rather neatly suggested by the pun in the title: the eternal flame has become the eternal frame. Kennedy's death is so thoroughly bound up with its representation that those who sought to find meaning or solace in his loss turned not to the Arlington grave site but to the grainy images of his assassination. The move from film to video replaces the temporal gap of photography — the time between exposure and development — with the simultaneity of televised transmission. Figured in that move is the negotiable status of the image as it was deployed in the assassination debates. The use of the Zapruder footage at the very beginning of the video briefly asserts the authority of film. The capacity of photography to register emotion is also inscribed toward the end, when the taped reenactments give way to a series of photographic stills, as the soundtrack's "Battle Hymn of the Republic" rises to its admittedly comic crescendo. Yet the intervening twenty-three minutes question the epistemological currency of the image. Mellencamp helps articulate the crucial point:

While Kennedy's death was, as the tape asserts, both a real death and an image death, far from liquidating representation it enthroned the film image. Eternal Frame critiques that powerful hold of the image as history on our memory and emotions.[4]

In *The Eternal Frame,* this critique of the "image as history" accentuates the gap between the event and its representation. Although this gap is underscored throughout the video — during interviews with the actors, motorcade rehearsals, the crew watching the rehearsals on a monitor and commenting on its bad taste — it is rendered most distinctly through a brief and hilarious chromakey image of the performers seated in the limousine in front of Dealey Plaza street signs. Here the video references the staged quality of Hollywood's rear-projection, implicating itself within conventions that acknowledge, while trying to disavow, the artifice of cinema. Elsewhere *The Eternal Frame* suggests the closing of that gap through the process of simulation. For example, the speech delivered by the actor-president near the beginning of the video identifies the reenacted killing as a consolidation of self and image, the conflation of reality and representation. Through a series of paradoxical statements, the actor-president announces both his death and rebirth as a function of image making:

It is truly fitting that I am only able to talk to you tonight via television, for like all Presidents in recent years, I am, in reality, nothing more than another image on your television sets. I am, in reality, only another face on your screens. I am, in reality, only another link in that chain of pictures which makes up the sum total of information accessible to us all as Americans. Like my predecessors, the content of the image I present is no different than the image itself.

Because I must function only as an image I have chosen in my career to begin with the end, and to be born in a sense even as I was dying. I suffered my image death on the streets of Dallas, Texas, August 10, 1975, in order to render my ultimate service to the media which created me and without which I would be nothing. I did this to emphasize the fact that no President can ever again be anything more than an image, and that no image could ever be in the past nor can ever be in the future anything but dead.[5]

Amid the actor-president's insistence that he is "in reality nothing more than an image," the video cuts away from his speech to show actor Doug Hall sitting before a mirror, ostensibly being made up for the scene. The assertion that image and identity are inseparable is thus questioned by a momentary reference to production processes at work beyond the appearance of the image.

Still, *The Eternal Frame* succeeds at eclipsing reliable markers between performance and authenticity, destabilizing categories such as model and representation. Event and image continually exchange status, as various film and video tropes complicate issues of transparency. Vérité camera work and the mixing of black-and-white images with color are used to differentiate performance modes, yet one suspects they are unreliable signifiers. When actor Doug Michaels is interviewed about playing the role of Jackie, his responses are juxtaposed with shots of him at the mirror getting into costume. While these cutaways suggest a clear break between actor and role, the fluidity with which the video moves between performative registers undermines the distinctions. The spectator grows unsure as to whether Michaels is acting the role of actor or speaking sincerely about his involvement in the project. The video appears to oscillate between a documentary of guerrilla theater and an element within the theatrical performance. Either way, the focus of the text remains not so much the assassination as its coded representation. The reenacted shooting in fact makes for a fairly unconvincing replication of the events of November 22, 1963, if such a thing is even possible, and its solitary limousine and performance of the wounds contribute to its status as comic imitation. Its impact therefore derives from its simulation of a set of images rather than from events, from its function as a remake of the Zapruder film, and from the acumen with which it copies the

Zapruder film's point of view, running speed, and distance from the limousine. The video trades on the repetition to which the Zapruder film was subjected and on its public circulation in both color and black-and-white formats. Thus the sequence entitled "November 22, 1975 Re-enactment" which comes near the end of the video is coordinated with the black-and-white print of the actual Zapruder film located at the very beginning. The text also references the point of view of other evidence, most notably the Nix film shot across Elm Street from Zapruder. It is alongside this shot that we hear one of the bystanders comment: "It looks so real now. The characters look so real." For spectators of the video, what appears so real is not how the performance reenacts the assassination, but how its images make for a nice imitation of older images.

Whereas the Warhol silkscreens and Conner's film used appropriation, Ant Farm/T. R. Uthco's video marks a more parodic gesture in its attempt to imitate an already-circulated and well-known piece of representation. Its efforts at distancing prevent it from approaching the parodic seamlessness of Krassner's assault on Manchester's *The Death of a President.* But the video was accompanied by a subsequent parody in the tradition of *The Realist,* printed in the pages of *National Lampoon* in January 1976.[6] Here photographs taken from *The Eternal Frame* and its image-assassination of the artist-president are situated like the stills of the Zapruder film as published by *Life* magazine. Four photos are numbered in the manner of the "original," and those that capture the simulated neck and head wounds, complete with the artist-Jackie retreating off the back of the limousine, are accompanied by captioned descriptions. These "as-yet-unreleased photos" are credited to amateur photographers, one of whom was standing on "the railroad overpass with a 300mm telephoto fisheye lens." Ant Farm/T. R. Uthco's critique of the transparency of images is thus extended to the textual supports in which it is framed, in this case its dissemination by the journalism community.

Both the video and the *Lampoon* parody extend the critique beyond the mainstream press or defenders of the Warren Commission to the buffs and their fetishization of the photographic evidence. The seemingly humorless assassination critics, their obsessive solemnity inscribed in the rhetoric of so many books and articles, are mocked throughout *The Eternal Frame.* Quite subtly, the beginning of the video comments on Dallas buffs' desire to construct a Kennedy imaginary and their efforts to rewrite the political biography of the cold war president. For many assassination critics this meant articulating a post-Dallas critique of federal institutions and practices and insisting that had JFK not been killed he would have embraced, indeed led, a similar reappraisal of governmental policy. In *The Eternal Frame,* the actor-president briefly figures this Kennedy makeover at a mock July 4th rally.

Asking "What has gone wrong with America?" he points to the crippling effects of "economic royalists, militarism, monopoly and the mass media." In fact, this makes up the enemies list for many assassination critics. By having a heavily made-up actor-president intone this list with a comically thick Boston accent, *The Eternal Frame* comments rather shrewdly on the revisionism enacted on JFK's political identity.[7]

By 1975 both Ant Farm and the *National Lampoon* were conscious of the camp elements of the assassination. Thus on the page following the *Lampoon*'s parody of the *Life*-Zapruder film layout is a reproduction of a "jumbo postcard," ostensibly meant to highlight the 1975 image death enacted by Ant Farm/T. R. Uthco. The postcard parodies the kind of Dallas souvenirs sold after the assassination which subsequently became part of the camp collectibles associated with the tragedy. Located on the card are the significant locales: the sixth-floor window of the Book Depository, the Dal-Tex Building, the motorcade route. But since the postcard is now a memento of the reenactment, its photo identifies the location of cameras rather than possible gunmen. Dealey Plaza is depicted as the site of a crossfire between super-8 cameras, video recorders, Nikon still cameras, and a Polaroid Colorpack. The space of the event is thus replaced by the space of the simulation, and the sources of that simulation — where photographers were located in the Plaza at the time of their shooting — are now understood as the important "points of interest." As with many of the Dealey Plaza postcards, an oval portrait in the corner is reserved for the slain president, but here JFK is replaced by artist-president Doug Hall.

Connoisseurs of assassination camp ultimately celebrated the bad taste implicit in commodifying a national tragedy. In the necrophilic aesthetics of Kennedy family merchandise after November 1963 — postcards, salt and pepper shakers, piggy banks — assassination "campers" found a subversive fashion where once there had been patriotic sentiment. The elegant first couple, the personification of style on the new frontier, became subject to the contradictions of offensive taste. The *Lampoon* articulated this process in one of their most notorious one-pagers: in a first-person paragraph, Jackie Kennedy describes her choice of the motorcade outfit. Pictured above are her pink suit, her bouquet of red roses and, drawn in a box, a piece of the president's scalp: "Soon I'll be waving to the people of Dallas from a motorcade as I ride through Dealey Plaza toward the triple underpass: I'd better hurry, because I don't want to be late for my . . . Date with Destiny."[8]

The formal and thematic issues raised by *The Eternal Frame* had been operating in earlier video work by Ant Farm. Eschewing the impulse of seventies' video intent on using the medium to cover social events or pursue anthropological documentaries, in *Media Burn* (1974) and *Cadillac Ranch Show* (1974) Ant Farm combined performance and video to document their own media spectacles.[9] In *Media Burn*, perhaps the group's best-known video, the artist-president assassinated in *The Eternal Frame* appears at a July 4th media event in which two "artist-dummies" drive a reconstituted Cadillac El Dorado through a wall of flaming televisions. The "event" is not only recorded by Ant Farm and integrated with interviews of supposedly authentic spectators, but is covered by the local television press as well. The press coverage is then integrated into the overall video so that *Media Burn* becomes a record of multiple performances reporting on each other. *Cadillac Ranch Show* documents the group's creation of a roadside attraction in which the front half of a dozen Cadillacs were buried in the ground and made into a literal piece of the Texas landscape. In both videos then, precise distinctions between the original events and their representations are dissolved, and the mutually enabling relationships between them, embedded in the term *spectacle*, are complexly articulated.

As with *The Eternal Frame*, *Media Burn* questions the implications for a culture thoroughly "informed" by image media and turns its critique on the icons of sixties' America. Explicit parallels are drawn between the Cadillac's trip through the television wall and the televised space launchings from the decade before. The artist-dummies play the role of astronauts, wedging themselves into their craft, communicating with the static-filled voices of "media control." The artist-president praises the Ant Farm artists as explorer-pioneers, and photographs of Apollo astronauts are briefly superimposed on the screen. Television as the central force in the era, as both mediator of experience and example of technological achievement, is linked with the culture's increasing fascination with the gadgetry of the new frontier: the design of the "fantasy dream car," with its internal cameras and monitor, as well as the technological wonders of space exploration. The presence of the artist-president further underscores the intersection of image technology and the operations of state because he represents the first product of a politics of television. This critique of the politics of television is then directly linked to *The Eternal Frame* in that both videos contain the July 4th speech delivered by the artist-president. In the version of this speech delivered in *Media Burn*, the artist-president tells his listeners: "The world may never understand what was done here today, but the image created here shall never be forgotten." He could just as well be describing the assassination as presented by *The Eternal Frame*. The historical footage will not guarantee knowledge or understanding, and the surface of the image may yield little beyond its infinite repetition.

The assassination, however, had a contradictory effect on the status of TV in 1963. The Kennedy-Nixon debates had testified to the power of the medium, and the weekend of televised coverage following JFK's death underscored its capacity to unify a national audience. But the assassination itself jolted television news into the future by registering its limitations, its inability in November 1963 to deliver images of the incident or to broadcast, during the first several hours, little more than anchormen in their New York studios.[10] Never again (with the help of developing technology) would television be caught without the apparatus to supply important images. The death of the first television president thus meant the birth of a sort of TV panopticism, a commitment by the networks to be constantly camera ready. Ant Farm/T. R. Uthco recreates the assassination almost exclusively for television by returning to Dallas rather than relying on found footage. *The Eternal Frame* could be understood, then, as television's revenge on the assassination, the increasing presence of cameras, professional and amateur, ready to capture (or produce) any potentially newsworthy event. Within any particular shot of *The Eternal Frame,* multiple cameras can be spotted recording the action from alternative angles as still photographers and videographers chase after the motorcade.

Ant Farms/T. R. Uthco's use of video instead of film also registers the movement of the assassination onto television in the mid-seventies, primarily the nationally televised broadcast of the Zapruder film on "Good Night America" in 1975. In fact, just as the debate was reemerging in the print and televised press and various critics were reinvesting their faith in the photographic recordings of Dealey Plaza, Ant Farm/T. R. Uthco's use of performance signaled a totally skeptical reply. The video makers' interest in vérité was directed not at the motorcade but at the reaction of its spectators and the surprisingly emotional responses generated by a simulation. While assassination buffs and their media supports still insisted on the transparency or legibility of the image, Ant Farm/T. R. Uthco employed the video image to record a form of street theater, implying that the investigators' search was essentially futile. When asked near the end of the video, "Who killed Kennedy?" Doug Hall responds, seemingly in earnest, "Who cares? We all killed Kennedy."

The Long Take

Had video production and distribution been readily available to assassination researchers in the mid-sixties, it would have served as an ideal vehicle for the kind of critique and analysis with which they were involved. By the eighties, that opportunity was taken up as critics began supplementing their written texts with video arguments.[11] In 1988, Gary Kibbons's *The Long Take,* produced outside the buff network, appeared as a reminder that some artists were still exploring the ontology of the image and its Bazinian potential as a tracing of phenomenal reality. As such, it revisited some of the theoretical terrain staked out by critics who had invested their faith in the visual evidence and struck a serious tone in consonance with the research community and at odds with the work of Ant Farm/T. R. Uthco.

The Long Take is a short video composed of four thematically related sections entitled: "film and death," "sex and death," "law and death," and "sex and law." A voice-over narration during the "sex and death" section paraphrases George Bataille's *Death and Sensuality,* commenting on the cultural organization of desire through the institution of taboos, the meaning of transgression, and the link between eroticism and death. The latter two segments address how the Canadian government presents a benign self-image through its rhetoric of opposition to the death penalty and how the state continues to police representation, either through legislation or through voyeuristic control of individual subjects. I want to focus, however, on the tape's first section, "film and death" which, although tangentially related to the other sections, engages more directly in a dialogue with two other discourses: phenomenological film theory and the Kennedy assassination.

The "film and death" section works by paraphrasing an essay by Pier Paolo Pasolini: "Observations on the Sequence Shot."[12] In this brief article Pasolini attempts to draw a parallel between death and filmic montage. Death, he notes, ultimately and exclusively brings meaning to life, settling the ambiguities and curtailing the potential for change that characterizes the sustaining of life. An individual cannot be judged honest, Pasolini notes in his example, until his or her life has ended and the potential for subsequent dishonesty has been eliminated. Only death confirms a kind of unity upon life which renders it meaningful. Pasolini argues that montage does the same for film by rendering the inherent present tense aspect of cinema, immanently located in the sequence shot, into the pastness created by editing. Borrowing Bazin's phenomenological approach to cinema, Pasolini writes: "The time of a sequence shot, understood as a schematic and primordial element of cinema — that is, as an infinite subjective — is therefore the present. Cinema, consequently, 'reproduces the present.'"[13] To exemplify this proposal, Pasolini chooses to discuss the Zapruder film, although he does not refer to it by this name, for he considers it the ideal sequence shot. He suggests we suppose that in our possession are a series of sequence shots, all of which capture Kennedy's death, but from differing angles: the perspectives of the alleged assassins, the witnesses, the police escorts. (No doubt Pasolini was unaware of the existence of just such a series of films.) Strung together, these fragments would offer up a "multiplication of presents," rather than an unfolding over time. He writes: "This multiplication of 'presents' in reality abolishes the present; it renders it useless, each of those presents postulating the relativity of the other, its unreliability, its lack of precision, its ambiguity."[14]

According to Pasolini, this juxtaposition of "presents," of fragments of what he calls reality's language of action, remain incomprehensible as long as they multiply the same action. What gives them meaning is their montaging into a coordination, an edited continuity that can render the present into the past tense. In this coordination the ambiguity of repetition is eliminated and replaced by the temporal meaning established through montage. This would mark a linguistic shift from cinema to film (in Pasolini's terminology) akin to the difference between langue and parole, whereby only the crucial moments of each perspective, each sequence shot, would be retained and the critical task would become that of ordering those moments into a single analytical reconstruction:

After this work of choice and coordination, the various visual angles would be dissolved, and the existential subjectivity would give way to objectivity; there would no longer be the pitiful pairs of eyes-ears (or cameras-recorders) to capture and reproduce the escaping and so scarcely cordial reality, but in their place there would be a narrator. This narrator transforms the present into the past.[15]

Pasolini's rhetoric is as extreme (if not more so) and as problematic as Bazin's in correlating film and the pro-filmic world. He writes: "this sequence shot, then, is nothing more than the reproduction (as I have repeatedly stated) of the language of reality; in other words it is the reproduction of the present."[16] But for Andre Bazin, editing introduced a degree of abstraction into the filmmaking process, in his words, an "unacceptable yet necessary" compromise of the ontology of the photographic image and its tracing of the phenomenal world. For Pasolini, the power of the sequence shot is reinforced through editing, dissolving "existential subjectivities" into objectivity. Ironically, this objectivity is created by yet another subjectivity, in this case, the editor of the existing sequence shots, what Pasolini refers to in this essay as a "clever analytical mind." The reality reproduced by the sequence shot is thus subjected to some Eisensteinian coordination, what Pasolini refers to as "choosing the truly meaningful moments" from among the available short films. Somewhat magically, it would seem, the editor is then able to discern the "real ordering" for these shots. For his mock investigation into the Kennedy assassination Pasolini has thus created evidence in the form of an ideal combination of image and montage. He is interested not in the moment but in the event, insisting on reconstruction rather than segmentation. Any repeated viewings of particular frames would be useless for Pasolini's mode of inquiry, and here, assuming that he was relatively unfamiliar with the details of the ongoing case, his thoughts anticipate the axis of crisis I have discussed elsewhere.

But more importantly, Pasolini's insistence on the immanent presentness of the medium and his theorizing of the ideal montaging of multiple sequence shots figures precisely the axis of faith which informed assassination critics. Although the critics relied on repetition as an important investigatory trope and Pasolini rejects that method as unreliable and ambiguous, his Bazinian trust in the apparatus and his utopian discussion of montage echo the approach assumed by many of the Dallas buffs. Writing this essay in 1967, Pasolini was in step, if not literally involved, with the second generation of Dallas researchers and the reconsideration of the Zapruder footage as analyzed by *Life* and Thompson's *Six Seconds in Dallas*.[17] Twenty years later, the axis of faith is rather blankly reinscribed in *The Long Take*. In the section titled "film and death," the video serves as an application of Pasolini's imaginary montage, a self-conscious suturing together of disparate materials into a continuous sequence. Accompanied by rather sinister background music, the sequence is narrated with a simplified paraphrasing of Pasolini's already-dubious association of death and montage:

Only when film is subjected to montage does the present become the past. Death and montage are therefore similar concepts. Death performs a lighting quick montage on the long take of our lives. It is thanks to death and montage that movies and life become meaningful and expressive. Montage accomplishes with the material of film what death accomplishes for life.[18]

Pasolini proposed coordinating various shots recorded in Dallas from the relevant "subjectivities." This is exactly how the first segment of *The Long Take* is structured. It opens with images of a library dedicated to the memory of JFK with large photographs of Kennedy mounted on the walls. The voice-over paraphrase reads: "It is absolutely necessary to die because while we are alive we lack meaning." This brief shot references the way the assassination contributed to or accelerated the struggle over the meaning of Kennedy's life and work. That such meaning is often conferred by institutions such as the library pictured here or the museum space is underscored by the content of the image. The video than takes up Pasolini's scenario, cutting between six color shots of the motorcade moving through the streets of Dallas. A series of views are juxtaposed: a shot from about five cars in back of the presidential limousine, then a reverse field shot of the motorcade, then two shots of the president taken from the sidewalk. A continuity is also established based on the various cameras' distances from Kennedy such that the sixth shot nearly approximates a medium closeup of him leaning on the car door and waving to the crowd. Over the course of these six shots JFK becomes more prominently centered in the frame. The video then cuts to a man looking into the viewfinder of an editing machine — Pasolini's narrator perhaps, the montagist able to transform "cinema" into "film." As if to show us exactly what this man is looking at, the next cut is to the Zapruder film and the voice-over reads the definition of the long take. Four stills from the Zapruder film are then momentarily on screen before the various alternative perspectives are reintegrated. Lee Harvey Oswald's alleged point of view, as rendered by the Warren Commission's reenactment, is shown, complete with the line of sight through a rifle scope. This angle is followed by two still photos of the railroad overpass, a spot at which several important eyewitnesses were located. Then comes footage of the grassy knoll shot from that overpass and, finally, footage of Elm Street taken from behind the picket fence, also a key location for both witnesses or a possible second gunman.

However, the ordered sequence orchestrated by *The Long Take* as prescribed by Pasolini hardly results in a montage that confirms ultimate meaning. Rather, it gestures in the direction of seamlessness without analysis. Like the essay on which it is based, the goal of the video, however skeletal its presentation, is closure through temporal continuity. In stark contrast to Conner's *Report,* the collage of Kibbon's video leans toward coherence and, in its serious application of the Pasolini text, accepts the ontology of the long take. Whereas *Report* frustrated temporal continuity and called into question the transparency of the documentary footage, *The Long Take* suggests the ordering capacity of narrative and, with its sound track given over to paraphrasing Pasolini, affirms the legibility of the image. Conner's act of appropriation not only challenged official sites of authorship but was aimed at critiquing the temporality imposed by those sites. Kibbon's film appropriation seeks to restore the "language of reality." It therefore leaves unchallenged Pasolini's notion of montage as guarantor of meaning, as translator of the incoherent. For Conner, the forces behind montage had to be uncovered — hence his references to Hollywood's horror genre and the IBM secretary. Their formal strategies had to be similarly interrupted through the exposure of frame lines, sprocket holes, or flipped frames. In Pasolini's scenario as enacted by *The Long Take,* montage appears anonymously articulated by nothing more distinct than the man viewing the Zapruder film.

In highly abbreviated form, the "film and death" segment of *The Long Take* resembles a compilation video produced and sold by the Collector's Archives, a Canadian company self-described as assassination research consultants. In their Kennedy Assassination Film Chronology tape distributed to Dallas buffs via the mail-order network, the Collector's Archives brings together perhaps all the existing footage of Kennedy's trip to Dallas. As Pasolini might have imagined, the tape montages into a thirty-minute chronology a reconstruction beginning with JFK's arrival at Love Field and ending with the limousine's high-speed run to Parkland Memorial Hospital. Here, then, is the master synthesis that *The Long Take* briefly implies. But contrary to Pasolini's speculation about the dissolving of "subjectivities" into objectivity, or the voice-over's assurance that montage brings meaning and expressiveness to film, the Assassination Film Chronology tape constructs a sequence, not a solution. It discards repetition, constantly rendering the present into the past, but despite Pasolini's rhetoric, neither it nor *The Long Take* result in "a clear, stable, certain, and therefore easily describable past."[19]

Much more expensive efforts to make that past more describable can be found in the narrative films produced during the thirty years following the assassination, to be discussed in Part Three of this book. Indeed, the role playing and reenactment of *The Eternal Frame* and the gesture toward temporal linearity of *The Long Take* point in the direction of these Hollywood films and their conventions of performance and continuity. These last four chapters, however, have sought to analyze a set of texts that share various historical reference points but have generally not been grouped together. When they are compared it is usually at the expense of any in-depth or specific discussion of the events they take as subject matter. Usually considered within authorship categories or the boundaries of a given medium, these texts have too seldom been investigated for how they precisely register the historical events and texts to which they are addressed. Important relationships can go unnoticed, in this case specifically the thematic and formal correspondences between the work of Andy Warhol and Bruce Conner.

What seems startling about the silkscreens, painting, sculpture, film, and videos considered here is just how precisely they are inscribed by the assassination debate, despite the apparent cultural gap between the investigators and the artists. Traced throughout these works are the same conditions that secured cultural meaning: the shifting legibility of the photographic image and its varying status as faithful record or unstable sign; the critique of authorship and the breakdown of information control brought on by the assassination inquiries; the frustration of narrative suffered by amateur and professional historians and figured in the tropes of repetition and metaperformance. Working within nonindustrial production contexts (Warhol is the possible exception here, but the medium in which he worked helped create similar results) allowed these artists to pursue formal strategies that could directly address these issues without having to conform to the demands of mainstream distribution channels. As a result, their work brings into sharp relief the activities pursued by assassination critics and the issues that resonated throughout the culture. Indeed, focusing on the Jackie portraits, *Instant On, Purple Ritual, Report, The Eternal Frame,* and *The Long Take,* one comes to understand the assassination debates not as a dialogue conducted by an increasingly closed circle, but as a confrontation with the same formal and epistemological questions explored simultaneously by the American avant-garde cinema, pop art, and postmodern video.

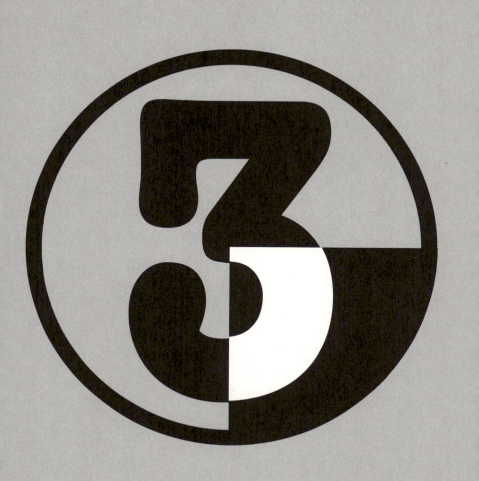

He felt connected to the events on the screen. It was like secret instructions entering the network of signals and broadcast bands, the whole busy air of transmission. Marina was asleep. They were running a message through the night into his skin. Frank Sinatra sets up a high-powered rifle in the window and waits for the train to arrive. Lee knew he would fail. It was, in the end, a movie.[1]

In *Libra*, his brilliant work of assassination fiction, Don DeLillo illustrates this often-remarked-upon incident of October 19, 1963. Lee Harvey Oswald, watching television with his wife on a Saturday night, sees *Suddenly*, Lewis Allen's 1954 film about an attempt to assassinate the president. The movie presents Frank Sinatra as a returned and troubled veteran, a would-be assassin who impersonates a Secret Service agent. Commandeering the house of a widowed mother whose husband has died in combat, the killers set up their shooter's nest in the family living room. Perched on a grassy knoll, the house overlooks the railroad station at which the president's train is scheduled to stop. Assassination critics on both sides of the conspiracy debate cited this historical coincidence, only implying what DeLillo openly imagined — the cinema as subtle motivator, source of identification, and ideological transmission.[2] In this case, the desire to assign the cinema some sinister psychic capacity may indeed be best suited to fiction, because subsequent research by assassination critics suggested that *Suddenly* was in fact not broadcast in the Dallas area on the night of October 19.[3] Nonetheless, the tantalizing coincidence this scene offered to writers and its presence in stories about Oswald registered a genuine faith in the suggestive powers of narrative film. It lent one more aspect to the cubist portrait of Oswald, here the impressionable movie watcher whose personal mission and historical identity are reflected back to him by the cinematic mirror.

Suddenly was not the only film reinvested with the meanings that emerged from the assassination debates. Indeed, while the buffs cited Oswald's possible connections to *Suddenly*, the producers of *The Manchurian Candidate* cited the approval bestowed on them by JFK.[4] Perhaps the outstanding example of Hollywood's returning vet and cold war scenarios, *The Manchurian Candidate* (1962) is as significant here for its exhibition history as

161

for its story of Raymond Shaw, the brainwashed assassin programmed to kill a presidential candidate. Kept off television for most of the two decades following its release, it was long rumored to be sequestered by its star, Frank Sinatra, ostensibly because its subject matter resonated too closely with the echoes of tragedy and conspiracy surrounding the death of JFK. It thus became something of a Hollywood equivalent to the Zapruder footage, its content considered too shocking for broadcast or too liable to reopen the nation's emotional wounds. When in 1988 the film was released in theaters nationwide and then cablecast on television, these reasons for its absence turned out to be apocryphal.[5] Still, this rationale for its status as absent text had clearly been influenced by the assassination debates. Not only its "suspicious" disappearance from the movie and television screen, but also the public's ability to contend with the inflammatory aspects of the film's plot became inseparable from questions about a possible conspiracy that were raised during the period of the film's absence. Indeed, the rerelease publicity used to market *The Manchurian Candidate* in 1988 played on these factors, declaring the film "Once Unbelievable, Now Unthinkable." The rhetoric of this publicity suggested that in the quarter-century that had passed, the sinister implications of the assassination literature had been sufficiently digested, if not legitimized, for the film's tale of conspiracy, incest, and internal subversion now to resemble shocking news more than science fiction.

Still other films, made after Kennedy's death, offered oblique references to the assassination or had their more violent moments read in hindsight through the prism of the JFK controversy. At the end of Arthur Penn's *The Chase* (1965), for example, Bubber Reeves is taken into custody by Sheriff Calder, only to be murdered Oswald-style on the courthouse steps. The film's narrative and mise-en-scène run parallel to aspects of the assassination: a southern town populated by hate and handguns, death at the police station, Calder's cowboy hat matching that worn by the deputy sheriff who accompanied Oswald, Calder's wife named Ruby, the grieving mother and widow left behind, the shots to the stomach in full public view.[6] In *Bonnie and Clyde* (1967) Penn returned to referencing Kennedy's death, although here his comment seems harder to grasp. In an interview with the *Cahiers du Cinema*, the director noted that the head wound inflicted on Clyde Barrow at film's end was intended as an illusion to JFK's head wound.[7]

Yet, despite the assassination narratives at the center of *Suddenly* and *The Manchurian Candidate*, they are not among the films I want to focus on in Part Three. Nor am I particularly interested in citing or interpreting every reference or possible allusion to the assassination or conspiracy in films made after the 1963 events in Dallas. Rather, I want to pursue close readings of five films. Three of these borrow narrative incidents from the assassination scenario but do not declare themselves as overtly about the investigation into a possible JFK conspiracy: *The Parallax View* (1971), *Winter Kills* (1979), and *Blow Out* (1981). The other two films mark explicit engagements with the JFK investigation: *Executive Action* (1973) and *JFK* (1991). Rather than using the assassination as narrative background, as in *In the Line of Fire* (1993), or as the dramatic setting for fictional biography, as in *Ruby* (1992), these films are thoroughly inscribed by the discourses of investigation, tapping deeply into the issues and problems discussed in Part One. No doubt such films as *In the Line of Fire* reflect certain contours of the thirty-year debate. The assassin as master of disguise takes its cue from the conspiracy literature's image of Oswald as changing man. The film also inscribes the master perspective fixed by the Zapruder imagery, most notably when Secret Service agent Eastwood recalls Dallas 1963 and the corresponding on-screen image, supposedly representing his own subjective view, shows the assassination from Zapruder's vantage point on the grassy knoll rather than that of someone running alongside the limousine.

Still, the films I want to consider make the investigation process the defining concept for their narratives. Although they extend and inflect questions pertaining to the epistemological status of the photographic/filmic image, their narrative formats produce a somewhat less direct encounter with these issues than those enacted by the pop and underground works analyzed in Part Two. A close reading of these films will take the analysis in directions unavailable to the Warhol silkscreens or the work of Bruce Conner, prompting considerations of narrative structure, character motivation, and the ways the assassination debate was fitted to the generic demands of commercial cinema. For DeLillo's Oswald, *Suddenly* was in the end more than a movie; it resonated beyond the television, it addressed his past, it warned of the future. So too, the meanings of these films extended beyond their commercial frame, linking up with and reformulating the historiographic issues and images which, as we have seen, informed diverse social settings and inspired artistic practice.

Before the issues of the assassination debate were featured as central narrative elements for a Hollywood film, they were deployed parodically in Brian De Palma's *Greetings* in 1968. There is an extraordinary scene partway through this film: Lloyd, one of the lead characters, is obsessed with the Kennedy assassination. In an attempt to verify or disprove the findings of the Warren Commission, he maps the bullet trajectories and the location of Kennedy's wounds on a live model, the naked body of a girlfriend. As she lies on her back apparently asleep, Lloyd reads aloud the wound measurements and affixes the precise markings to her body. He then removes his own shirt, already prepared with the bullet holes in place, and fits it onto the prone woman, discovering, to his delight, that the shirt holes and wound markings do not match up. "The whole thing is a blatant falsification!" he shouts. "I'll crack this case wide open!"

De Palma plays the scene for laughs, mocking Lloyd's obsessive enthusiasm for conspiracy, just as elsewhere in *Greetings* he somewhat benignly ridicules Lloyd's interest in the grassy knoll photographs and his bookstore encounter with a conspiracy buff. Indeed, one senses that had a more mature De Palma used the scene in a later film, the emphasis would have been on pathology rather than prank, its menacing implications more fully explored. Still, in uncanny fashion, the scene figures the intersection of discourses that informed the assassination debate in 1968: the amateur sleuth, the semiotics of entrance and exit wounds, the displacement of bodies, and the cohabitation of assassination and soft-core images. Surrounding Lloyd on his bed is the relevant literature: the "Reasonable Doubt" issue of *Life* magazine from 1966, Harold Weisberg's *Whitewash*, the *New York Review of Books*, a bogus issue of *Film Comment* with the phallic magic bullet on its cover. The principle of maximum visibility has been pursued to its extreme conclusion, the coroner's slab having been replaced by the bed. The concealed body of the president, knowable only through autopsy materials, has been replaced by a live female body, the truths of which have been culturally guaranteed by porn's epistemology of the visible.

Although De Palma's Greenwich Village frolic may reside on the margins of mainstream cinema, it marked one of the first direct incorporations of assassination discourse in American narrative film. Despite its mocking gesture toward the buffs, it captured the overlapping social spaces of assassination researchers and other strains of the sixties' counterculture. In *Greetings*, the assassination becomes one of several historical signifiers — Vietnam, draft evasion, Antonioni's *Blow-Up* — which punctuate a series of comic episodes. By the early seventies, however, the climate had been created for feature-length films fully organized around the dissent of assassination critics, a climate that ushered in a far more serious tone than accompanied the images of *Greetings*.

Seventies' Conspiracy Cinema

Several films produced in the seventies have in fact been assigned by other critics to a genre of conspiracy cinema. In their book *Camera Politica*, Michael Ryan and Douglas Kellner situate *Executive Action* and *The Parallax View* alongside such films as *Klute* (1971), *Three Days of the Condor* (1975), *All the President's Men* (1976), and *Twilight's Last Gleaming* (1977) in a group that represents the efforts and failures of seventies' American liberalism.[1] Inscribed in these films, they argue, is the dilemma of a liberal social critique which persists in privileging the individual over the structure in its assessment of power and its story of the causes of and solutions to social and economic problems. For these writers, the seventies were characterized by a "liberal statism," best exemplified by a reformist approach to social welfare which collided with a reemerging populist movement suspicious of big government. Without the inclination or the vocabulary to call for changes in the system, liberalism could offer no radical alternative to the statist approaches that had alienated many and that could not, given its focus on the individual, effect the necessary political transformations. Kellner and Ryan thus argue that conspiracy films present power in one of two ways, neither of which grasps its specific structure, but both of which conform to the liberal view. These films "turn the systemic concealment of real power structures into a personalized account of secret intrigue," often by reducing large power blocs or particular interests to the motives of a criminal few.[2] Furthermore, these films also depict the object of critique as some opaque or ultimately unnamable agent, such that "there is no recognizable enemy that the audience can identify as a nemesis or against whom negative emotion can be mobilized."[3] For these critics, such films may legitimately focus on the conspiratorial aspects of power in America, be it governmental or corporate, but they play to and inspire paranoia more often than analysis.

The scope of their study forces Ryan and Kellner to articulate general theses about the ideological tenor of a given period and restricts the specificity of their textual analysis. The discussion of the politics of representation seems rarely to move beyond the common dichotomy of liberal versus conservative. They begin the more specific analysis of *Executive Action* by noting that "the film successfully transcodes the popular discourse of conspiracy around the Kennedy assassination that thrived in the early seventies, but it also instantiates a problem of the left-liberal genre as a whole."[4] They are right to imply that much of the JFK literature was nested within a liberal agenda, which, as noted in Part One, clung to a faith in institutions while targeting the sinister forces manipulating them. Indeed, the critique of the state — its secrecy, its function as author of history — that issued from many assassination critics frequently remained fixated on the tragic event rather than on the discursive procedures with which they engaged. This fixation ultimately aborted its potential for more comprehensive or radical analysis.

Yet I would suggest that the specific content and the social effects of the JFK debate were more significant than Ryan and Kellner's reference to "the popular discourse" would imply. Moreover, one needs to register more precisely the relationship between this discourse and notions of conspiracy theory in general. The debate surrounding Kennedy's assassination should not simply be conflated with a conspiracy genre, to the extent that such a thing existed, despite the partial overlapping of their social spheres and markets of distribution. The conspiracy theories specific to Kennedy's death, outlined in Part One, were, I would argue, strongly responsible for the conspiracy narratives Hollywood articulated in the seventies and eighties. Occasionally intertwined but also distinctly separate from this literature were other notions of what might be termed postmodern conspiracy theory — a nexus of discourses related to science fiction which combine political intrigue, image technologies, and apocalyptic visions and which are perhaps best represented by the fiction of William Burroughs.[5]

For the most part, the JFK literature, especially that produced during the sixties, did not take part in the kind of sweeping gestures characteristic of postmodern conspiracy theory. However, its relationship to a politics of paranoia is more difficult to articulate. On the one hand, the work of the most important critics — such writers as Sylvia Meagher and Josiah Thompson — did not spring from paranoid fantasies whereby a sweeping theory of conspiracy developed from a sense of personal persecution. On the other hand, elements within the anti–Warren Report debate came to be characterized by several traits outlined by Richard Hofstadter in his essay "The Paranoid Style in American Politics."[6] For Hofstadter, an extremist strain has recurred throughout American history, a "paranoid" understanding of history and politics that focuses its attack on some enemy conspiracy set on undermining the fundamentals of American civilization. Whether it be the threat posed by the eighteenth-century Illuminati, the Masons, or the Communists, the paranoid style has consistently displayed a conspiratorial understanding of history, an attitude toward politics based on crusade rather than compromise. Two aspects of the paranoid style are especially applicable to JFK assassination critics: the tendency to view historical conflict as struggles between absolute good and absolute evil, and a related tendency that "traffics in the birth and death of whole worlds, whole political orders, whole systems of human values."[7] Hofstadter suggests that "the central preconception of the paranoid style" is "the existence of a vast, insidious, preternaturally effective international conspiratorial network designed to perpetrate acts of the most fiendish character."[8] That this description seems to characterize the JFK conspiracy debate is in fact the cumulative result of thirty years of social dialogue, for in and of themselves most investigations into or essays on the assassination did not put forth any overarching theory. Most were content (or discontent) with raising particular objections about the official version or the work of other critics. Furthermore, those longer studies that did offer coherent theories did not always insist on some "vast . . . conspiratorial network."

It is precisely here, with the perception of the all-encompassing conspiracy theory, that two narrative films have played decisive roles, the two films that will serve to frame Part Three of my study: *Executive Action* and *JFK*. Both films revolve around scenarios implicating large or opaque conspiracies, either between former government agents and powerful business interests, as in *Executive Action,* or among an array of government and former government agents, as in *JFK*. This is largely due, however, to the historical burden carried by both films. Each functions less as a "transcoding" of the popular assassination discourse than as a summary of it. *Executive Action* represented assassination critics' first opportunity to have access to a major audience through a Hollywood feature film and box office stars. It became necessary, through the work of one film, to sum up or at least reference the critical inroads established by a range of critics during the decade following Kennedy's death. The results thus reflect some compendium of Dallas research, less an indictment of particular historical forces than the promotion of a vague image of conspiracy within the paranoid style.

JFK emerged under similar demands. Its tremendous budget and celebrity director would guarantee its exposure, if not its impact, so that it came to appear the last great hope of assassination critics for an unprecedented public forum. Given the relative obscurity of *Executive Action* and the fictional premises of films like *The Parallax View* and *Winter Kills,* it became *JFK*'s responsibility to devise a narrative that could contain and transmit thirty years of assassination research. Under this pressure, how could anything short of a super conspiracy narrative be possible or acceptable? Thus the courtroom speech delivered by Jim Garrison/Kevin Costner at the end of *JFK* functions not as closing arguments against Clay Shaw but as summary arguments on behalf of the diverse network of researchers against the Warren Report. Through *JFK,* the multilevel process of investigation becomes imaged not as discursive struggle but as the formulation of one massive conspiracy theory.

A sense that the JFK debate was characterized by the paranoid style was further enhanced by the films to be discussed in the following chapter. Indeed, the appearance of paranoia is due not only to the presence of certain narrative factors but also to a mise-en-scène. The shadowy scenes of *The Parallax View,* the canted angles of *Blow Out,* and the icy vision of a psycho (Anthony Perkins) at the center of a conspiracy in *Winter Kills* helped define the identity of assassination buffs with an imagery that often dwarfed the writings and research they had produced. This image could then be used in turn against those who argued for a conspiratorial understanding of the assassination. As Christopher Lasch has written, "Hofstadter's work, in particular, was later cited so often by defenders of the Warren Report, in an attempt both to characterize the 'climate of hate' that led to the murder of President Kennedy and to disparage the people's belief in conspiratorial explanations of how it happened."[9] Questions of theorizing conspiracy would, in fact, become something of a double bind for assassination critics. The best of them resisted inflating their findings into broad theories of political manipulation. And yet their critique's efficacy was minimized if their focus remained on the assassination and did not extend to other abuses of power. Whenever critics sought to include their work in the overall challenge to the state and its efforts to muffle dissent, assassination critics ran the risk of being labeled conspiracy nuts in the paranoid style.[10]

The Cinema of Pathos

It seems of little use to insist that the films under consideration be categorized as a genre, despite whatever thematic and structural similarities they may possess. Rather, I want to situate them within the terms laid out by Thomas Elsaesser and Robin Wood in their work on American film in the seventies. The terms they outline will be especially relevant to my subsequent discussion of *The Parallax View, Winter Kills,* and *Blow Out.* In a speculative essay from 1975, "The Pathos of Failure," Elsaesser suggests that a defining feature of the seventies' liberal cinema is a lack of motives on the part of its heroes, one that results in a "fading confidence in being able to tell a story."[11] If there is an ideological critique being carried out by these films, it lies in their resistance to causality and its implied sense of progress. The classical cinema, Elsaesser notes, maintained "a fundamentally affirmative attitude to the world it depicts, a kind of a-priori optimism located in the very structure of the narrative about the usefulness of positive action."[12] The cinema of pathos, on the other hand, offers no such optimism about personal action's ability to resolve social problems. "Their liberal outlook, their unsentimental approach to American society makes them reject affirmation on the level of ideology, a rejection which has rendered problematic the dramaturgy and film-language developed within the context of an affirmative culture."[13]

Elsaesser searches for a mise-en-scène in these films that can render this rejection of affirmation. He locates it somewhat tentatively in a new realism, a visual concentration on nonpicturesque American detail: "stretches of barren roadside, its drive-ins, petrol-stations and hick town main-streets — the kind of scenery precisely nowhere and everywhere in America, and therefore furnishing an important element of abstraction without being itself abstract."[14] This mise-en-scène can also center on specific locales which serve as dominant metaphors: the theater in *The Last Picture Show,* the dance hall in *They Shoot Horses, Don't They?* These spaces and the unglamorous ways in which they are imaged successfully transmit "the almost physical sense of inconsequential action, of pointlessness and uselessness, a radical scepticism, in short, about the American virtues of ambition, vision, drive."[15]

Whereas the films in Elsaesser's study, many of them structured around the motif of the journey, register a plotlessness and a resistance to classical causality and conflict resolution, the films of my study are structured by complex plots and feature narratives driven by a search for solutions. The crisis of narrative figured by assassination films stems from plot situations that totally overwhelm their main characters, often through a form that foregrounds the untellability (and the related unintelligibility) of their stories. Thus, whereas the heroes of Elsaesser's cinema of pathos inscribe a mood of indifference through lack of motivation, the heroes of *The Parallax View, Blow Out,* and *Winter Kills* are strongly motivated by a mystery to solve or an ideal to redeem. What assigns them ultimately to the cinema of pathos is the total frustration waiting for these characters at the conclusion of each film and the thorough pessimism about the purpose of their missions. These films, while far from a stance of indifference, represent individuals whose total commitment meets only with tragic consequences. Their seventies' counterparts' (played by Clint Eastwood or Charles Bronson) determination was redeemed through a narrative closure of catharsis or violent satisfaction. But Joe Frady, Jack Terry, and Nick Kegan conform to the despair and the narrative failure that Elsaesser attributes to a cinema of pathos.

Elsaesser acknowledges that any narrative experimentation present in these films is limited still by the "audience-oriented" demands of the American film marketplace. Unlike European filmmaking, where the limits of narrative can be explored without the familiar forms of melodrama or the investigation, building an innovative cinema in the climate of the American sixties and seventies was a matter of "modifying traditional genres and themes."[16] Indeed, Elsaesser's fragmentary speculation (at best) about the historical causes of this cinema refers to the changed conditions of Hollywood production, primarily the alternative posed by television. Seemingly outside television's mainstream address, "ideologically less representative groups" still turned to the cinema for cultural representations with which they could identify. Here, then, was an audience for independent filmmakers whose own interests may have rested outside the boundaries defined by the newer medium and whose films could image issues or action unavailable to the small screen. The results, suggests Elsaesser, were films that could "reflect stances of dissent typical among minority groups."[17]

That Elsaesser falls back on familiar yet vague explanations (for example, these "movies reflect the moral and emotional gestures of a defeated generation") signifies less a failure of analysis than the difficulty of articulating specific historical influences. Robin Wood echoed and extended the work of Elsaesser's essay. In the same year, Wood observed significant overlaps between Altman's films and the "dominant themes of the American cinema today" — "the growing sense of disorientation and confusion of values, with the consequent sapping of any possibilities for affirmation."[18] Whereas Elsaesser had focused on a set of films concerned primarily with the motif of the journey, Wood examined the work of significant auteurs and a range of generic forms. The crisis of the family was inscribed in the horror film (*The Exorcist, Rosemary's Baby*), while the struggle with social decay was realized quite literally in the disaster and survival genre (*Earthquake, The Towering Inferno*). But in the films of Arthur Penn, Jerry Schatzberg, and especially Robert Altman, Wood found the most compelling evidence that "the central theme of the American cinema has been, increasingly, disintegration and breakdown."[19] His characterization of the structuring dynamic in Altman's films applies equally well to *The Parallax View, Winter Kills,* and *Blow Out:* "The protagonist embarks on an undertaking he is confident he can control; the sense of control is progressively revealed as illusory; the protagonist is trapped in a course of events that culminate in disaster (frequently death)."[20]

Although he cautions against simple cause-and-effect explanations, Wood suggests that the struggle over the war in Vietnam precipitated the dominant themes of seventies' cinema. In the course of this struggle, a range of ideological supports were torn from under the social structure, as the legitimacy of various forms of authority was questioned. Liberation movements initiated before and during the war thrived in this atmosphere of critique, challenging the racist and sexist structures that accompanied the traditional order. "What one can attribute to Vietnam," writes Wood, "is the sudden confidence and assertiveness of these movements, as if they could suddenly believe, not merely in the rightness of their causes, but in the possibility of their realization."[21] Like Elsaesser, Wood situates these general historical arguments alongside the transformation of the classic Hollywood system. The stylistic elements that forced seventies' narratives into a certain "incoherency" were in part the result of changes in the regulating function of studio production, the rise of television, and the demise of the Hays code.[22]

Context and Text

Wood's observations, like Elsaesser's, are crucial points of context within the film criticism literature of this period, and their general sketches of the dominant thematic structures of American cinema form the background for a closer look at the films I will discuss in detail. However, by relating the historical issues outlined in Part One to the narrative films that focus on assassination discourses, I hope to go beyond the general aspects of their discussions and articulate more specific linkages between context and text. My interest in establishing these closer relationships, however, is not intended as an overvaluation of context, my goal not simply to register how general discursive tendencies or historical events were inscribed in specific films.

Writing on historiography, Dominick LaCapra has warned against sacrificing the specifics of the individual text to contextualism, which results in a type of history by association that connects different levels or artifacts of culture by a simple juxtaposition, a "weak montage."[23] One problem with this associative approach is its tendency to minimize the resistant or contestatory aspects of particular works, consistently reading a film or a novel as emblematic of a larger dominant system. LaCapra is more articulate in critiquing the contextualist approach than in offering an alternative or efficient model for correctly elaborating the text to context relationship. He does suggest that terms such as *culture* or *society,* what is typically implied by context, be broken down or at least conceptualized according to its multilevel complexity. It was precisely toward those ends that Part One of this study was addressed. He writes: "One such requirement would be an account of the nature and relations of levels of culture and society — of elite, middle-class, and popular cultures; their links with a commodity system; and the manner in which they are embedded in social groups and structures."[24]

With this requirement in mind, I want to note the mass culture status of the narrative films being taken up here. Their situation within the commodity system and the ways that system circulates and advertises the images it sells strongly distinguished these films from the experimental works discussed in Part Two. These narratives operated on roughly the same plane as many of the mass-marketed books and articles at the center of the assassination debates. Moreover, they exerted a defining influence on the identity of that debate, a status not shared by the pop and underground texts. These films contributed to, even if they did not directly help construct a sense that the JFK assassination was a piece in some larger historical intrigue, its investigation exploring an environment also inhabited by the assassination of Robert Kennedy, the incident at Chappaquidick, and covert activities by secret government agencies. Like various aspects of the assassination literature, several of these films strayed from the specificity of Dallas, turning its details into transportable parts. In particular, it is in the fashioning of a certain "paranoid" image that film texts appear to have transformed context, helping to create, as mentioned above, the mise-en-scène for a social phenomenon many critics tried to describe in the mid-seventies under the heading "paranoia."[25]

Their status as Hollywood productions ensured that these films presented a more consolidated image of the investigatory process, combining narrative elements from the buff literature with the generic formulas attending the commodity cinema. As mentioned with respect to *Executive Action* and *JFK,* the conditions of production for these films demanded that their narratives sum up the conspiracy literature. They also came to register that literature's increasing legitimacy by the mid-seventies and the relative safety of the producers' investment in films that criticized or mocked the Warren Commission (as in *The Parallax View*) or the quasi-royal American family (as in *Winter Kills*). Ultimately it is impossible (and unnecessary) to say whether some vague sense of paranoia permeated aspects of the culture before the appearance of these films, or vice versa. Rather, one can try to specify the ways these films engaged with, responded to, and refigured the discourses operating elsewhere in the assassination debates.

At this point any clear distinctions between texts and context break down. LaCapra is correct to insist that individual works are not simple containers for dominant ideology, but notions of the resistant text ultimately speak to contextual questions. Qualities of contestation do not reside autonomously in a given film. His cautionary remarks serve best, then, as a guide to noting how certain films appear to reconstitute the frames in which they operate. For example, several assassination films succeed at transferring the focus of inquiry from government activities to individual interests and corporate criminality. Whereas the assassination literature sought out and partially exposed clandestine operations, the narrative films present, if not insist upon, the opacity of sinister power. Equally important is the representation of the assassination critic as lone investigator, effacing any sense of the collective inquiry that really characterized the buff network, in order to conform to the narrative economy that stresses individual action and lone heroes. Ironically, although the very existence of these films testified to a certain success on the part of Warren Report critics, the films themselves depicted the investigatory struggle as consistently doomed to frustration and defeat. As this and subsequent chapters turn to a more specific analysis of assassination films, I will mark not only inscription of their social context, but also how individual films refigured the prevailing discourse, issuing an image of the assassination debates as they developed through their second and third decades.

Inside Executive Action

Although much of this film is fiction, much of it is also based on documented historical fact. Did the conspiracy we describe actually exist? We do not know. We merely suggest that it could have existed.

When in 1974 the makers of *Executive Action* attached this statement to the beginning of their film, they admitted, in their stance of modest honesty, to the minor aspirations and severe limitations attending their assassination narrative. Seventeen years before *JFK*, *Executive Action* functioned as the first film with national distribution to organize its narrative explicitly around the JFK assassination, directly engaging the questions raised by the growing network of critics. Like Oliver Stone, director David Miller and screenwriter Dalton Trumbo chose a form of documentary fiction, combining historical names with characters of their own creation, integrating archival imagery from the sixties with filmed reenactments, and juxtaposing color with black-and-white photography in the reconstructed depiction of historical events.

In *Executive Action,* a right-wing extremist named Foster (Robert Ryan) recruits the services of James Farrington (Burt Lancaster), an ex–CIA operative who organizes and executes clandestine activities. This time Farrington's assignment is the assassination of JFK, an operation he successfully carries out with the assistance of professional hit men who had been involved in the Bay of Pigs invasion. Foster's motives for wanting to kill JFK are underscored in the film's opening scene, a meeting of co-conspirators with vague ties to government intelligence agencies and their corporate fronts. The Kennedy family is poised to become a political dynasty, they and the audience are told, the first president-brother set on using the powers of his office to advance a liberal agenda. This includes a test ban treaty with the Soviet Union, taking a leadership role in the civil rights movement, a cut in the oil depletion allowance, invoking antitrust laws to stop corporate mergers, and pulling out of Vietnam, thereby handing Southeast Asia over to the Communists. Without considering the political consequences of a Johnson presidency, these men assume that the removal of JFK will reverse the direction of American policy, ensuring the continuation of cold war support for the Pentagon and accelerating the demise of minority cultures within American borders.[26]

Unlike the assassination films that followed it, *Executive Action* does not revolve around the individual investigator. If the film can be said to have a central hero, it would be the slain president. As a result, the film is neither a mystery nor a quest narrative. The plot momentum is almost entirely determined by the inevitability of the events it tries to explain. Indeed, for a film purporting to depict the development and execution of the assassination, *Executive Action* represents conspirators who are essentially static, witnesses to history rather than agents of its change. Their passivity is established through the film's primary structuring principle: the act of watching images. Rather than represent the implementation of their plan, the film is crowded with scenes of Foster and Farrington in the observer's role, their identities determined by the passivity of continuous reaction shots.

The narrative is in fact structured according to a series of history lessons, each accompanied by visual aids supplied by the film's main characters. At the secret meeting that opens the film, Farrington narrates a slide presentation on the history of assassination in America. The deaths of Lincoln, Garfield, and McKinley and the attempts on Teddy Roosevelt and FDR are analyzed. Each time, the viewer is reminded, the official explanation certified the killer as a solitary madman, and Farrington assures his co-conspirators that the assassination of 1963 will follow the established historical pattern. Even before this minilecture, the roundtable discussion about the feasibility of the murder functions as a civics primer on the procedures of federal security agencies: Secret Service men are paid less than the FBI and practice their marksmanship only twice a year; the FBI does not work with other agencies; hundreds of American companies front for the CIA. The audience is further reminded that J. Edgar Hoover dislikes the Kennedys and that CIA director Dulles and his deputy director were forced out by JFK after the Bay of Pigs.

The lesson is picked up again when an unseen computer picks out Lee Harvey Oswald as the ideal patsy for the assassination. Again the co-conspirators huddle in the dark to watch a slide show, this time the biography of Oswald, complete with archival images of him in the Marines and with Marina in Minsk. Once Oswald is working with Farrington's contact and is being set up to take the fall, Foster is informed of his progress through another film screening, this time images of Oswald handing out Fair Play for Cuba Committee literature on the street. Finally, and most importantly, the conspirator-as-witness motif is inscribed during the reenactments of the deaths of Kennedy and Oswald. Farrington and Foster sit immobile in front of their TV screens. Their status as perpetrators is almost dissolved by the crosscutting, as the tense motion of the motorcade enroute to the fatal bullets is juxtaposed with the stasis of each man staring at his TV. At this point they hardly seem players in their own event, resembling just another pair of film spectators, assuming the same stance with respect to assassination images as that of the 1974 audience.

Quite fittingly, even the gunmen are briefly represented as witnesses just prior to their executive action. Before Kennedy comes to Dallas, the hit team is dispatched to rehearse their mission, a rehearsal that involves their attendance at a presidential rally. Located in positions that approximate their future shooting sites, the gunmen focus on JFK, this time with cameras rather than rifles. (The scene nicely parallels the bogus postcard of Dealey Plaza created by *National Lampoon*). Here *Executive Action* underscores the enfolded relationship between assassination and image making. In the following scene, the assassin-photographers study their results — images of JFK with cross hairs trained on his head — in anticipation of the shooting to come. The effect is one of the killers' appearing to glimpse the past, studying the assassination as already a piece of representation.

At only one point in the narrative does either mastermind take a hands-on approach to the assassination plot. To learn the progress of shooting teams training with mock victims in the desert, Farrington travels out west to the practice site. Yet in this brief scene actor Lancaster appears ridiculous, almost hilariously out of place. Dressed in jeans and a shirt that (one assumes) unwittingly display an aging paunch, Farrington meets his lead man at a roadside diner. He is an almost comic spectacle, the football cap on his head combining absurdly with the black horn-rimmed glasses on his face. Outside the wood-paneled library screening room, Farrington has no accommodating space in the film, nowhere he is able to appear an active part of his own conspiracy. Indeed, for both Farrington and Foster, physicality reinforces a sense of their own inactivity, their lack of agency. This is especially the case with Robert Ryan. *Executive Action* would be his last film, and here the often-menacing bodily presence that accentuated his brilliant career is gone, his movements confined to a lumber.

Farrington and Foster assume the role of witnesses despite the film's insistence that they are spearheading the assassination. In fact, the film's narrative strategy reserves yet another character for the crucial role of witness. Throughout the first half of *Executive Action,* Farrington and Foster repeatedly seek the tacit approval of a man named Ferguson (Will Geer). Ferguson is the president of TransJordanian Oil, a conservative representative of the business community who is at first reluctant to lend his endorsement to the murder. He is skeptical of the Kennedy dynasty theory, declaring to the co-conspirators that JFK's old man "was farther to the right than I am." Yet Ferguson is in no way instrumental to the assassination. He functions largely as the spectator's surrogate, the on-screen vehicle by which the identity of JFK as liberal can be substantiated. Ferguson's activities consist almost entirely of watching television news reports about JFK. Each step in the film's argument about Kennedy's liberal agenda is accompanied by a scene that opens with archival images of him addressing some policy matter. The camera then pulls back or cuts to reveal Ferguson watching the same image: JFK insisting that the general welfare is served by furthering the cause of civil rights and later images of Kennedy meeting with Martin Luther King at the White House; footage of Kennedy announcing that he supports a test ban treaty; and finally a bogus news broadcast intercut with a Kennedy press conference in which the anchorman reports sources' saying that Kennedy plans to remove all U.S. troops from Vietnam by 1965. This last viewing experience convinces Ferguson that the conspirators are correct, and he immediately phones them to confer his blessing on the murder plot.

Ferguson is therefore far more relevant to the film's social address than he is to the conspiracy within its narrative. His vague identity as a southern oil man conforms to elements within the buff network that sought connections between Texas conservatives and the assassination, characters who represented the antithesis of Kennedy's eastern establishment background but who were never successfully linked to any conspiracy. Ferguson suits the profile, constructed by the early sixties' discourse, of powerful interests who, despite their lack of direct involvement, were seen as profiting from JFK's death.[27] Moreover, Ferguson functions as the spectator's surrogate witness, an excuse for the image track to be devoted to archival footage of JFK sounding liberal themes. It is here that the film reveals a disregard for narrative economy and for the logic of adequately explaining the presence of certain characters. Rather than functioning as a story about a possible conspiracy (and here the crucial notion rests in the term *story*), the film works as a series of lectures, a summary of various issues and details raised by assassination critics. In the process, it reinscribes the assassination literature's tendency to place its epistemological faith in the photographic image.

In *Executive Action*, historical truth resides in the black-and-white footage of JFK, offered as incontestable evidence of the film's political interpretation of the sixties. Two formal strategies in the film serve to privilege the archival footage in this way. First is the montaging of historical film clips which the narrative subsequently situates as images being watched on television. Yet it is clear from the structure of these montages that they could not belong to a standard TV news broadcast, that the filmmakers have taken a liberty that violates realist conventions in order to focus on the subjects of civil rights or the test ban treaty. Thus the shot of JFK with Martin Luther King is preceded by a series of images drawn from the civil rights movement, images of protest marchers accompanied on the soundtrack by the singing of "We Shall Overcome." Similarly, images of JFK signing the test ban are preceded by excerpts of congressional testimony, in this case footage of Edward Teller and retired Navy Admiral Lewis Strauss testifying against the treaty. Although the spectator is supposed to believe that these images belong to a newscast being watched by Foster and Farrington, the montage is completed by the seemingly unrealistic dubbing of a Kennedy peace speech over the image of him signing the treaty. Thus, despite attempts to make archival footage fit within its narrative, the film succumbs to its authority. Once again *Executive Action* articulates itself as a fragmented historical lecture struggling to conform to the contours of fictional narrative.

The second formal technique that privileges the archival imagery has already been briefly mentioned. As the film follows its chronological trajectory through the summer of 1963, it increasingly relies on the introduction of scenes by way of historical footage. It then underwrites the truth of these images by attaching specific dates to them. In place of establishing shots, the screen is given over to images of Kennedy making some statement of policy. Only after the liberal message has been signaled and Kennedy's ideological identity secured does a second shot reveal on whose television these images are being broadcast. The second shots in these sequences (most of the time they are reaction shots of Ferguson or Foster) work to signify the preceding images as "unmediated" while also integrating them into the space of the narrative. That is, once these images are located as being watched by Ferguson in his study, they are set within a frame, literally that of his TV. Before that frame is introduced, these documentary images are privileged as conveying historical truth. As such, the technique rather simplistically reinscribes the reading of Kennedy's politics as put forth by some critics, ignoring revisionist critiques of his civil rights record and insisting that JFK thought and acted outside the cold war tradition.

In Part One I suggested that the critics' faith in the power of camera vision and the truth-bearing potential of the photographic image had to negotiate with a crisis of legibility, either through the overwhelming accumulation of representations and multiple interpretations or through the buffs' skeptical interrogation of the visual evidence as presented by the Warren Commission. This latter tendency is similarly inscribed in *Executive Action*. One aspect of the assassination literature incorporated into the Farrington-Foster plot is the doctoring of the Oswald backyard photos, the ones that show the alleged assassin holding a rifle and wearing a pistol. For Farrington these photos will be useful in framing their patsy, and the film devotes an extended sequence to the forgery process. Thus, while the narrative acknowledges the manipulation of images, suggesting in the manner of the buff's skepticism that things are often not as they appear, it insists that the spectator accept its own archival imagery as sound evidence.

Based on a story by Mark Lane and Donald Freed and crediting as researchers several assassination critics, including Penn Jones, Jr., and David

Lifton, it is not surprising that *Executive Action* is littered with details from the buff literature.[28] In addition to the Kennedy-as-liberal thesis and the doctored backyard photographs, the film puts forth the theory that an Oswald double was used to create eyewitnesses to his leftist learnings and interest in riflery. Furthermore, the film subscribes to the three-gunman four-shot theory which places a gunman in the School Book Depository, one on the Dallas County Records Building just south and east of the Depository, and one on the grassy knoll to the front of the motorcade. *Executive Action* also repeats the buffs' tendency to rely on the federal government for final sanctioning of the conspiracy thesis. According to the rhetoric of many critics, closure could be reached only by the government's acknowledging its own wrongdoing, either its own involvement in the killing or the cover-up maintained by the Warren Commission. Despite the assassination researchers' undercutting the government's authorial role, they still looked to Washington for a procedural end to the investigation. The film subscribes to this rhetoric through its prologue: a voice-over narration reads an on-screen text informing the spectator that, in one of his last interviews, Lyndon Johnson told a prominent reporter that he doubted the lone assassin theory which had targeted Oswald, but that right before the interview was aired, Johnson had requested that these comments be edited from the broadcast. Here, then, is the high-level approval the buffs had constantly sought.

The incorporation of assassination literature into the film's narrative ultimately achieves a transferential relationship. I would suggest that the filmmakers, acting as surrogates for the research community, articulate an image of the conspirators that comes to closely resemble the buff network itself. The identity of many assassination critics hinged on their role as analysts of imagery, and in *Executive Action* that role is transferred to the conspirators and assassins. Farrington and Foster are characterized essentially as men who display and analyze representation. They study maps of Dealey Plaza, they order Oswald handing out literature on the street to be filmed with a camera hidden in a van, they help train the voice of an Oswald double, they devise an elaborate code to send orders to the assassin team. Like the critics who tried to expose the conspiracy, the film's conspirators can be characterized as interpreters and manufacturers of imagery.

This transference then plays a crucial role in effacing any specific political identity for the conspirators. Indeed, for all its referencing of the assassination literature, *Executive Action* fails to indict any group or agency of the government, refusing to put forth any political theory of conspiracy echoing from the critical literature. As Joan Mellen points out in her essay "The Politics of Distortion," the film's opening scene serves to exonerate federal intelligence agencies.[29] The Secret Service is written off as incompetent, its agents having been to a late party the night before the assassination and its security plans totally inadequate. It is also clear from this scene that the group's intelligence comes from ex–CIA operatives or a contact who has infiltrated the White House staff. The FBI and CIA are not implicated in the plan, although it is implied that their methods of operation will add to the investigative confusion immediately following the murder, ensuring a safe getaway for the real culprits. Mellen argues that, rather than being affiliated with any existing or plausible political force within the United States, the conspirators of *Executive Action* are located on the ideological fringe: "Foster's views take him completely out of any viable American reality and into the realm of a proto-fascism removed from the modus operandi of American imperialism."[30]

Mellen's article, in many ways an incisive analysis of the ideological contradictions that structure *Executive Action,* is itself informed by the dual tendencies of faith and crisis in the photographic evidence. Like assassination critics, Mellen insists on the absolute legibility of the visual evidence, the Zapruder film in particular, and argues that the filmmakers' efforts fail because they refuse to let the famous 8mm film speak its truths.

These few seconds of the Zapruder footage alone destroy the Warren Report, the fiction of Oswald as the lone assassin and the lie that Kennedy was shot only from the rear. It indicates a conspiracy. And the cover-up of the Zapruder film by the FBI itself represents proof at the very least of a conspiracy to destroy evidence in the Kennedy killing.

Yet, although moments of the Zapruder footage are intercut in Executive Action, this one crucial sequence is omitted. We see in the re-enactment riflemen training their telescopic sights, but only on the back of the head of Kennedy. We see them shooting from behind and they hit "Kennedy" from behind. The moment of frontal impact from the Zapruder film is left out![31]

Mellen concludes by claiming that the film's intercutting of reenactment with Zapruder imagery undermines the latter's documentary capacity, guaranteeing that "so few, least of all an uninitiated audience, could distinguish the actual footage from the simulation." "It seems almost unbelievable," she continues, "that in making this film the Zapruder footage should be so used as to remove the one scene which would leave everyone shattered and convinced."[32] However, Mellen's admonition would appear to apply best to herself, for the crisis of legibility informs her own analysis. Zapruder's film is in fact not present at all in *Executive Action!* The sequence does integrate historical footage with reenactment, but the documentary films appear to be taken from the 8mm footage shot by Robert Hughes or Orville Nix. Both of these photographers were standing south of Elm Street, on the other side of the motorcade from Zapruder, and their angles of shooting were generally to the side or behind the presidential limousine. Apparently investing epistemological faith in *any* of the footage shot in Dallas on November 22, 1963, Mellen readily transfers identity from one piece of evidence to another. Furthermore, Mellen insists that the film undermines its own grassy knoll thesis by representing all the shots as coming from the rear. Once again the sequence is misread, for the head wound is clearly depicted as coming from the front, the camera approximating the point of view of a gunman on an incline in front of the limousine. Thus her description of a distortion via omission is in fact a symptomatic misreading which underscores the overvaluation of the historical image and its legibility.

As the first mainstream film to specifically address the debate surrounding Kennedy's assassination, *Executive Action* figured the problematic fit between the discourses of investigation, as constructed by Warren Commission critics, and the narrative format. More fragmented lecture than drama, the film argued for conspiracy in only the vaguest sense, positing the criminals as purveyors of representation, referencing details of the case as if a thin compilation of the assassination literature. However, that literature and the debate it informed supplied the basis for three assassination thrillers, films that discarded the historical names and archival footage structuring *Executive Action*. As we will see in the following chapter, in their quest narratives, their image of the investigator / amateur sleuth, and their climactic mise-en-scène, *The Parallax View, Winter Kills,* and *Blow Out* resembled one another, conforming in part to Elsaesser's outline for a cinema of pathos and to Wood's profile for a cinema of breakdown.

T he final image of *Executive Action* comprises a postscript: the eighteen photographs that appear on the screen are the faces of material witnesses to JFK's murder who died, many under mysterious circumstances, between 1963 and 1967. Written text informs the viewer that the odds of these people's dying during this time, as calculated by Lloyds of London, were one hundred thousand trillion to one.

The Parallax View

After its opening scene of political assassination, this is precisely where the narrative of *The Parallax View* picks up: with the fear of an eyewitness, horribly confident that such odds exclude her, that of the one hundred thousand trillion she is the one. Alan J. Pakula's 1974 film has two beginnings. The first is set atop the Seattle space needle where Senator Charles Carroll, a promising political figure and a narrative surrogate for both JFK and Robert Kennedy, is assassinated by two gunmen. Present during the shooting are Lee Carter (Paula Prentiss), a television reporter; and Joe Frady (Warren Beatty), a rogue newspaper writer. From the chaos of the murder scene there is a cut to a long shot which slowly tracks in toward the image of the blue ribbon government commission appointed to investigate the senator's death. It is of course the film's version of the Warren Commission, and its chairman solemnly announces that Senator Carroll was killed by a lone gunman who acted out of a "misguided sense of patriotism and a psychotic desire for public recognition." In hopes of putting an end to the "irresponsible exploitative speculations put forward by the press," the commission declares there was no conspiracy.

The narrative begins again three years later, when Carter shows up at Frady's door. She is terrified that someone is trying to kill her, that the next mysterious death to claim a witness to the Carroll assassination is earmarked for her. This scene initiates the film's central discourse on vision, one figured primarily by a mise-en-scène that obscures dramatic action through intervening glass, curtains, fences, and most importantly, a consistently shadow-soaked frame. Carter is targeted because she appears in photographs taken at the scene of the assassination, the film's equivalent to the Zapruder footage, and she tells Frady that the deaths of those pictured has risen to six.

183

Referring to the space needle, he says to her: "Did you see anything up there? Well either did I. And believe me I looked. We all looked." She then replies with a question that haunts the rest of the film: "You mean, if you didn't see it, it's not there?"[1]

When Carter is in fact the next to die, Frady's quest, and the film's structuring trajectory, are set in motion—to identify and then to infiltrate the agency or organization (Parallax) responsible for the murders of the assassination witnesses. Moreover, her death, and the narrative issuing from this scene, constitute the film's primary statement concerning the assassination debate: the suggestion that the criminal source of the JFK assassination continues to function, that the case is still open, not because the Warren Commission offered an inadequate solution to the crime, but because the conspiracy itself was not a solitary murder of a president. The conspiracy remains ongoing, informing, if not dictating, the contemporary political process.

The film suggests this toward the beginning by juxtaposing elements that refer to both Kennedy assassinations. Senator Carroll dies on the floor and is framed in a pose that deliberately mimics that of Robert Kennedy lying on the kitchen floor at the Ambassador Hotel.[2] The message is clear: the assassinations that characterized the decade were not separate incidents, but rather a continuing line of political subversion. That line began in Dallas. The film's reference to the JFK assassination is not achieved by so literal a parallel, but rather through a peculiar scene which appears to have little relevance to the mystery about to unfold. Frady ventures to a small northwestern town to learn about the death of another eyewitness, who allegedly drowned while salmon fishing. Within minutes he is goaded into a barroom brawl with the sheriff's deputy, a fight that succeeds in destroying half the tavern. Significantly, it is a western-style saloon with the men in cowboy hats and bolo ties and waitress-hookers outfitted as cowgirls. It is, in other words, Frady's encounter with Dallas justice, a trip back in time to some menacing place. Frady's long hair and hip individualism are immediately at odds with those in the bar, and the confrontation begins when the deputy suggests that Frady's appearance is feminine. It is in this small town that the narrative floodgates are quite literally opened when Frady almost dies in the dammed river in which Arthur Bridges allegedly drowned. It is furthermore the first locale in which Parallax or one of its agents tries to kill Frady. But, unlike Lee Harvey Oswald, the patsy with whom he will be paralleled at film's end, Frady escapes from this version of a Dallas sheriff. Finally, this is the place where Frady gets his first lead about Parallax. His finding their literature in the sheriff's home only serves to confirm the linkages between the surrogate Dallas and the ongoing organization of conspiracy.

By suggesting that the murder of JFK was only one event in a still-active war of subversion, *The Parallax View* coincided with certain tendencies within the assassination literature. As discussed in Part One, during the mid-seventies conspiracy theorists showed renewed energy, some critics expanding the scope of their hypothesis by trying to establish connections between Dallas and the deaths of RFK, MLK, and Malcolm X. Moreover, critics worked to discern linkages between the Dallas killing and clandestine government activities, primarily the Watergate break-in and cover-up.[3] Indeed, these critics argued, as one of them puts it, that "the cover-ups are more important than the original assassinations."[4] Thus the buffs understood their investigative work not simply as an act of historiography, but as a political intervention with relevant implications. In isolating connections between the JFK assassination and current government affairs, some critics identified a secret cabal which functioned to maintain the military-interventionist state. They argued that a second government existed, a shadowy and fluctuating enterprise made up of top-level intelligence agents, national security officials, and affiliates of the Pentagon. This cabal, alternately referred to as the Secret Team or the Power Control Group, not only had Kennedy executed but maintained the cover-up in order to protect its clandestine power.[5] Subscribers to theories about the Secret Team did not make up the majority of assassination critics. However, the growing presence of such ideas in the buff literature would be one of the defining characteristics of seventies' research.

The Parallax View incorporates this tendency but jettisons whatever was specifically political about it. Like *Executive Action,* the film makes a point of exonerating particular government agencies. Frady in fact tells his editor that he has no information that could link the government to the murders. Furthermore, the two assassination victims are rendered essentially apolitical; the film never articulates what they stand for or what their assailants are trying to silence. The film instead constructs and then indicts some vague image of the corporation, focusing Frady's search on a company that recruits assassins for assignments engineered by various business interests, whose ideological positions are never revealed. The politics of Parallax are characterized solely as profit oriented, and Frady's contact within the corporation informs him that "Parallax receives demands from all phases of industry." Thus, whereas certain assassination critics sought to expose a government ruled by gunplay, *The Parallax View* suggested that the principle was applicable to the general economy. The government itself, represented here by the pseudo–Warren Commissions that bookend the film, lends official (if not ignorant) cover to the criminal machinations of business.

Yet the structures of economic power go unaddressed in *The Parallax View,* as plot combines with mise-en-scène to keep the specific character of such forces visually obscure. Rather, the film both fuels and would appear to be reinforced by the seventies' growing distrust of the corporation. In their discussion of "conspiracy films," Ryan and Kellner suggest that filmmakers such as Pakula successfully approximated the public's attitude toward big business.[6] According to at least one comprehensive study of popular opinion regarding the status of corporations in American life, the mid-seventies marked perhaps the most profound lack of confidence in business since before World War II. Analyzing nearly twenty years of data, sociologists Seymour Martin Lipset and William Schneider concluded:

Thus a significant loss of faith in industries and companies took place between 1965 and 1975—precisely the years when anti-business attitudes and political distrust were increasing most rapidly. The collapse of confidence in business appears to have been quite broad; it applied to business in general and to every major part of the business community.[7]

The Parallax Corporation does business out of an opaque office building, and Frady is distinctly framed so that its glass walls dwarf him with their huge grid patterns. Parallax shares this ominous space with a gas and oil company and a chemical supply firm. Each despoils the cultural environment in its own way. The sinister powers of Parallax are rendered most explicitly perhaps through the scene in which Frady, trying to infiltrate the corporation, is tested for employment. Seated in a dark room, the test measures his physical reactions as he is confronted with a dense montage of familiar or generic imagery: political figures such as Washington, Lincoln, Kennedy, Nixon, Hitler; a comic book hero; happy families; romantic couples; historical photographs of civil rights violence and Vietnam; patriotic icons such as flags, the White House, an Uncle Sam poster. Intercut with these and many other images are single words: GOD, LOVE, COUNTRY, FATHER, HAPPINESS.[8] Perhaps the most significant juxtaposition joins a photograph of Lee Harvey Oswald with the word ME, a linkage that not only suggests the type of personality sought by Parallax but anticipates the way the corporation will ultimately employ Frady.

As Andrew Horton points out in his analysis of the film, the montage of this scene establishes "concepts of self, family, country, God, and love, and then subtly twists them towards their opposites. The ideal family is contrasted with the starving, disturbed family, love becomes hatred, sex becomes pornography, Lincoln and Washington are supplanted by Hitler and Nixon, and the Nazi and American flags appear in the same frame."[9] As a result, general connotations are stripped from the images, and their accelerated montage ultimately frustrates attempts to make sense of their interrelationships. In other words, this scene subtly registers the negotiable status of the image as it operated in the assassination debates, its tendency to slip into illegibility or be forced into opposite interpretations. The scene of the test radically interrupts the narrative, as if the social reality existing outside the film, but about which the film is directly concerned, seizes momentary control of the frame, spilling out its clusters of imagery and symbol across an otherwise dark mise-en-scène. The montage overwhelms the screen, operating without the frame of point of view and with a tenuous connection to narrative space, but its presentation may be no less opaque than the other images encountered by Frady.

Throughout the montage, Frady's point of view is merged with that of the audience; the film insists on their mutual identity as targets of visual assault. "At this level Parallax can be seen as the whole system of persuasion and ideological indoctrination that embraces both the entertainment industry and Madison Avenue style politics."[10] Indeed, as was the case with *Executive Action,* the conspirators are portrayed through this scene as manipulators of imagery, capable of registering (and perhaps instilling) the qualifications of an assassin based on the arrangement of strategic montage. The film thus depicts the killers as media experts, functioning, in the words of one contemporary reviewer, as the "new fantasy villains, corporate men in elevator shoes with technology at their finger tips."[11]

In the test montage scene those "fantasy villains" are invisible, confined to a voice that tells Frady when to leave the room. But this is only one of many scenes constructed around a mise-en-scène of paranoia, visual environments in which characters do not know they are under surveillance or in which apparently empty spaces turn out to be sites of concealed presence. This is generally the case with Frady's contact agent from Parallax. He appears one night at Frady's door, cloaked in the darkness of the hallway, and in a subsequent scene is found waiting in the deep shadows that constantly fill Frady's apartment. From the very beginning, intervening objects which obscure vision are associated with death. The Carroll assassination on the inside of the space needle is shot with the camera positioned on the outside, the gunshots muffled by the glass onto which the senator's blood splatters. The scene in which Carter comes to Frady for help ends with a shot of her on his balcony, her body partially blocked from view by flowing curtains. There is then a cut to her corpse in the morgue, the curtains having been replaced by a plastic death sheet.

The final scene and its two murders articulate most explicitly the film's thesis on vision and power. The rehearsal for a speech by George Hammond, the next victim of the Parallax assassins, is being held on the convention floor — the very site of official political discourse and the process of campaign rhetoric. Its artifice is underlined by the nationalist imagery of placards of presidential faces and by Hammond's prepared remarks echoing over the public address system while he practices his golf swing. This space is rendered in bright light. Conversely, the rafters in the ceiling and the catwalk from which the shooting takes place are the site of genuine political power, the space of clandestine activity. This space is rendered in darkness, the faces and arrangement of gunmen concealed. It is here that the evidence to frame Frady is planted, the rifle with its viewing scope a clear reference to Oswald's alleged murder weapon. Frady's attempt to escape the scene is depicted quite literally as a race toward light, the tall white rectangle of a doorframe, but before he can reach it he is gunned down.

During the Parallax test scene there is a sense that Frady has begun to lose control of the narrative, that the successes of his early work — the discovery of Parallax, his averting an airplane explosion, the confidence shown in him by his originally skeptical editor — are giving way to plot complexity on a par with the density of the montage. It is a process that can be traced through his shifting identities. When the boat owned by Alston Tucker (Carroll's campaign manager who has gone into hiding) is sabotaged and it appears that Frady has been killed by the explosion, he is free to construct a new identity for himself, so he instructs his editor to print his obituary. At the lab where he has the Parallax written exam filled out by a psychopath, Frady gives his name as Harry Nelson. When the Parallax agent first calls on him he still appears to be in control of his own destiny and operates under the name Richard Paley. But when Parallax learns that the real Paley is dead, Frady is forced to employ another alias, Richard Parton, the identity he got from an old friend and former FBI contact just after Carter was killed. The narrative gives no substantive clue as to when Parallax sees through Frady's cover, but by film's end, when he has been set up as the patsy for the Hammond assassination, it becomes clear that Frady had lost the power to author his own identity at about the time he believed he was successfully infiltrating the corporation. All that is returned to him by the second blue ribbon commission is his name, for somewhere in his transition from Paley to Parton, Parallax took charge of constructing his identity. Frady will be written into history as another Lee Harvey Oswald, as the lone, antisocial killer of George Hammond. The commission, in fact, rightly characterizes Frady as a man obsessed with the Carroll assassination but then perversely twists this identity, citing it as his motive for committing the crime.

In its presentation of the doomed hero, *The Parallax View* conforms precisely to Robin Wood's characterization of the seventies' protagonist, the confident individual whose "sense of control is progressively revealed as illusory . . . trapped in a course of events that culminate in disaster (frequently death)."[12] The film works to refigure the identity of the assassination buff, registering his or her inquest as essentially futile. Like the other films to be discussed in this chapter, *The Parallax View* presents the investigator as clinging to a naive faith in the power of the individual. Again the point is driven home by reference to the control of images. Both Carter and Alston

Tucker carry with them photographs from the Seattle murder. When Frady is on Tucker's boat, Tucker hands Frady a slide viewer containing two images from the crime. One of them captures the face of a Parallax gunman, but neither Frady nor Tucker knows enough to identify the man. Rather, the slide viewer serves only as a pathetic index of the imbalance between Parallax and its victim-critics, a piece of low tech equipment clung to by an amateur living under a death warrant. Even the name of the corporation suggests its power over visual perspective: invoking its powers of parallax, it is capable of creating slightly varied points of view on the same set of events.

Furthermore, *The Parallax View*, like *Blow Out* and *JFK* to follow, radically alters the politics of inquest, offering a public image of the post–Warren Commission investigations that is far more amenable to its narrative format than the historical record. Indeed, each film effaces the collective aspects of the assassination research by presenting the historiographic challenges of the period as essentially the work of one man. The Hollywood cinema's reliance on the individual protagonist is certainly a determining factor on this point, but in *The Parallax View,* as in *JFK,* this process is foregrounded by a specific line of dialogue. When Frady returns from Tucker's boat and asks his editor not to call the police or the FBI, the editor shoots back: "You alone can uncover what all these agencies couldn't?" Frady replies "Maybe," but the narrative replies "no." Under the generic constraints of the thriller, the political struggle to uncover Parallax or conspiracy is represented as a singular act and in that singularity there is failure. Imaging the buff as a hip individualist, *The Parallax View* constructs the political world as outside his grasp, transmitting, in its limited notion of critique, a pessimism about social change. The conspiracy theorist finds his diagnosis at odds with his political efficacy, and the conflict is figured in a mise-en-scène of visual uncertainty.

To several critics in 1974, that mise-en-scène, and the intrigue with which it was enfolded, seemed as justified as it was generic. For them, the reality of political events had finally caught up with the pessimistic screen images that had informed film noir and cold war spy thrillers. Joseph Kanon told readers of *Atlantic* that "what gives the movie its real force is the way its menace keeps absorbing material from contemporary life." As opposed to the era of *North by Northwest,* he wrote, now "the stuff of suspense thrillers has entered the mainstream of national life."[13] George Wead struck a similar note in his discussion of "filmnoia" in *The Velvet Light Trap:*

Our clichés have all come true in the 70s. We now have only our most cynical metaphors to live with. . . . At no period since Prohibition has it been so easy to establish immediate paranoia simply by reconstructing or referring to actual events which the audience has lived through. Executive Action uses film clips of Kennedy's assassination and The Parallax View opens with an

adaptation of Robert Kennedy's assassination. They make us paranoid by recalling our own past.[14]

The climate of intrigue or paranoia into which *The Parallax View* successfully tapped was not simply the product of contemporary tragedies. Rather it was an ongoing construct, the result of various discursive struggles which contextualized "our own past" and gave wider meaning to individual events. In fact, the very struggles the film was so pessimistic about helped create the conditions of its own production. Despite its representation of the investigator as doomed figure, the film remains indebted to the process of critique generated by government critics. Part of the film's social resonance is owed not simply to its "reconstructing or referring to actual events," but to its narrative engagement with the mostly amateur investigative process by which those events were continually reframed.

When George Hammond is assassinated toward the end of *The Parallax View,* the golf cart he is driving along the floor of the convention center veers off path and into a row of tables in place for that evening's speech. The red-white-and-blue tables are arranged in formation like some national symbol. To its end, the film remains vague about specific political sources for assassination, instead constructing a limited critique of power that fixes its sights on faceless business interests but can only really locate their agents of violence. That violence and its fragmenting effect on the country are figured in this scene as the golf cart smashes over tables and tears through the national colors. At the end of *Winter Kills,* originally released in 1979 and rereleased in 1983, a similar metaphor is suggested. Thomas "Pa" Kegan (John Huston), patriarch to the film's surrogate Kennedy family, flees onto the balcony of his own office. High above the streets of New York, he momentarily clings to life by holding onto a giant horizontal flagpole. When he falls to his death, his body tears through a huge American flag draped outside the Pan-Am Building. Again the fragmenting of patriotic symbol is offered as one of the final images for a film that attempts to tear away some national facade.

Winter Kills

Whereas *The Parallax View* offers a mysterious yet essentially coherent story of conspiracy, one in which the audience and its surrogate—in the figure of Joe Frady—can find focus and a basis for progressive action, *Winter Kills* insists on the uncertainty of focus, the unstable ground on which its investigator (and audience) move. Amid the darkness of mise-en-scène and the intricacies of plot, Frady was still able to uncover information that could form a solid basis for investigation, despite his inability to understand the larger picture. In *Winter Kills,* Nick Kegan (Jeff Bridges) is confronted with such a multiplicity of scenarios, false identities, and conflicting motives that whatever he uncovers only succeeds at undermining his fragile knowledge. Whereas *The Parallax View* maintained a seriousness about its foreboding mood, *Winter Kills* presents a conspiratorial narrative rife with generic parody and hyperbolic characterization. Indeed, these latter qualities allow the film to resist simple classification. In its exaggeration of performance and its foregrounding of generic clichés, *Winter Kills* resists categorization as straight thriller. Just as each new encounter forces Nick Kegan to reassess his previous experience, the film's tonal variations constantly force the audience to reconsider its narrative identifications. In its challenge to conventional expectations lies its threat. Its melodramatic mixture of menace and parody may well permit *Winter Kills* a more critical stance than the other films discussed in this chapter.

To what extent that threat was reflected in the film's mysterious exhibition history is difficult to know, but like *The Manchurian Candidate,* another film based on a novel by Richard Condon, *Winter Kills* became strangely absent between 1979 and 1983.[15] The film began production in late 1976 but was shut down by union representatives four months later for failure to pay crew salaries. In fact, during most of the time the film was in production, stars and staff worked without pay, and when work stopped in 1976, its producers had a creditors' list that numbered four hundred. The project lay dormant for two years while writer-director William Richert and various lawyers sought new financing. After filing for Chapter XI bankruptcy protection and contracting with Avco-Embassy to release the film, they resumed production in December 1978. After a three-week run in a limited number of showcase theaters, the film was removed from exhibition without explanation, preventing its next move to thousands of nationwide theaters. Furthermore, the film's exhibition in the Rank theater circuit in England was similarly canceled.

Both Richert and Condon have speculated about the film's disappearance in 1979. Richert recalls being refused access to shooting at the Pan-Am Building, ostensibly because the Kennedys had offices there. Condon, referring to theories advanced by others but implying his assent, wrote in the year of the film's rerelease:

It was 1979; a presidential election was coming up. Avco, which was the parent company of Avco-Embassy (distributor of <u>Winter Kills</u>), had revenues of 864,646,000 that year for its products and services, and these included important contracts with the U.S. Departments of Labor, State and Defense. It is tempting to speculate that Avco might have felt it expedient to please powerful political friends. And <u>Winter Kills</u> was, after all, just a drop in Avco's bucket. Mysteries are never mysterious if one has the right seat at the proceedings, but we don't.[16]

Here, then, is a case in which a film's original release dates paralleled a resurgence of the assassination debate, but its makers were prevented from cashing in. Condon's suspicions may be justified. It could well be that a rookie director, combined with first-time producers Leonard Goldberg and Robert Stirling, lacked the power to override the film's opponents.[17] By 1982, however, with Avco out of the film business, Richert succeeded in purchasing the distribution rights to his film and, after a brief showing in Seattle, opened *Winter Kills* once again in New York in January 1983.

Had the film remained in theaters in 1979 it could have provided an outrageous companion piece to the House assassinations committee report. For the film's narrative functions as a young investigator's odyssey through a collage of conspiracy theories culled from the literature of assassination critics. As the film begins, Nick Kegan, the half-brother of a former president who was assassinated in the streets of Philadelphia in 1960, hears the deathbed confession of a man who claims to have been second gunman for the infamous murder. Armed with new evidence of a conspiracy, Nick reports the news to his father — the film's approximation of Joseph Kennedy, Sr. — a lewd and eccentric patriarch in control of a vast corporate network and an immense private fortune. The parallels with the JFK case are established in the first several scenes: over sixteen innocent people have died under mysterious circumstances; a government inquiry — the Pickering Commission — concluded that a lone gunman named Willie Arnold acted alone; Arnold was killed Oswald-style while in police custody by a small time mobster named Joe Diamond.

Parallels between the Kegans and Kennedys could hardly be more thinly veiled. Pa Kegan is an unabashed womanizer, more than willing to pimp for his sons, and he gloats over the 1,072 sexual trysts President Kegan enjoyed while in the White House. Allegations about mob assistance for the JFK campaign are echoed throughout the story. The rhetoric of the new frontier returns in the Kegans' version of Hyannisport, a desert estate called Rockrimmon, and in Pa Kegan's imploring Nick to get on the case: "We got to be pioneers, son."

Winter Kills articulates the assassination debates as a series of narrative encounters, a telling and retelling in which multiple scenarios work to negate rather than reinforce one another. The film therefore registers the very dilemma that had stricken the historiographic efforts of the Dallas literature. But whereas *Executive Action*, and subsequently *JFK*, would negotiate this problem through conglomeration, the summarizing of previous research into a supertheory of conspiracy, *Winter Kills* structures its narrative around competing theories and multiple authors. Here, each new scenario displaces rather than incorporates its predecessor, producing a paranoia by subtraction. Nick Kegan's quest is fashioned as a series of visits with men alleged by one source or another to have been involved in the assassination. These visits comprise, in essence, a researcher's guide to the major theories constructed by assassination critics during the first decade of their investigation.

Thus the narrative starts with an indictment of the Philadelphia (read Dallas) police. In the figure of Captain Heller, local law enforcement is caricatured as idiotic, pratfalling its way through the investigation in the great tradition of Mack Sennett. To underscore the theory of police incompetence, Heller assures Nick that the force did everything it could to protect his brother on the day of the assassination. Nick then meets Z. K. Dawson (Sterling Hayden), an arms builder and rival of the Kegans. Dawson is self-conscious about the role cast for him by, in his words, "conspiracy lovers in this conspiracy-loving country"; namely, the cold warrior whose motive for the murder lay in the president's alleged gestures toward disarmament. Like Heller, Dawson, too, is hyperbolized, not only in Hayden's star intertext with *Strangelove's* Jack Ripper, but by the war games he plays on his land. The film registers him not only as a figure within the assassination plot, but as a character within the conventionalized plots of the cold war genre. It is as if Nick has stumbled onto another film set, his small car being absurdly chased and fired upon by Dawson and his men in their tanks. The point is reinscribed toward the end when Nick learns that Pa's right-hand man, John Cerutti, engineered the whole encounter with Dawson as a "little scene, a skit."

Dawson counters his own insertion into the conspiracy plot by contradicting what Nick thinks he has learned in Philadelphia. It was the Philadelphia police who killed the president, Dawson tells Nick, and he sends the confused investigator to see Ray Doty, former assistant to Captain Heller. Doty then functions as narrator for conspiracy number three, the Mafia connection, in which theories about Jack Ruby's relationship to the mob are presented though the character of Joe Diamond (Eli Wallach). Like Ruby, Diamond is a small club owner who fawns over the local police, has ties to the Cuban crime world, and is given the Arnold-Oswald contract to pay back a debt. Doty enunciates the mob motive as it was suggested by Dallas buffs: $2 million in contributions went from the mob to the Kegan campaign, but the president did not keep his end of the bargain.

Conspiracy theory number four is articulated in Cleveland, where Nick goes to visit Irving Mentor, another mob *capo*. The diner where the meeting takes place is stuffed with caricatured gangsters, men smoking fat cigars, wearing nearly identical fedoras and black overcoats. Mentor speaks the clichéd dialogue — "These are my boys . . . Joe was from the old neighborhood." He then proceeds to give the Marilyn Monroe scenario: the president was killed because he stopped sleeping with Ella May Irving, who then killed herself. The actress's death, Mentor tells Nick, cost Federal Studios $150 million. Mentor's story displaces Doty's until Nick meets next with mob boss Frank Mayo. The scene with Mayo in the back end of a prison van serves primarily to undermine the knowledge gained up to this point. Diamond never had Cuban connections, Mayo tells Nick, and Irving Mentor, whoever he was, was not a known member of organized crime.

Thus the narrative which progressively overwhelms the film's protagonist positions the assassination as a pretext for immersion into the texture of deceit that surrounds power. Early in the film, Pa Kegan insists to Nick that information is power, and yet the ensuing investigation challenges simple linkages between information and truth. The greatest weapon for the concealment of truth appears to be misinformation, and Nick's odyssey becomes increasingly characterized by revelations about false identity. Captain Heller, he learns, actually died years earlier, so the uniformed buffoon he met in Philadelphia was an impostor. The man he thought was Z. K. Dawson was merely playing the part assigned by Cerutti's little skit. Most damaging for Nick is the revelation that his lover, Yvette Malone, was an actress, apparently employed by Cerutti to distract him throughout his search. The film's deployment of false identity thus joins up with the hyperbolized characters and the parodied plot to suggest how the discourse of the assassination debates had become enfolded with the tropes of genre convention and performance. This is foregrounded primarily by Richert's use of fifties' Hollywood stars. Sterling Hayden, Eli Wallach, Ralph Meeker, Dorothy Malone, Elizabeth Taylor, Richard Boone, even Anthony Perkins allow the narrative's fixation on politics and the family to resonate with the cold war thriller and the domestic melodrama.

Nick's investigation is associated with a third fifties' genre toward the end of his search: science fiction. Indeed, the cinematic intertext is so potent with respect to the character of Cerutti that the narrative isolates him in a single space, and he is confined throughout the film to the family's corporate control center. The exact location of that center is left deliberately ambiguous, as it is represented as a windowless, futuristic building through an extreme low-angle shot that severs it from any surrounding terrain. (It is, in fact, a building located toward the south end of Manhattan.) Anthony Perkins plays Cerutti as a high-tech Norman Bates, his psychosis hinted at early in the film but then fully exposed through the close-up of his face after Nick has left the control center. But rather than peeking through a hole in the wall at women about to take showers, Cerutti is a global voyeur with state-of-the-art surveillance methods at his disposal. He is the film's glimpse into the future, but here the sci-fi nightmare is not the invading monster but the invisible gaze, the man behind the celebrity leaders, in charge of the corporate panopticon. With its huge-screen projection of the earth as seen from outer space and its cavernous rooms with panels of flashing lights, Cerutti's control center once again underscores the intersection of Hollywood and assassination discourses.

Furthermore, from *Executive Action* to *The Parallax View* to *Winter Kills*, the identification of criminality with the manipulation of representation has grown increasingly sophisticated. Like Farrington and Ferguson and the Parallax Corporation, the Kegan empire, under Cerutti's guidance, testifies to the political power invested in machines of the visible. Cerutti explains it to Nick as the two walk through the control center:

Visuals, pictures on microfilm, movies, video, marvelous little gadgets that document verbatim all your father's conversations with all his people and his people's conversations with others. From our satellite we can watch everything, nasty little wars in Africa, troop movements, ship movements, nuclear tests, the Sinai, the Panama Canal, every little thing to check out an investment, buy us in or out.

But Cerutti does not function to make the interlocking conspiracy theories more legible. Rather, his implication with the intertexts of science fiction support him as agent of confusion. For during Nick's visit to the control center, Cerutti offers three more scenarios for him and the audience to consider. First, Cerutti explains that it was Lola Camonte, actress and madame, played in a silent cameo by Elizabeth Taylor, who arranged the assassination with the help of Frank Mayo. Lola had arranged a large contribution from the mob in return for the elimination of Castro and had also provided President Kegan with a steady supply of women. Pa Kegan had also accepted Lola's favors and had agreed to the contribution deal. But when the president refused the deal and, according to Cerutti, broke all ties to his father and Lola, Mayo put out the assassination contract.

Cerutti, however, administers the site of information; he is a storehouse of conspiracy theories and, like the machines he oversees, he automatically calls up another scenario when Nick appears unconvinced. Next he tells the increasingly perplexed investigator that it was the daughter of Z. K. Dawson, a former lover of the president—who just happens also to be Yvette Malone, Nick's lover—who arranged the assassination. "Your attraction to Yvette becomes positively Romeo and Julietteish," Cerutti tells Nick, a love between rival families, the Dawsons and the Kegans. But again, Nick is not buying. Suddenly it dawns on Nick that the only one not indicted by any existing scenario, the one person essentially responsible for the narrative chaos he has encountered and amazingly survived, now appears the most likely suspect: Pa Kegan himself. The facade of openness represented by the Kegans' incestuous family relationships—the shared lovers, the father pimping for his sons—now appears as a front for the crime of filicide. The motive was business, in particular the family finances. Pa Kegan had purchased the White House for his son because, in Cerutti's words, "that's where you can generate the most cash. A cold-ass business proposition like everything else in this society." But when the president started actually to believe the national rhetoric about democracy, he had to be stopped, and so the old man carried out the assassination of his own son.

The assassination of JFK is thus written as the revenge of the older generation on the sixties' "new generation of leadership." The emotional substance of so much of the assassination literature, with its lamenting of murdered youth and lost idealism, is literalized in this last scenario through the violent retaliation of the old order. Once again, the casting figures the conflict: Jeff Bridges misled at every point by the performers of a previous era; John Huston, the one director among them, orchestrating the menace to ensure his survival. Writing off the renewed faith in civic life shared by many sixties' liberals and, in the years after the assassination, written into history as JFK's legacy, Cerutti also dismisses Nick as naive. In this he reinforces the criticism leveled by Pa Kegan throughout the film. Yvette regards Nick's marriage proposals as similarly unsophisticated. Within the logic of the older generation, Nick's naiveté raises questions about both his masculinity and his sexual orientation. Pa Kegan persists in asking about Nick's sex life and tells his son he used to worry that Nick would turn out to be gay. Nick refuses his father's gun as well as his invitation to enjoy the company of the hospital nurses.

The Oedipal violence at the center of this conspiracy theory destroys Pa Kegan's appeals to family unity, calls that ring hollow anyway given the portrayal of Nick's mother (Dorothy Malone) as mentally unstable and out of the family loop. Even in its minor narrative details *Winter Kills* hints at the violence associated with home and family. Nick's mother accidentally suffocates her little dog while asleep at Rockrimmon. The hotel in which Nick lives is staffed by eccentrics, his private servant in particular appearing as if he were better suited for a horror film. Finally, Nick is forced to struggle for his life when he is attacked by a maid in his bedroom. The film reserves its most peculiar moments of violence, however, for symbolic images of idyllic childhood. I refer to scenes in which an unidentified woman and her little boy suddenly appear, first on a bicycle in Philadelphia and later at Irving Mentor's diner in Cleveland. Accompanied by music that might be associated with a child's song and which gives their appearance the quality of a dream, the woman and her child serve, in fact, as killers, snuffing out those who have just met with Nick. The woman and child are not connected to anyone else in the story, and Cerutti does not even account for them. Rather, they suggest the reversal of conventional appearances. Thus there is violence lurking behind the facade of family, as dreamlike images of mother and child suddenly turn murderous. Meanwhile, figures of violence, such as Joe Diamond, Irving Mentor and Frank Mayo, are presented as somewhat benign.

Outside the text this Oedipal violence targets the popular notion of Kennedy unity, of family as the final protector of loyalty—whether in public appeals for privacy, in the family's control over autopsy materials, or in the endorsed version of history published in Manchester's book. But drawing simple connections between the narrative and the real-life family to which it may refer is inadequate. It is perhaps more useful to see *Winter Kills* in the terms Robin Wood lays out for seventies' cinema. The film explicitly images Wood's assessment of a society in decay, one in which "the questioning of authority spread logically to a questioning of the entire social structure that validated it, and ultimately to patriarchy itself: social institutions, the family, the symbolic figure of the Father in all its manifestations, the Father interiorized as superego."[18] However neither Wood nor the film argues that the patriarchal institutions have collapsed, only that a process of questioning, perhaps critique, has been initiated. For all the talk about crisis, Wood must also acknowledge the failures of social transformation. "Society appeared to be in a state of advanced disintegration," he writes, "yet there was no serious possibility of the emergence of a coherent and comprehensive alternative."[19] *Winter Kills* suggests this impossibility in its closing scene.

When Nick leaves the control center and confronts the old man with the conspiracy theory given to him by Cerutti, Pa Kegan at first tries to shift the burden of guilt with a final scenario, an amendment to Cerutti's version. He tells Nick that the corporation grew into a monster he could no longer control. It was Cerutti, the employee for whom the survival of the empire always came first, who had the president assassinated. But he did it with Kegan resources so that all incriminating fingers would point back to the father. "I'm just a god damn figurehead," he tells his son. But the shoot-out between Nick and Keifetz during this scene appears to confirm Pa Kegan's version as a lie, exposing the old man's willingness to kill his other son to maintain the cover-up. Yet when the father falls to his death and Nick is left the sole surviving Kegan, the film underscores his lack of alternative roles. He instructs the secretary to call the police rather than Cerutti, but when she asks Nick if he is coming back, he responds mechanically, "I'm part of the family." The limited social alternatives and the overdetermination of Nick's choices are also signaled by the soundtrack as it brings up the same version of "Hail to the Chief" first used to introduce the father.

The patriarchal law, imposed to maintain the mythic ideal of family, is thus exposed as homicidal, and the economic component of familial relations is placed at the scene of the crime. The alternatives seem bleak: there is the police force, an inept extension of the state, itself propped up by such fictions as the Pickering Commission; there is John Cerutti and the corporate apparatus; there is the myth of the pioneering family. With the past unreadable and the future uncertain, Nick makes his own peace with the dead. He calls Yvette's answering machine. His first move, and the film's last, is to leave a message that may never be heard.

Blow Out

There are two striking similarities between the end of *Winter Kills* and the end of Brian De Palma's *Blow Out* from 1981; one of them extends to *The Parallax View* as well. Like the Richert and Pakula films, *Blow Out* climaxes with the fragmentation of a patriotic emblem. Here it is the image of Jack Terry (John Travolta), in pursuit of a psychotic assassin, driving his Land Rover the wrong way through a Liberty Day parade in downtown Philadelphia. Jack's investigation into the assassination of Governor George McRyan, a journey that has brought him face to face with political cover-up, blackmail, and a complicit police force, culminates as he literally drives a wedge through the facade of American history. Marching bands and patriotic floats are mowed down before Jack's ride ends with a crash into a modern American icon: the department store. In the shattered display window are mannequins outfitted in colonial dress, symbols of the ossification afflicting once-revolutionary ideals. Those ideals are then transferred to Jack through costume, specifically the bloodied bandage wrapped around his head in the ambulance. When Jack returns to the chase, he momentarily retains the bandage and therefore the classic image associated with the colonial fife and drum. Thus *Blow Out*, like *Winter Kills* and *The Parallax View*, summarizes its message of dissent through the mise-en-scène of its climactic scene. Unlike the discourse of assassination critics, these films insist on conspiracy and cover-up as fundamental elements of the political process — without the compensating faith in or promise of national institutions. Indeed, in these scenes of fragmentation, the films image, despite (or perhaps in lieu of) their limited critiques, a profound cynicism and a stark pessimism about national rehabilitation.

That cynicism is also inscribed through the failure of their protagonist-investigators, a failure that resonates, in both *Winter Kills* and *Blow Out*, through the voices of murdered women. Significantly, both films also conclude with their male heroes, destroyed by narrative events, listening to the recorded voices of women whose lives were sacrificed in the course of investigation. Nick Kegan hears Yvette's phone machine message one last time. Jack Terry sits in a snowy park listening to the audiotape of Sally and then in the screening room watching the film into which her scream has been dubbed. Their inability to control narrative events has resulted in a loss exacted on women's bodies. Indeed, in uncanny fashion these films figure that intersection of discourses discussed in Chapter 2: the cohabitation of assassination imagery and soft-core pornography, the way the epistemology of the visible underwrote scrutiny of assassination imagery in a manner like the "principle of maximum visibility" operating in hard core and slasher film.

At this point of intersection the body of Yvette Malone comes to rest at the end of *Winter Kills*. Not only does the narrative mandate her death, but it features her nude display on the hospital slab, her cadaver prepared for the dissection used in medical school training. In *Blow Out*, the utilization of Sally's death scream figures a similar process. "Like pornography," Linda Williams writes, "the slasher film pries open the fleshy secrets of normally hidden things."[20] When Jack is left with nothing but a recording of Sally being murdered, he returns to his job as a sound man for slasher films and inserts her voice into his current project, *Co-Ed Frenzy*. The assassination of McRyan and the slasher film are thus clearly paralleled. Both concern murders to which Jack was an earwitness, which can only be made visible by the subsequent addition of the image. In the first case that image is supplied by the footage shot by Manny Karp, in the second case by that supplied by his partner making *Co-Ed Frenzy*. As with the assassination literature, struggles to discern the truth from representation result in the investigation or its violence being inscribed upon a female body.

In the closing scenes in which Nick and Jack listen to recorded voices, there is a momentary reinscription of death, a return to the violence, and in this return each man's failure is conspicuously underscored. This failure is accompanied by an image of figurative impotence. In *The Parallax View*, when Carter arrives at Frady's apartment and rekindles his interest in the Carroll assassination, it is made clear that he has just had sex with an unidentified woman. In fact, this woman's momentary presence and her disappearance from the rest of the narrative underlines the way in which the investigation displaces sex in Frady's life. Given Warren Beatty's persona, *The Parallax View* utilizes him anomalously more as solitary rather than leading man. Jack Terry is represented as similarly uninterested in sex. His relationship to women is defined primarily through a job that involves presenting images of bodies for consumption by and the arousal of others.

In his discussion of *Blow Out*, Robin Wood suggests that Jack be understood as symbolically castrated, pointing to the scene in which Jack takes Sally from the hospital to a motel room. Rather than following the conventional pickup scenario, Jack puts Sally to bed and spends the night with his audio equipment, studying the recordings of the fatal blow out. Like other critics, Wood reads Jack's microphone as phallic symbol, the source of his "compensatory power."[21] But it is, I would suggest, a signifier of his impotence, since during the course of the narrative it provides Jack with a false sense of adequacy. The power Jack thinks he has, located primarily in his recording apparatus and his skill at wiring people for sound, is revealed as illusory and destructive of those it is intended to protect. In fact, his work as a sound effects man serves to highlight his lack of vision in pursuit of Burke and in seeing the danger in which he puts Sally. In this lack of vision lies his symbolic castration. Freud's essay on "The Uncanny" is again the text that makes the link: "A study of dreams, phantasies and myths," Freud writes, "has taught us that a morbid anxiety connected with the eyes and with going blind is often enough a substitute for the dread of castration."[22]

Jack's reliance on sound and its implication with impotence is best exemplified by the chase scene through the train station. Although he is ultimately able to relocate Sally and Burke, it is here that Jack really loses them. The scene is punctuated by repeated shots of Jack immobile on the station floor, his disorientation a result of his privileging of sound over sight. Jack's impotence is not a one-time accident, but rather a defining aspect of character, for his use of Sally as bait is a repetition of an earlier wiring gone bad, the death of Freddie Corvo. But even before these events, the film hints at the linkages between knowledge and the visible while suggesting the gap between knowledge and the aural. When Jack first listens to his recordings in the motel, the editing establishes a difference between what the spectator knows and what Jack can only surmise. The scene cuts from close-ups of Jack's eyes to the familiar images of the car going into the creek. The alternation of shots suggests his attempts to visualize the events from nonvisual evidence. But the third time Jack repeats the recording, De Palma cuts to an as-yet-unseen image, a slow motion close-up of the tire being punctured by a gunshot coming from the nearby bushes. This close-up, no doubt meant to confirm Jack's suspicion, is jarring in its revelation of information, and rather than forging identification it serves to separate the audience from Jack. Certain knowledge is established by visible evidence reserved for the audience. Jack will have access to such certainty only after he sees the film shot by Manny Karp. De Palma's insertion of this close-up positions the film as thriller rather than mystery, but it also indicates the presumption of historical knowledge. De Palma is not giving the plot away with this close-up because he can assume the audience's familiarity with narratives of political assassination.

Jack's association with sound over image is posited as one reason for his inability to control events. That loss of control is signaled by repeated 180-degree pans roughly halfway through the film, when Jack discovers that all of his audiotapes have been erased. Suddenly his apartment seems like a trap, its walls encircling him. During the scene in the motel, when Jack realizes the importance of what he has recorded, De Palma's camera follows the audiotape through the machine in disciplined fashion, tracking the tape's movements past sound heads and onto the takeup reel. But when his tapes are erased, the camera spins momentarily out of control, its gaze unable to fix on Jack as he searches through his library.

As I have organized this discussion of *The Parallax View, Winter Kills,* and *Blow Out,* a thematic trajectory through the motives of investigation could be read, a movement from the social concerns of Joe Frady to the familial / social concerns of Nick Kegan to the personal motives of Jack Terry. It is not necessary to insist on the chronological importance of this trajectory to see how these films present three related but different attitudes toward the politics of investigation. The representation of the assassination buff in the form of Frady and Kegan serves to highlight the ambivalent character of De Palma's failed hero and the cynical strain running through *Blow Out.* Jack comes to his commitment to the truth only after Karp's film is reprinted in *News Today* magazine. But his continued perseverance appears motivated more by resentment toward the disbelieving Officer Mackey and the recuperation of ego in light of the Freddie Corvo death.

Nonetheless, compared with Frady and Kegan, it is Jack Terry who does the work of the conspiracy researcher, clipping the Karp frames and reshooting them into his own film. De Palma constructs Jack as an amateur sleuth by having him function as a surrogate Zapruder, an unsuspecting witness at the scene of the crime, and an assassination critic who uses Zapruderlike imagery (the Karp footage) to carry out his own analysis. Indeed, the pessimism conveyed by the film is reinforced by the agency with which Jack is invested. The narrative makes a point of acknowledging that Jack is essentially self-taught. Whereas Frady in *The Parallax View* and Kegan in *Winter Kills* conduct investigations in which they are primarily acted upon, Jack Terry constructs the crucial evidence by creating a sound version of the Zapruder film, something that the House assassinations committee had done with the recently discovered Dallas police dictabelt recording. His failure is perhaps all the more painful given the time devoted to depicting his skills and the substantive results of his investigation.

Throughout *Blow Out* Jack Terry is at work on two films: the Karp footage of the assassination and *Co-Ed Frenzy.* The former is understood to contain some truth, some crucial evidence in a political assassination; here *Blow Out* shares the buff's faith in the epistemological status of the image. What it does not share is any faith in the society into which that truth can be circulated. Indeed, the television news media, as represented in the character of Jack Donahue, is depicted as slick and self-promoting. Donahue's on-the-air vocal inflection is easy enough for Burke to imitate. Furthermore, the first images of television news reporting on McRyan are rendered through a split screen, the left half of the frame devoted to Jack at work with his audio equipment. The depthless quality of the television, its status as all surface, is juxtaposed with the apparatus and the work process, represented here by Jack on the left half of the frame. *Blow Out* thus suggests that, whereas the Karp footage is the politically urgent film, *Co-Ed Frenzy* is the politically acceptable one, suitable for viewing by a society that throughout the film comes to appear unredeemable.

Toward which of these films does *Blow Out* itself gravitate? Does it pursue the politics of conspiracy or fall in the generic category of slasher film? While *Blow Out* constructs an image of the buff that more closely resembles the practices of assassination critics, it devotes minimal attention to the issue of conspiracy. In fact, the idea of conspiracy is invoked as if some vague gesture to popular thinking but is dismissed in favor of De Palma's generic concerns. In the character of Burke, *Blow Out* returns to theories of the deranged lone assassin. Indeed, the narrative makes it clear that McRyan's political rivals wanted him embarrassed, not killed, and that Burke exceeded his orders when the job assignment ended in the governor's death. Here political violence is written as psychological violence, and as with *Winter Kills, Psycho* is the filmic intertext. Burke is paralleled with Norman Bates toward the end, when he stabs Sally and when Jack and he strike a pose identical with that of Sam Loomis and Norman in the Bates's fruit cellar at the end of *Psycho*.

As with *The Parallax View* and *Winter Kills, Blow Out*'s critique focuses less on the execution and logistics of assassination than with the sources of social violence that shape the political process. Set together, these films take some notion of conspiracy for granted, using it as a starting point for explorations into corporate criminality, familial power, and gender violence. In the process they refigure the assassination debate by relating its critique of the state to other dominant institutions. Still, these films register that critique as doomed to failure, even though they had been made possible by a series of successful discursive struggles. Indeed, the scant critical attention paid to these films generally questions their political efficacy on the grounds that they are unable to image social alternatives. For Robin Wood the problem is symptomatic of the "progressive Hollywood cinema" in general: "the blockage of thought arising from the taboo on imaging alternatives to a system that can be exposed as monstrous, oppressive and unworkable but which must nevertheless not be *constructively* challenged."[23] But Wood is unable to define what he means by the term *constructively*, except to go on to say that De Palma seems unable to "believe" in "any imaginable alternative." A similar critique, but one explicitly fixed on audience action, is advanced by Chris Hugo in his auteurist analysis of De Palma: "The sad ending implicates the audience in an aura of defeatism — better to *watch* a film about political corruption and murder and cry at the hopelessness of taking action than to *do* anything about it."[24]

These arguments strike me as problematic not because of some failure to characterize these films accurately, for in their representation of investigation these films certainly border on defeatist. Rather, the problem lies in the implication that individual films could have the power to move viewers to political action, especially films operating, for whatever reasons, within the dominant narrative format. I do not care to outline some theory of political cinema that can be used to test the efficacy of the films under discussion. Indeed, a cinema becomes political only within a wider network of social relations and representational forms which are exerting a political force in conjunction with the cinema. The struggle around the Kennedy assassination, to take the most relevant example, suggests that the construction of alternatives — a public rather than a secret dialogue, efforts to reform government activity — gets generated by political actions operating across diverse social locales and a range of media practices. I am reluctant to assign a rigid political value to any of these films individually, one that could measure their capacity to "move" audiences to a new level of consciousness or political action. To what extent such a shift in consciousness might be ascribed to a given film text or is in fact the result of extratextual factors is a question problematized by a film such as *JFK,* the next and final film I want to consider. For, after several years of (relative) dormancy, the assassination debate was renewed under the gaze of both the cinema and society as each cooperated with the production and release of Oliver Stone's film in 1991.

Few contemporary American films have attracted the attention and animosity directed at Oliver Stone's fictional reconstruction of the late sixties' New Orleans conspiracy trial. Though *JFK* was not released until December 1991, skeptical articles began to appear in May and June of that year, their criticism based on an early draft of the script allegedly obtained by a disapproving assassination critic.[1] Upon the film's release, the criticism continued along two fronts: Stone's decision to base his narrative on the much-discredited Jim Garrison, former New Orleans district attorney, and the film's visual strategy of intercutting archival footage with reenactments of alleged events. Also the focus of media attacks were the dramatic liberties Stone took with Garrison's story, primarily his inclusion of the character called X and the broad theory of conspiracy articulated by Stone's Garrison. This particular conspiracy theory portrayed JFK as attempting to end the cold war while it implicated in the assassination elements within the Pentagon, the CIA, the Mafia, the Texas oil industry, anti-Castro Cubans and, subsequent to the shooting, the cover-up enacted by the Warren Commission and the White House.[2] When in January 1992 the *New York Times* accused Stone of employing "trick photography," it was echoing an almost year-long attack which had reached its apex on the cover of *Newsweek* with the headline: "The Twisted Truth of 'JFK'/Why Oliver Stone's New Movie Can't Be Trusted."[3]

Yet mainstream periodicals like *Newsweek* were somewhat split in their judgment. Although its news writers identified the film as a distortion, its film critic, David Anson, could still praise its dramatic impact and "charged" style: "But it is possible to remain skeptical of 'JFK's' Edenic notions of its heroes and still find this movie a remarkable, necessary provocation."[4] *Time*'s film critic advanced a similar argument: "Whatever one's suspicions about its use or abuse of the evidence, *JFK* is a knockout. . . . In its bravura and breadth, *JFK* is seditiously enthralling; in its craft, wondrously complex."[5] Undoubtedly the ferocity of the attack mounted against *JFK* assisted its box office appeal, but its cultural impact, to the extent this can be measured, was also enhanced by the journalistic space turned over to Oliver Stone. Rarely, of course, does a film text speak for itself, given the diverse channels of publicity made available to it. But, in the case of *JFK,* its director was afforded something like a second soundtrack, an almost weekly opportunity to counter the critics and reinterpret the film.[6]

To fend off criticism during production, Stone told critics that his film's structure would resemble that of Kurosawa's *Rashomon*. Although ultimately no such form would organize the film, Stone's suggestion of multiple interpretations succeeded at defending a script that was itself going through multiple drafts. Invoking Kurosawa could also attach a serious, art cinema aura to the project, distinguishing Stone's involvement with the assassination from the tabloid media which had rediscovered the assassination several years earlier during the twenty-fifth anniversary of Kennedy's death. Once the film was released, Stone continually invoked some vague notion of historical myth to justify the dramatic license taken with otherwise well-documented events. "Our film's mythology is different," wrote the director, "and, hopefully, it will replace the *Warren Commission Report*, as *Gone with the Wind* replaced *Uncle Tom's Cabin* and was in turn replaced by *Roots* and *The Civil War*."[7] Surprisingly, Stone seemed content to give his film the same historical status as the Warren Report, appearing more interested in claiming for his film the same epic breadth that he believed had helped solidify the Warren Report's position as dominant text.

Moreover, Stone's remarks register his limited understanding of historical myth, which has severe consequences for his treatment of the assassination. His *Gone with the Wind* approach posits myth as the product of a singular phenomenon — a book, a film — rather than the result of accretion, the position of any given text within wider discursive fields which over time amass a substantial cultural force. Indeed, for all his talk about the powers of conspiracy, Stone relies frequently on a historiography of great individuals — Kennedy as fallen king is the most often repeated image — or of singular events. Registering the impact of *JFK* certainly requires moving beyond Stone's conservative formula in order to recognize the impact of factors beyond the text itself: the $40 million budget to underwrite the production values carried by the casting of major stars and the elaborate reconstruction of historical events and settings; the power of the celebrity auteur with a strong box office record; and the preconstituted audience (and culture) already invested in the subject matter and its submarkets in publishing and television.

These elements coalesced around *JFK* in 1991 to function as both amplifiers and catalysts for the assassination debate, returning the research and speculations of Warren Report critics to various channels of discourse. This renewal took the form of republication, as books such as *Rush to Judgment* and *Best Evidence* returned to bookstore shelves in fresh volumes. Critics who had spent nearly thirty years on the case found themselves once again on the lecture / conference circuit. The JFK Assassination Information Center, a research repository founded in 1989, was host to an Assassination Symposium in Dallas in November 1991 and again in 1993, and the Assassination Archives and Research Center of Washington, D.C., went there for their own conference in October 1992. Regional symposia began to convene on a regular basis, featuring not only lectures concerning the major conspiracy theories, but also workshops on research and investigative techniques.[8] In March 1991 Stone joined Norman Mailer, Edward J. Epstein, and others at a forum titled "Hollywood and History: The Debate over JFK" sponsored by the Nation Institute. The event signified the partial return of the left-liberal press to the assassination controversy and the standing-room-only crowd it drew to New York City's Town Hall suggested the scope of that return even for those outside the circle of hard-core assassination buffs.[9]

Indeed, the controversy surrounding *JFK* also rekindled disagreements over the debate within the left-liberal media. As noted in the Introduction, publications such as *Minority of One* and *Ramparts* took the lead in critiquing the government's version of the assassination. Yet there was also a sustained skepticism for some on the left, a contention that energy spent investigating conspiracy theories not only courted questionable historiography but displaced attention from a more systematic and structurally oriented social critique. This clash was rearticulated during 1991, the same month as the Nation Institute's forum.[10] The editors of *Tikkun* suggested that critics of *JFK* suffered from an apolitical skepticism.

"I haven't seen JFK, but I suspect the whole fuss comes from simple-minded people looking for conspiracies because they can't handle the complexities of politics." This response is as likely to arise on the Left these days as on the Right. Such thinking comes in part out of the fear among former social-change activists that reminding themselves of how democratic politics in this country has been subverted—from the Kennedy assassination to the Iran-Contra scandal—will force them to rethink the various life-choices that led them away from political involvement.[11]

Erwin Knoll, editor of *The Progressive,* summarized an opposing view in his editorial for that same month. After noting that assassination manuscripts had generally not met the magazine's standards for "accuracy" and "plausibility," yet stating his own belief that Kennedy "may have fallen victim to a plot that encompassed more than a 'lone assassin,'" he concluded:

I believe it is no service to raise important questions and then provide false answers. I don't believe anyone's consciousness is raised by still another attempt to perpetuate the Camelot myth. I don't question Stone's right to turn a buck by pandering to the emotions of a gullible audience, but I insist on my right to despise him for doing so. Please don't write to tell me I'm participating in a conspiracy. I know. I know.[12]

The release of *JFK* expanded the readership for a new installment of assassination books as well. The point of greatest contestation, however, emanated from a nonassassination book, John Newman's *JFK and Vietnam,* which argued that by 1963 Kennedy was coming to the conclusion that the Indochina war was unwinnable.[13] Newman, a U.S. Army major specializing in intelligence, claimed that evidence of Kennedy's intent to scale back rather than escalate U.S. involvement was located in a top secret National Security Action Memorandum (NSAM 263). In that memorandum Kennedy authorizes the withdrawal of one thousand military advisors. NSAM 273, signed by Lyndon Johnson within a week of the assassination, is also concerned with the U.S. role in Vietnam, but any mention of the advisor withdrawal has been removed from it. Furthermore, Newman argued that foreign policy officials systematically misled JFK about conditions in Southeast Asia in an effort to make him believe a conclusion to the conflict was closer than it really was. Although Newman's book did not link its argument about Kennedy's evolving antiwar stance to a conspiracy for his assassination, its conclusions provided Stone with the "credible" research he needed to defend his portrait of JFK.[14]

Riding the coattails of *JFK*'s popularity, the television talk and tabloid shows returned to the assassination as well. These programs, in addition to advertising Stone's film, did little more than allow assassination researchers to repeat the claims they had been making for years.[15] Once again, the substantive debate was carried on in the print press, and it was here that the call for opening House assassination committee files was tracked and Stone's conspiracy claims rebutted. In January 1992 it looked as if renewed interest in the assassination might prompt the release of files accumulated during the House investigation of the late seventies, documents sealed until the year 2029. That month both Louis Stokes, former chairman of the House assassinations committee, and Senator Edward Kennedy endorsed efforts to make those files public.[16] Coincident with these developments were reports in which Jimmy Hoffa's former attorney claimed to have delivered a note to mob bosses Carlos Marcello and Santos Trafficante ordering a hit on President Kennedy. This prompted further calls for the release of government-held materials, in particular some 1,300 tape recordings made by undercover FBI agents investigating organized crime and its relationship to CIA efforts to overthrow Castro.[17]

In May of 1992 assassination critics were being rebutted, this time in the pages of the *Journal of the American Medical Association.* JAMA's editors held a press conference to announce publication of an interview with autopsy doctors James J. Humes and J. Thornton Boswell, in which both defended their original findings regarding Kennedy's throat and head wounds. This interview, said the editors, was the culmination of a seven-year effort "to help calm the ardor of the honest conspiracy theorists who have simply not had access to the facts."[18] The following day, the *New York Times* editorial page expressed essentially the same schizophrenic opinion it had articulated for almost the last twenty-five years. It declared that the AMA had "performed a service for reasonable people and reason," one that offered "proof against paranoia." The editors then concluded that, because conspiracy buffs, Stone included, had been successfully refuted, the government should "declassify and publish reams of still-secret information."[19] One might infer that, had proconspiracy evidence been published by *JAMA*, the *Times* would not have found cause to make the files public. Once again the paper maintained a firm distinction between calls for government disclosure and critics of the Warren Report, concluding: "Students of the assassination who are neither hysterical nor paranoid believe there's still much to learn about the *assassin* [italics mine] and about the actions of intelligence agencies."[20]

Efforts to encourage the government to release assassination documents were finally rewarded in August 1993. The National Archives unsealed over 90,000 pages of CIA papers, investigation documents, and photographs, evidence ranging from ballistics tests on the alleged murder rifle to interagency memoranda to newspaper clippings. Then, in May of 1994, the archives released another 50,000 documents, most of which had pertained to Senate committee inquiries into the work of intelligence agencies. Files from the FBI offices in Washington, Dallas, and New Orleans were made public, as were further autopsy photographs and evidence related to the presidential limousine. Still, as of May 1994, at least 100,000 CIA papers and 100 boxes of FBI materials were as yet unreleased.[21]

The Lone Investigator

Like the discourse of the Dallas critics from which it sprung, *JFK* insists alternately that the assassination debate requires government sanction for investigative closure and that government efforts have been repeatedly compromised, leaving the historiographic challenge in the hands of the citizen-critic. The point is driven home in Garrison's climactic courtroom speech, an emotional indictment of various elements within and associated with the federal government that ends with an appeal to the jury, and to the film's audience, to sort out the truth and render their own verdict. "Do not forget your dying king," Garrison tells the jury in rhetoric consistent with the narrative's mythologizing of JFK. "Show this world that this is still a government of the people, for the people and by the people." At this point Garrison pauses and Stone's camera drops down to meet his gaze. Directly addressing the audience, he says, "It's up to you."

Stone's camera placement reinforces his dialogue as a call to action, which gains even greater urgency when the jury returns a verdict of not guilty. Reserving Garrison's final oration as a summation of the conspiracy evidence accumulated before and after the actual New Orleans trial, *JFK* attempts to achieve a more general victory from a specific defeat. It inscribes this victory at the end when one of the jurors tells reporters, "We believe there was a conspiracy but whether Clay Shaw was a part of it is another kettle of fish." In this sense *JFK*'s method seems similar to that of a wartime film genre that historian Richard Lingeman has called the "last stand" picture. In films like *Bataan* and *So Proudly We Hail*, individual wartime losses are represented in order to arouse sympathy for the general cause.[22] Whereas in 1969 the Garrison trial served to divide assassination buffs and send the anti–Warren Commission critics temporarily into retreat, its courtroom failures are resurrected in *JFK* to suggest the power of the cover-up and the loneliness of the investigator.

Indeed, it is the isolation of the Warren Commission critic, as represented by *JFK,* that compromises the film's political critique and prevents it, in at least one respect, from moving beyond the limitations hampering *The Parallax View* and *Blow Out.* Like Joe Frady and Jack Terry, Garrison's quest meets with defeat, and the cracking of his voice toward the end of his speech suggests his frustration in taking on forces that David Ferrie earlier refers to as "untouchable." Garrison's closing admonition, "It's up to you," is significant in its address to the individual. He does not say, "It's up to us." Rather, his call to action punctuates a narrative that has effectively effaced the collective aspect of the anti–Warren Commission discourse, the multivoiced dialogue and critique that defined the politics of assassination inquiry. Indeed, in replacing the lone assassin theory with a theory of the lone investigator, the film diminishes, at the level of narration though not at the level of imagery, what is so historiographically important about the assassination debate.

Although in interviews Stone acknowledged the collective efforts of assassination critics and argued that the dramatic format required their consolidation within the figure of Garrison, his failure to challenge the conventions of that format reinscribes the simple approach to causality that elsewhere *JFK* attempts to counter. In several scenes Liz Garrison (Sissy Spacek) is made to speak lines that insist on the great-man approach to history. "Are you going to stay up all night, every night," she asks her husband, "so you'll be the only man in America that's read all twenty-six volumes of the Warren Report?" When Garrison chooses to spend Easter interrogating Clay Shaw rather than going to Antoine's with his family, Liz tells him, "You're not the only one who can sacrifice." Garrison's reply is that of the lonely critic: "Somebody's got to try, God dammit." It is Garrison who notices that the address of Oswald's Fair Play for Cuba Committee occupies the same building as Guy Bannister's office. It is Garrison who articulates the head-snap reading of the Zapruder film. It is Garrison who amasses the wealth of evidence regarding Oswald's and Ruby's actions which questions the conclusions of the Warren Report. Within the logic of the narrative, confirmation that Garrison is on the right track comes not from others working on the case (there is no acknowledgment that anyone has worked on the case outside New Orleans), but from news of Robert Kennedy's assassination. When Jim tells Liz that Bobby Kennedy has been shot, she symbolically concedes that his mission goes beyond yet includes the family's welfare, extending to that of the nation. With his political instincts ratified by history, Garrison's mission and his role as provider merge, as the couple is reunited in bed.

Telescoping the process of inquiry contributes to the black-and-white oppositions between good and evil that the film struggles to maintain despite (or perhaps because of) its narrative complexity. When Garrison tells his staff that their investigation has taken them "through the looking glass," his understanding is still summed up with the binary of black versus white, even if those values now seem to be reversed. Garrison's cautionary declaration that "black is white and white is black" sounds like an attempt to maintain some orientation amid the image track's fluid montaging of color stocks and filmic registers. Such binaries are maintained when *JFK* assigns the formulation of its vast conspiracy theory to the work of one man. Competing theories or alternative interpretations are thus depicted as the result of saboteurs. This is figured primarily by the character of Bill Newman, the staff member who argues against Garrison's theory, but who the spectator knows has had clandestine contact with an FBI agent.

In one of his published defenses of the film, Stone makes the point explicit:

the film brings together several layers of research from the '60s, '70s and '80s, we hope, in a seamless jigsaw puzzle that will allow the audience, for the first time, to understand what happened and why. As an outsider to conspiracy theories until the late '80s, I was always confused by competing theories—involving the Mafia, the CIA, Castro, anti-Castro Cubans, etc.— which, of course, allow the Lie to continue.[23]

According to these terms, complexity or ambiguity supports the cover-up. History, the truth of which is presumably accompanied by clarity, is understood as seamless. Although it may be a concession to convention, the figure of the lone investigator rewrites the post-Dallas history in a way that denies collective action. More than the montaging of archival footage with filmed reenactments, it is the representation of the inquiry process that distorts the historical field and limits the political critique of *JFK*.

As with certain segments of the buff literature, *JFK* writes Kennedy's political biography with an adoring pen, and the binary of good versus evil informs its construction of the slain president as, in the words of Garrison, "so dangerous to the establishment." The construction of Kennedy the liberal, preparing to pull out of Vietnam, reinforces the lone investigator model. In his closing speech, Garrison insists that the assassination be seen in terms of tragic drama: "We've all become Hamlets in our country. Children of a slain father leader whose killers still possess the throne. The ghost of John F. Kennedy confronts us with the secret murder at the heart of the American dream. He forces upon us the appalling questions of what is our constitution made. . . . " Thus it is Kennedy who compels the citizen to become an investigator. Garrison's rhetoric about the ghosts of kings masks the critical agency and the struggle waged by the very community of which he is a part. *JFK* suggests that the Warren Commission critic finds motivation in some identification with the "slain father" rather than with a community of political skeptics. The point is inscribed in the film by the parallels established between Garrison and Kennedy: footage of JFK with his children juxtaposed with shots of Garrison and his family and the image of Garrison standing over the grave at Arlington National Cemetery.

Montaging History

Through the figure of the lone investigator, *JFK* attempts to make the narrative complexity of the assassination case cohere within a stable address. Yet the intricate and varied collage of images that makes up the film, its montaging of disparate time frames and its rapid alternation of visual perspectives, frequently functions as a destabilizing counterpoint to a narration that strives for intelligibility. While the voice-over monologues delivered by X (Donald Sutherland) and Garrison attempt to gather the narrative strands into a seamless continuity, the images sutured together in support of them push ambiguity to the foreground. Indeed, the negotiation between epistemological certainty and anxiety which I have traced throughout various assassination texts is inscribed in this tension between voice track and image track, between the unifying force of the single investigator and the montaging of filmic registers. The instability of the image track is sustained by there being no consistent pattern for the deployment of black-and-white versus color film. Flashbacks that speculate on possible events — Ruby being admitted to the Dallas police station or Oswald's palmprints being pressed onto the alleged murder rifle — are rendered in black and white, while other speculations — Oswald with David Ferrie at the Carousel Club or the forging of the backyard photos — are rendered in color. In her analysis of the film, Pat Dowell makes a similar point: "Stone tries to put the pieces together again, but lets each one keep its provenance — each one is tagged vi-

sually with its place of origin, appearing in a different color, size, or grain —
so that the audience will not mistake the screen for a window on the past."[24]

The epistemological instability of the montages, not confined to the film's
two long monologues, is reinforced by Garrison's use of the Zapruder film
in the courtroom. In this scene, the famous amateur footage is assigned to a
specific on-screen author/interpreter, whereas earlier in the film it was part
of a larger montage sequence that reconstructed the assassination. Tethered
to the narrative space of the courtroom and under the control of Garrison,
the Zapruder imagery functions in the service of epistemological certainty.
Thus Garrison can identify each of the six shots on which his theory insists,
using the Z footage as both film and still frame to establish certain knowledge. It is important to note that Stone waits to use (or to reveal) frame 313,
the moment of the head wound, until the courtroom scene. During the
earlier reconstruction of the motorcade, frame 313 is strategically omitted
and is in fact replaced by the CBS News Bulletin placard, a juxtaposition
that comments on the media's role in blocking the transmission of evidence
during the sixties. Saving frame 313 until Garrison's speech to the jury authorizes his interpretation with all the reliability guaranteed by the one image that transmits the truth in all its graphic horror. His control over this
image, and hence of the narrative chaos emanating from it, is underscored
by repetition. Three times the courtroom and theater audience is subjected
to a close-up of the head wound, and three times Garrison describes the
movement of Kennedy's body as "back and to the left." By the third repetition, many in the courtroom (and perhaps many in the theater) have turned
away from the image, certifying that the knowledge it contains is painfully
evident.

The containment of the Zapruder film within the courtroom scene allows
JFK to rehearse the tendency in the assassination debate that maintained a
faith in the powers of camera vision. Thus the film revived in 1991 an approach to representation and an argument about the assassination evidence
that had been called into serious question during the previous decade. It
signified that, despite the epistemological crisis that characterized the image
after years of contradictory interpretation, the impulse toward affirmation
and a faith in the image still informed the investigation. A similar faith
underwrites the film's opening montage of sixties' imagery. Here an author-
itative voice-over, never again heard throughout the film, articulates the
"true" interpretation of Kennedy's political history and identity. Supported
by an image track consisting exclusively of archival footage — JFK with John
Foster Dulles, Eisenhower warning of the military-industrial complex, Castro at a political rally — the narration establishes Kennedy's relationship
to three subjects which will resurface as assassination motives: the policy
on Cuba and the Bay of Pigs disaster; Kennedy's "secret deal" with Khru-

shchev to end the missile crisis (which some took as a sign that JFK was soft on communism); and Kennedy's reservations about U.S. involvement in Southeast Asia.

This faith in the image is underscored by notes from the diary kept by cinematographer Robert Richardson during production: "Utilize the opening documentary material to establish a concrete foundation of factual reality. Let the audience move through the material, never doubting its authenticity."[25] Sharing the soundtrack with the omniscient narrator during this sequence is Kennedy's voice. He tells Walter Cronkite that he doubts whether the war in Vietnam can be won. He tells an audience at American University that the United States must reconsider its attitude toward the world. That these fragments are reliable signifiers of Kennedy's politics is implied through their juxtaposition with images of Kennedy as a young man. These home movies, coded as innocent and authentically autobiographical, serve to legitimize the history lesson being elaborated throughout the sequence. These images speak the "truth" about JFK, helping to establish the film's thesis of conspiratorial motive even before Garrison's investigation is introduced. Of course the subsequent three hours elaborate a fictional scenario, but its crucial components have now been verified by the prologue's deployment of historical footage. This "nonfiction" sequence is also combined with the film's opening credits; that is, with signifiers of the world outside the film. These credits, which cite the stable identities behind various characters or roles, help register the prologue as fact, as a piece of the text given over to unquestioned knowledge. When the credits end, the story begins, but only after the text has begun the process of self-legitimation.

For assassination critics, a faith in the epistemological powers of the image could go only so far in solving the case, for much of the evidence relied on the testimony of human rather than camera witnesses. Whereas Conner's *Report,* with its flicker sequences and repetition, suggests the gaps or lapses in vision that frustrate the writing of this history, the narrative films discussed in Part Three use the power of their format to supply the kind of visual evidence the case has always lacked. In particular, *JFK*'s use of historical identities and densely layered flashbacks echo the problems of reconstruction and reenactment that informed the debates. For many newswriters, this was the most dangerous aspect of Stone's work: "This is a film in which the real and the imagined, fact and fiction, keep shading into one another."[26] As I have suggested, the suturing of reenactment and voice-over frequently does serve a persuasive function, delivering visual corroboration for the multiple speculations that make up Garrison's case and the film's narrative. But the mixing of film stocks, chromatics, and visual perspective also frays the ties between knowledge and the visible. *Newsweek*'s charge that "Only the alert viewer will be able to distinguish real documentary footage from reconstructed scenes" serves better as a commentary on the anaesthe-tized state of American film audiences, or at least the magazine's view of them, than as a critique of the film's visual strategies. Alert viewers do not just exist; they are made. Though its director may speak of history as seam-less, *JFK*'s visual quilt, punctuated throughout by star cameos, challenges the spectator to confront the simple and problematic distinction between documentary and fiction.[27] Indeed, the film's political implications reside in part in how it succeeds at posing this challenge, in whether it prompts view-ers to consider how central to the writing of history are questions about access to and organization of images. The assassination investigation is so fraught with the blending of media that what some critics feared to be a dangerous technique — the mixing of archival footage and reconstructed scenes — may in fact be a built-in necessity for any film that takes the as-sassination as its primary subject.

Throughout much of the film, Garrison and his staff are fueled by the assumption that things are not as they appear (a rule the audience could apply while watching the film), a point made repeatedly by images of an unidentified pair of hands constructing the famous backyard photos. In fact, these images are intercut with a meeting in which Garrison's staff is piecing together its own collage of Oswald, a conversation over a montage of archi-val footage of U2 planes, still photos of Lee Harvey Oswald, and reenact-ments of Oswald's life in the Soviet Union and Dallas. Whether the work of Garrison's staff or of mysterious conspirators, *JFK* implies here that ques-tions of historical identity are enfolded with the arrangement of imagery. This is especially the case with its representation of the alleged assassin. Although footage of Oswald in the Dallas Police Department exists and was widely broadcast on television in the years preceding *JFK*, Stone chooses to reenact the brief interview between Oswald and the press. Similarly, the director forsakes the famous television footage of Ruby shooting Oswald for a black-and-white reconstruction. Actor Gary Oldman recites line for line Oswald's remarks in the station basement, and elsewhere Stone uses only a few photographs of the "real" Oswald, images published in *Life* after the assassination. *JFK* is able to make its case that Oswald's identity is more difficult to document with certainty, underscoring the way theories about doubles and stand-ins have complicated the evidence surrounding the al-leged assassin.

Whereas Garrison's closing speech and Stone's editing are perhaps barely able to keep the Zapruder film from slipping toward ambiguity, the flash-back montages elsewhere splinter the conspiracy evidence in a way that can-not be contained by voice-over narration. Although the montages gener-ated to accompany Dealey Plaza eyewitnesses, X, and the anti-Castro New Orleans underground are assigned a source, their gradual accumulation eventually frustrates their fit within a stable form. In addition, flashbacks like the one in which Ruby asks Earl Warren to take him to Washington, D.C., are motivated by neither a voice-over nor an interview. Finally, after Garrison stays up late to read the Warren Report, his reading gives way to images of the motorcade — a blowup of the Zapruder film which focuses on Jackie, with rifle fire on the soundtrack — images then revealed to be part of Garrison's dream. As in the dream work, the montages that structure so much of *JFK* resist linearity, pivoting on so many conflicts of scale and texture, color and temporality as to form any investigator's worst nightmare.

The film's flashback montages thus serve both to illustrate and to overwhelm the arguments of their principal organizer. But unlike those of Frady, Kegan, and Terry, Garrison's journey does not conform to the cinema of pathos. Indeed, Garrison's critique of the government is balanced by the film's celebration of the patriarchal family and the virtues of heterosexuality.[28] Whereas the investigators from the seventies' cinema were all in some sense social outsiders, men defined in part by their isolation, Garrison is constructed as a socially integrated hero, a model for the rhetoric of family values. The investigative impotence of Frady, Kegan, and Terry, as has been discussed, was variously portrayed through narratives that questioned their sexual interests. But in *JFK* homosexuality forms the basis of conspiracy, serving to fix the identities of Clay Shaw and David Ferrie no matter what mysteries surround their political affiliations. While Garrison momentarily sublimates his sexual energy for the larger cause of the nation, and is later rewarded for it by his wife, Shaw and Ferrie romp decadently with the prostitute Willie O'Keefe adorned in eighteenth-century costume and wigs. While Shaw and Ferrie were historical figures involved in the Garrison trial, O'Keefe is a fictional construct. His character serves as a replacement for the much-discredited actual witness used by Garrison, a man named Perry Russo, in order to establish a connection between Shaw and Oswald. Moreover, O'Keefe allows the film to both image the secret cabal as gay and depict the gay narrator of this scene as delusional. Thus, when O'Keefe begins ranting about JFK's being a Communist, the flashback images stop and Garrison is afforded a reaction shot that confirms the gay source as untrustworthy.

Despite O'Keefe's apparent unreliability, the images accompanying his story only reinforce the links between "the murder at the heart of the American dream," as Garrison puts it, and a sexuality that does not reproduce the traditional family. Indeed, the film suggests that Garrison's failure to grasp the evil forces behind the assassination result from his inability to understand two secret and corrupt practices: homosexuality and the Pentagon. O'Keefe suggests the former when he shouts, "You're a God damn liberal, Mr. Garrison, you don't know shit because you've never been fucked in the ass." But when David Ferrie is found dead, Garrison must forgo a prosecution based on the gay/anti-Castro underground. It is at this point that the narrative expands its conspiracy theory and Garrison travels to Washington, D.C. It is here that the character called X, the film's stand-in for Fletcher Prouty, must educate Garrison about that other clandestine practice, military intelligence. Sitting on a park bench, X tells Garrison, through an extended monologue, that the assassination was masterminded by high-ranking Pentagon officials and defense industrialists who were unhappy about Kennedy's foreign policy. After explaining the history of U.S. covert activity since World War II and suggesting that JFK wanted to bring an end to the "black ops," X tells Garrison, "I think it started like that, in the wind, defense contractors, big oil bankers, just conversations, nothing more, then a call is made." While X stops just short of naming LBJ as a co-conspirator, Stone's flashback imagery does not. When X uses the words *perpetrators* and *coup d'état,* black-and-white photographs of LBJ are on screen; in the second one, as if caught in the act, he is looking straight into the camera.

Garrison's talk with X is punctuated throughout with long shots, several of which include the Washington Monument in the background. In fact, the stark contrast between this scene, with its daylight and shot scale, and the cramped, dimly lit spaces of the New Orleans investigation suggests the dissociation of conspiracy theories being made to fit within a single scenario. As Garrison's research continues, the film abandons questions of how, questions addressed by the gay/anti-Castro theory, to pursue questions of why, questions presumably answered by X's theory of black ops. But, as Michael Rogin has noted, Stone "provides no characters whose actions connect his sordid New Orleans revelations to the Washington scene of the crime."[29] Instead, the introduction of X allows the film to return to the thesis mapped out during its prologue, a theory of motive extending beyond the Cuban connection to include Kennedy's policy in Vietnam. Like the prologue, X's monologue addresses itself to the sixties in general, suggesting that the assassination cut short a new liberal agenda and ushered in a decade of social turmoil.

X's Pentagon theory works to eliminate the importance of the on-screen New Orleans jury and its subsequent verdict, speaking instead to the jury sitting in the theater. If X's thesis can achieve legitimacy for the audience, then Garrison's failure to convict Clay Shaw hardly matters. *JFK* can remain faithful to this part of the Garrison affair (where it otherwise is seldom faithful) and still celebrate its individual hero. Unlike his filmic predecessors, Garrison survives the narrative into which he is set because he is permitted to momentarily step outside it. In Washington, D.C., where history is as fixed as the stone monuments where Garrison and X walk, the uncertainty plaguing the investigator's project is removed. Gay men in New Orleans may be unreliable, but not this oracle met on the steps of the Lincoln Memorial. The illegible films and suspicious autopsy are cleared away, and the truth emanates from the nation's capital just as it did five years before with the Warren Commission's report. When Garrison travels to Washington, he reinscribes the tendency within the assassination literature that looked to the federal government for authorization of closure, for the seal of truth. For *JFK* it is a return visit, with footage of Eisenhower conferring approval on its thesis at the very beginning of the film.

Summation and Continuation

When *JFK* was released in 1991, it functioned as both a summation and a continuation. In one sense it appeared isolated on the political landscape, not only as one of the few mainstream American films to pose questions critical of government operations, but also as a text that articulated a set of arguments belonging to an earlier period in recent history. The assassination literature on which it drew had exerted its greatest impact during the sixties and then again during the mid-seventies, with ideas that had struggled into public discourse alongside other critical interrogations of the state and its practices. No such environment surrounded Stone's film. As Michael Rogin has noted, Oliver Stone "is a product not of the rise of the New Left but of its demise." The earliest criticism of the Warren Commission may have been in kinship with New Left ideology, although by the mid-seventies that ideology had splintered, been refigured, or in some cases dissipated. But *JFK*'s celebration of Kennedy as civil rights icon with designs on ending the cold war place it squarely within a post-Reagan version of liberalism, as does Stone's embracing of Camelot and his desire for an assassination countermyth. The scope of its narrative fashions *JFK* as a summary, an impression reinforced by the fact that its critique of federal intelligence authorities remained widely unsustained elsewhere in the culture.

Yet the film also functioned as a continuation of the assassination debate, one that not only revived old arguments but also contributed to renewed discursive activity with the release of government documents. From this perspective, *JFK* punctuated but did not end the eighties, a decade that witnessed ongoing work by assassination critics. Stone's film contributed best to those critical efforts through the boldness of its visual strategy and registered its worst tendencies through the organization of its conspiracy theory. Central to its own impact was the enlistment of archival footage, post-Conner and Warhol, rather than its muddled fixation on motives, its unsatisfactory narrative shift from questions of how Kennedy was killed to questions of why.

Throughout this study, I have referred to the assassination debates, but as the book's three-part structure would imply, that debate contains within it several continuing discourses, each defined by the specific media forms that give it shape. Thus, one could speak of a journalistic discourse, an experimental practice discourse, and a Hollywood narrative discourse, each with its own history within the wider field. *JFK* reverberates with a structural tension: a movement toward the experimental discourse, figured by its complex montage, but arrested by narrative conventions that insist on an individualized and myth-centered approach to political history, conventions that guarantee its place within a commercial and formal economy. The challenge posed to subsequent Hollywood films that engage the discourses of the assassination will be to confront that tension with a text that organizes a similarly rigorous and provocative montage but in conjunction with a narrative that reflects the collective skepticism and critique generated by the JFK assassination inquiries.

Epilogue

This project really began when I saw Bruce Conner's *Report* for the first time. For years I had been reading about the assassination of JFK, casually studying its imagery and keeping pace with emerging developments. With this book coming to a close, what is so striking to me now is the way a particular text made it possible for me to see and construct a tropology for a body of literature with which I had worked for years but had never recognized. With a sudden, startling comprehension, I saw in Conner's use of repetition and his strategy of appropriation a pattern in the JFK inquiries that refigured my understanding of the assassination discourse. When I decided to write about *Report,* it was in conjunction with the Warhol silkscreens, which developed into the core of Part Two. I began, in other words, by moving from text to text, a method that consistently resulted in surprises about a given work and its articulation of the assassination debates. Indeed, throughout my writing, the structure of a particular film or art work prevented me from easily imposing a conceptual model on any individual text, forcing me to rethink if not always to adequately refigure my frames of intelligibility.

Yet this project was motivated by and remains a call for context, a call for history. For at the same time I began writing about Conner and Warhol, the mainstream media were marking yet another anniversary of the assassination, and the airwaves were cluttered with fragments of assassination footage. I wanted to offer some resistance to the idea that these images were free-floating signifiers by establishing and arguing for a discursive context that could situate them within a history of representation. It was clear that assassination imagery had been made to appear in a wide variety of social locales—the mainstream and marginal press, soft-core pornography, pop art, the underground, and commodity cinema—but questions remained about the intertextual relations, both ideological and formal, among these various practices.

These varied locations suggest the diversity of the audience working with and making sense of assassination imagery, an audience splintered among disciplines: assassination critics, art historians, film scholars, collectors of camp. My purpose has been not so much to address each of these audiences separately as to attempt to construct an audience for whom conceptual and textual connections did not previously exist. I hope that readers in this audience will now understand the assassination debates as a historiographic struggle and an aspect of social history thoroughly bound up with film and the arts during the sixties and after.

As a call for context, I have tried to maintain that concept in all its complexity, for the assassination debates, understood as encompassing the arts, not simply reflected through them, are far from monolithic. Indeed, the debates are not only complex but ongoing, and as this study concludes, one cannot help but take note of the leads still worth pursuing. Undoubtedly, an analysis of the literary fiction produced around the assassination would add a crucial piece to the structure suggested here. As Warren Commission critics and contemporary artists continue to explore the offerings of video and as current avant-garde filmmakers continue to experiment with found footage strategies, their work will also contribute to the ever-expanding collage of assassination documents.

Notes

Introduction **The Assassination Debates**

1. Michel Foucault, *Discipline and Punish: The Birth of the Prison,* trans. Alan Sheridan (New York: Pantheon Books, 1978; Vintage Books, 1979), 202.

2. Roland Barthes, *S/Z,* trans. Richard Miller, with a preface by Richard Howard (New York: Hill and Wang, 1985), 105.

3. This subject really deserves separate treatment elsewhere, where a historical review of the response of Hollywood and television to current events could be detailed without sidetracking the subject at hand. However, it seems worth noting that, despite the growing capacity of television news to cover the globe (although not to analyze its developments adequately), its docudramas continue to focus on the privately scandalous — preppie murders, Long Island love affairs, sensational murder trials. Current events topicality seems little more than an advertising hook for such programming.

4. Frederic Jameson, "Periodizing the Sixties," in *The 60s Without Apology,* ed. Sohnya Sayers et al. (Minneapolis: University of Minnesota Press, 1985), 182.

5. Christopher Lasch, "The Life of Kennedy's Death," *Harper's,* October 1983, 32.

6. Gerald Posner, *Case Closed* (New York: Random House, 1993).

7. Dominic LaCapra, *Soundings in Critical Theory* (Ithaca: Cornell University Press, 1989), 37.

8. This list does not include those congressional committees whose work overlapped with the assassination investigation: the Edwards Committee in the House and the Schweiker Committee in the Senate, both undertaken in the fall of 1975, or the Church Committee of the same year, devoted to CIA activities.

9. For the most thorough cataloguing of these materials, see DeLloyd J. Guth and David R. Wrone, comps., *The Assassination of John F. Kennedy: A Comprehensive Historical and Legal Bibliography, 1963–1979* (Westport, Conn.: Greenwood Press, 1980). The figure 2,300 is taken from this source and includes items issued in the foreign press of western Europe.

10. For more on these organizations, see *Skeptic* 9 (September/October 1975), 41–42.

11. Among these are Citizens for Truth About the Kennedy Assassination, located in Hollywood, California, and the JFK Assassination Information Center. The latter, founded in 1989, is located near Dealey Plaza in Dallas and was cosponsor of the ASK assassination symposium held November 18–22, 1993.

12. For a more general discussion of this culture of skepticism, see Morris Dickstein, *Gates of Eden: American Culture in the Sixties* (New York: Penguin, 1989), 248–251.

13. Sayres et al., *The 60s Without Apology,* 8.

14. The most comprehensive single source detailing the activities of the media and how they covered the assassination is Barbie Zelizer, *Covering the Body: The Kennedy Assassination, the Media, and the Shaping of Collective Memory* (Chicago: University of Chicago Press, 1992). In her history of the journalistic coverage, Zelizer attempts to demonstrate how the press consistently worked at self-legitimation. However, she does not discuss all aspects of the underground press nor does she consider the presence of assassination literature in soft-core pornography. Still, no other source comes close to Zelizer's thorough analysis. Several other sources provide brief chronologies of the press/media reporting. See, for example, Sylvia Meagher, *Accessories After the Fact: The Warren Commission, the Authorities and the Report,* with an introduction by Peter Dale Scott, preface by Richard S. Schweiker (New York: Vintage Books, 1976), 458–464; Guth and Wrone, *The Assassination of John F. Kennedy,* xi–xxxiv; Martin Shackelford, "What We Were Told About the Assassination of John F. Kennedy: A Weekend of Newspapers, a Decade of Magazines," in Ian MacFarlane, *Proof of Conspiracy* (Australia: Book Distributors, 1975), 131–140.

15. I will discuss the sale and possession of the Zapruder film and its deployment by *Life* in a subsequent chapter.

16. Joachim Joesten, *Oswald: Assassin or Fall Guy?* (New York: Marzani and Munsell, 1964).

17. Thomas Buchanan, *Who Killed Kennedy?* (New York: Putnam, 1964).

18. The House Select Committee on Assassinations also failed to produce an index for the fourteen volumes accompanying its final report. See Sylvia Meagher and Gary Owens, *Master Index to the J.F.K. Assassination Investigations: The Reports and Supporting Volumes of the House Select Committee on Assassinations and the Warren Commission* (Metuchen, N.J.: Scarecrow Press, 1980).

19. David S. Lifton, *Best Evidence: Disguise and Deception in the Assassination of John F. Kennedy* (New York: Carroll & Graf 1980), 15. I take Lifton's reference to ordinary folk to be more accurate than sappy. For more on the assassination buffs see Trillin, cited below.

20. Calvin Trillin, "The Buffs," *The New Yorker,* 7 June 1967, 41. I will refer to these independent researchers by several names, primarily *critics* and *buffs.* Many within this network disapprove of the term *buff,* believing that its casual, hobbyist connotation belies the serious nature of their work. Obviously this project takes much of their work seriously, and my use of the term *buff* is not meant condescendingly.

21. Michel Foucault, *Language, Counter-Memory, Practice,* edited and with an introduction by Donald F. Bouchard, trans. Donald F. Bouchard and Sherry Simon (Ithaca: Cornell University Press, 1977; Cornell Paperbacks, 1980), 138.

22. Edward Jay Epstein, *Inquest* (New York: Viking, 1966).

23. Harold Weisberg, *Whitewash* (Hyattstown, Md.: Harold Weisberg, 1965).

24. See as an example Anthony Lewis, "Panel to Reject Theories of Plot in Kennedy's Death," *New York Times,* 1 June 1964. Lewis's column appeared almost four months before the Warren Report was released.

25. Quoted in Jerry Policoff, "The Second Dallas Casualty, the Media and the Assassination of Truth," in *Government by Gunplay: Assassination Conspiracy Theories from Dallas to Today,* ed. Sid Blumenthal and Harvey Yazijian (New York: Signet, 1976), 211.

26. Gerald Ford, "How the Commission Pieced Together the Evidence," *Life,* 2 October 1964, 42. This article will be discussed in more depth in the following chapter.

27. For this study see *Psychiatric Quarterly* 40 (1966): 737–755.

28. Mark Lane, *Rush to Judgment* (New York: Holt, Rinehart & Winston, 1966; Dell, 1975).

29. Josiah Thompson, *Six Seconds in Dallas* (New York: Bernard Geis Associates with Random House, 1967; Berkeley Publishing, 1976).

30. "Did Oswald Act Alone? A Matter of Reasonable Doubt," *Life,* 25 November 1966, 53.

31. "The Assassination, the Phantasmagoria," *Time,* 25 November 1966, 34–35.

32. *New York Times,* 25 November 1966, 36.

33. The 70 percent figure is taken from MacFarlane, *Proof of Conspiracy,* 127. The 54 percent is from *Time,* 25 November 1966, 34.

34. For a detailed discussion of the dispute over Manchester's book and its author's working relationship with the Kennedys, see John Corry, *The Manchester Affair* (New York: G. P. Putnam's Sons, 1967).

35. See Sylvia Meagher, "The Kennedy Conspiracy by Paris Flammonde," *Commonweal*, 7 March 1969, 712–714; Edward Jay Epstein, *Counterplot* (New York: Viking Press, 1969); James Phelan, "A Plot to Kill Kennedy? Rush to Judgment in New Orleans," *The Saturday Evening Post*, 6 May 1967, 21–25. For a brief but informative account of the Garrison affair, see Robert Sam Anson, *They've Killed the President: The Search for the Murderers of John F. Kennedy* (New York: Bantam Books, 1975), 102–128.

36. Richard Sprague, "The Assassination of President John F. Kennedy: The Application of Computers to the Photographic Evidence," *Computers and Automation* 19 (May 1970): 29–60; (June 1970): 7; 19 (July 1970): 36; 20 (March 1971): 44; 20 (May 1971): 27–29.

37. For a more detailed discussion of CTIA, see Fred Cook, "Assassination Investigations: The Irregulars Take the Field," *The Nation*, 19 July 1971, 40–46.

38. A specific account of the origins of the AIB can be found in MacFarlane, *Proof of Conspiracy*, 131–134.

39. Quoted in MacFarlane, *Proof of Conspiracy*, 134.

40. See "*Life* Sues to Enjoin Book on Assassination of Kennedy," *Publisher's Weekly*, 25 December 1967, 32. This case will be discussed further in the following chapter.

41. Robert Blair Kaiser, "The JFK Assassination: Why Congress Should Reopen the Investigation," *Rolling Stone*, 24 April 1975, 27–38; Robert Sam Anson, "The Man Who Never Was," *New Times*, 19 September 1975, 14–25; Jerry Policoff, "The Media and the Murder of John Kennedy," *New Times*, 8 August 1975, 28–36; Forum for Contemporary History, *Skeptic*, September/October 1975.

42. Quoted in Martin Waldron, "Schweiker Joins Attack on Warren Report as Clamor for New Inquiry Rises," *New York Times*, 20 October 1975, sec. B, 1.

43. *New York Times*, 1 December 1975, 30.

44. Quoted from Assassination Information Bureau Position Paper, reprinted in Blumenthal and Yazijian, *Government by Gunplay*, 260.

45. See U.S. House of Representatives, *The Final Assassinations Report, Report of the Select Committee on Assassinations*, by Louis Stokes, chairman, with a forward by Tom Wicker and introduction by G. Robert Blakey (New York: Bantam Books, 1979). Hereafter I will refer to this report as the HSCA Final Report.

46. This, of course, is only the most partial of lists concerning the specific questions raised by assassination critics. Some of these points will be discussed in more detail in the following chapter.

47. HSCA Final Report, 329.

48. HSCA Final Report, 104.

49. HSCA Final Report, 63–103. In 1980 the U.S. Justice Department asked the National Research Council to set up a committee to review studies of the acoustics evidence. This committee followed a lead suggested by an assassination critic who believed the police dictabelt had recorded the voice of a sheriff giving orders to officers, orders reportedly not issued until after the shots had been fired. Based on their own testing, the committee concluded that the tape was not acoustical evidence of a second gunman. For a detailed discussion of this point, see Richard B. Trask, *Pictures of the Pain: Photography and the Assassination of President Kennedy* (Danvers, Mass.: Yeoman Press, 1994), 139–141.

50. HSCA Final Report, 104–288.

51. G. Robert Blakey and Richard N. Billings, *The Plot to Kill the President* (New York: Times Books, 1981).

52. David E. Scheim, *Contract on America* (New York: Zebra Books, 1989).

53. For a more concise description of the various mob connections to the case published at this time, see Carl Oglesby and Jeff Goldberg, "Did the Mob Kill Kennedy?" *Washington Post*, 25 February 1979, B1, B4.

54. The term *secret team* refers to an alleged government group in charge of clandestine operations. The theory holds that agents within this team, and thus within the government, were given orders to kill or acted autonomously in killing JFK. For the best defense of the theory offered by Stone, arguing it "makes us contemplate political assassination in clandestine America . . . rather than various, cabalistic notions of 'conspiracy' articulated by the media in a grab bag, inchoate form," see Christopher Sharrett, "Debunking the Official History: The Conspiracy Theory in *JFK*," *Cineaste* 19 (1992): 11–14.

55. Chapter 10 will undertake a detailed discussion of *JFK* and the public response it generated.

56. The most straightforward warning came on the cover of *Newsweek*, December 23, 1991, with its headline "The Twisted Truth of 'JFK': Why Oliver Stone's New Movie Can't Be Trusted."

57. On the release of government files, see Tim Weiner, "Papers on Kennedy Assassination Are Unsealed, and '63 Is Revisited," *New York Times*, 24 August 1993, A1, A11. The context for further research was also enhanced by the declassification of National Archives files relevant to the presidency of Lyndon Johnson and the public release of KGB files after the transformation of the Soviet Union. See "Johnson Balked at Panel on Kennedy Killing,"

New York Times, 23 September 1993, B13, and David Wise, "Was Oswald a Spy, and Other Cold War Mysteries," *New York Times Magazine*, 6 December 1992, 42–48.

58. Some of the specifics of Posner's argument will be discussed in the following chapter. Media approval for *Case Closed* came from both the print and television press. See *U.S. News and Weekly Report*, 6 September 1993, 62–98. The cover of this issue declares *Case Closed* "Finally Proves Who Killed Kennedy." The ultimate showcasing of Posner's book came on a broadcast of CBS Reports: "Who Killed JFK?" 19 November 1993.

59. Evan Thomas, "The Real Cover-Up," *Newsweek*, 22 November 1993, 67.

60. *Newsweek*, 22 November 1963, 57.

61. Michael Beschloss, "The Day That Changed America," *Newsweek*, 22 November 1993, 62. As will be discussed in a subsequent chapter, the infantilizing of conspiracy theorists unable to cope with the tragic implications of a lone assassin had been a frequent explanation of and defense against assassination critics.

62. For more on how the buffs felt at this point, see Neal Karlen's report on the ASK assassination symposium, "Jack in the Box," *City Pages*, 15 December 1993, 10–11.

63. Transcripts of executive sessions held by the Warren Commission were made public in 1968. In November 1966, the Kennedy family donated autopsy photos and x rays to the National Archives with strict instructions that only under exceptional circumstances could they be examined within the first five years of their donation and then only by official federal investigators. Subsequently, permission to see these items had to be requested from and granted by Burke Marshal, close family associate and former assistant attorney general. In January 1978 over 100,000 pages of FBI records were declassified. In 1975 the National Archives made available information pertaining to the chain of possession for autopsy photos and x rays. These staggered developments hint at the complex chronology subtending the case.

64. According to Penn Jones, Jr., editor of the *Midlothian Mirror*, who has devoted the years since the assassination to investigating possible conspiracy, eighty-five individuals with some connection to the case have met with sudden or unnatural death. See Anson, *They've Killed the President*, 137–138, for a discussion of the deaths of Jim Koethe of the *Dallas Times Herald* and Bill Hunter of the *Long Beach Press-Telegram*. See Blakey, *The Plot to Kill the President*, 152–153, for references to statements allegedly made to columnist Jack Anderson by John Roselli directly incriminating organized crime in the assassination.

65. Perhaps most immediately relevant to this point are Bruce Conner's remarks in a 1969 interview. When asked why he made ten versions of *Report*, Conner responded, "I was obsessed." When asked about his strategic intentions for the film, whether he was conscious of looking for a certain effect, he responded, "Yes, I know what I was doing. I was obsessed." See "Bruce Conner," *Film Comment* 5 (Winter 1969): 16–25.

66. See any number of works that make up the anti–Warren Report literature for the minibiographies or testimonials concerning the involvement of various authors. See especially Lifton cited above. Elsewhere see Bob Katz, "Still on the Case," *Boston Globe Magazine*, 13 November 1988, 44.

67. Michel Foucault, *Language, Counter-Memory, Practice*, 154.

Part One

1. Hollis Frampton *(nostalgia)*, voice-over narration for film of that name. 1 January 1971.

Chapter 1 **The Zapruder Film**

1. The "story," as I put it, is told in greater detail in Robert Sam Anson, *"They've Killed the President!"* (New York: Bantam Books, 1975), 15–20. Perhaps the most thorough account of the Zapruder film and its journey through the government and critical communities is found in Richard B. Trask, *Pictures of the Pain: Photography and the Assassination of President Kennedy,* (Danvers, Mass.: 1994), 57–153.

2. Rick Friedman, "Pictures of Assassination Fall to Amateurs on the Street," *Editor and Publisher,* 30 November 1963, 16–17, 67.

3. Trask, *Pictures of the Pain,* 107. Several critics, suspicious of the CIA's possession of the film, have suggested that the agency may have obtained a copy as early as the night of the assassination, giving them grounds to declare the film evidence compromised. Trask asserts that the CIA tests on the Zapruder film took place no earlier than November 29. For a discussion of possible CIA possession of the Zapruder film on November 22, see Philip H. Melanson, "Hidden Exposure: Cover-up and Intrigue in the CIA's Secret Possession of the Zapruder film," *The Third Decade* 1 (November 1984): 13–21.

4. Zapruder received $50,000 for print publication rights. Two days later the deal came to $150,000, when movie and television rights were secured by Time-Life. For an extended account of the transaction, see Loudon Wainright, *The Great American Magazine* (New York: Knopf, 1968), 308–333. Wainright, however, incorrectly states that, as of 1986, "the viewing public

has never been shown" the Zapruder film. This error plus his long-time position as editor at *Life* may cast some doubt on his mininarrative.

5. I am indebted to Paul Arthur for his helpful comments concerning my discussion of *Life* and its use of assassination imagery.

6. Wainright, *The Great American Magazine,* xvii.

7. For a more detailed discussion of how the Zapruder film was handled by Time-Life during this period, see Jerry Policoff, "The Media and the Murder of John Kennedy," *New Times,* 8 August 1975, 28–36. See also Robert Hennelly and Jerry Policoff, "JFK: How the Media Assassinated the Real Story," *Village Voice,* 31 March 1992, 33–39.

8. This memorandum is reprinted in Harold Weisberg, *Photographic Whitewash* (Hyattstown, Md.: Harold Weisberg, 1967), 142.

9. Exactly who saw what print of the film seems a bit unclear. The one source referred to above is Edward J. Epstein, *Inquest* (New York: Viking, 1966). However, Thompson notes only Shaneyfelt viewing the original print on January 25. In *They've Killed the President,* Anson reports that in January a copy of the film and a full set of slides were turned over to the commission, but this would seem to be contradicted by the Shaneyfelt testimony cited above. Furthermore, while the FBI analysis of their working print consisted of studying 35mm slides made from each frame, Thompson suggests that these were still smaller than the four-by-five-inch enlargements he examined at *Life*'s offices. See Josiah Thompson, *Six Seconds in Dallas* (New York: Bernard Geis Associates with Random House, 1967; Berkeley Publishing, 1976), 9–12.

10. For a discussion of how the commission used this evidence, see Epstein, *Inquest,* 122–126.

11. My use of the term *dialogic* is influenced by Dominick LaCapra's usage in several essays in *Soundings in Critical Theory* (Ithaca: Cornell University Press, 1989). LaCapra speaks of the dialogic relation between historian and object of inquiry in an attempt to stress the historically specific uses of the language or perspectives employed in historiography. LaCapra makes a similar point in his discussion of Freud, in which he suggests that historian and subject can be seen in terms of a transferential relationship. For a further discussion of dialogism in historiography, see Dominick LaCapra, *Rethinking Intellectual History* (Ithaca: Cornell University Press, 1983), 50–52.

12. This letter is reprinted in Thompson, *Six Seconds in Dallas,* app. F.

13. Throughout this discussion, when I refer to the commission's reprinting the Zapruder film, I am referring to its frame-by-frame publication in Volume 18 of its exhibits.

14. Sylvia Meagher, *Accessories After the Fact: The Warren Commission, the Authorities and the Report,* with an introduction by Peter Dale Scott, preface by Richard S. Schweiker (New York: Vintage Books, 1976), 22.

15. Vincent J. Salandria, "LIFE Magazine and the Warren Commission," *Liberation* 11 (October 1966): 44.

16. Ibid.

17. "A Matter of Reasonable Doubt," *Life,* 25 November 1966, 38–53.

18. Ibid., 41.

19. The phrase "instantly democratize" belongs to Salandria in "Life Magazine and the Warren Commission." Thompson refers to the photos as "inviolable" in *Six Seconds in Dallas,* 17.

20. Quoted in Thompson, *Six Seconds In Dallas,* 17.

21. Time Inc. v. Bernard Geis, Josiah Thompson and Random House Inc., 67 Civ. 4736 U.S. District Court, Southern District of New York.

22. Harriet F. Pilpel with Kenneth P. Norwick, " 'Fair Use' Protects Zapruder Film Copies," *Publishers' Weekly,* 28 October 1968, 26–27. See this article also for a summary discussion of the case.

23. L. Fletcher Prouty, "The Guns of Dallas," *Gallery,* October 1975, 87. Prouty's rhetoric aptly characterizes the critic's desire for a time clock of the shooting. For the film not only supplies the kind of evidence available through its still frames but also serves as a temporal measure which can be compared to the speed with which three shots can be fired from the alleged murder rifle.

24. Trask, *Pictures of the Pain,* 269–275. In his history of assassinations, James McKinley points out that the Itek findings were read with a certain suspicion by critics because Itek's president was a former CIA employee and because 60 percent of Itek's business was with the government. James McKinley, *Assassination in America* (New York: Harper & Row, 1977), 139.

25. This conference was held in Boston on January 31, 1975. Two months later, Groden's version of the Zapruder film was aired on national television for the first time on Geraldo Rivera's "Goodnight America." In his review of Rivera's two assassination programs, John J. O'Connor mildly chastises Rivera for sensationalism. See *New York Times,* 27 March 1975.

26. Robert Groden, "A New Look at the Zapruder Film," *Rolling Stone,* 24 April 1975, 35.

27. *CBS Reports Inquiry: The American Assassins,* 25, 26 November 1975.

28. Trask, *Pictures of the Pain,* 275. Trask states this point more in terms of a fact made clear by the Aerospace study. I have framed his comment as a

suggestive insight because, not having seen the Aerospace research, I am not in a position to speak with such certainty. Trask is in a sense paraphrasing what Wolf told Rather on the CBS broadcast in response to Rather's comment about the impression that JFK only moves backward. Wolf says: "My answer to your implied question is I don't know what I see, I know what I measure." Trask quotes at some length from the transcript of the CBS broadcast on pages 126–127 of his book.

29. Trask, *Pictures of the Pain*, 275.

30. David E. James, *Allegories of Cinema* (Princeton, N.J.: Princeton University Press, 1989), 244.

31. Ibid.

32. Lois Mendelson and Bill Simon, "Tom, Tom, The Piper's Son," ART-FORUM, September 1971, 47.

33. For quality blowups of these frames, see *Rolling Stone*, 24 April 1975, 34.

34. The multitude of ways the Zapruder film called into question the government's history of the event are too numerous to list here. My point is not to repeat all the criticisms of the Warren Report that access to the film made possible but to mention the following key example. Many critics argued that the time frame established by the film allows for questions concerning the commission's single bullet hypothesis in that it sets a limit on Oswald's alleged firing time. Figuring the time it takes to fire the Mannlicher-Carcano rifle and the time elapsed on film between when Kennedy is first struck, when Connally appears struck, and when Kennedy is fatally struck, the film forces any lone assassin scenario to account for all the wounds in just three shots. Four shots in that time frame necessitates adding a second gunman. Any number of books by assassination critics discuss this issue in detail. See Thompson, *Six Seconds in Dallas*, ch. 3–5.

35. The Moorman photo was taken by Mary Moorman immediately after the fatal shot. It corresponds to Zapruder frames 313–315 and has been used to study the direction in which Kennedy's body was driven upon impact. James Altgens was an AP photographer who photographed JFK immediately after what most agree was the first shot. His photo, published in the commission's report with much of its right side cropped, allows for a precise marking of where the limousine was on Elm Street at the time of this shot. This marking can in turn be coordinated with the angle from the Depository window to show whether Oswald's alleged line of sight was clear or obstructed at the time of the shot.

36. The Collector's Archive markets an extensive array of assassination imagery and texts. At the time of this writing they were still operating out of Box 2 Beaconsfield, Quebec H9W 5T6.

37. For more on this latter process, see Thompson, *Six Seconds in Dallas*, app. B and C.

38. The detailed analysis of each theorist can be found in Groden, "A New Look," 35–36, and Thompson, *Six Seconds in Dallas*, 32–151. Both authors, it is fair to say, look to and cite eyewitness testimony to corroborate their readings of the film.

39. For a detailed discussion of these findings, see HSCA Final Report, 31–103.

40. Luis W. Alvarez, "A Physicist Examines the Kennedy Assassination Film," *American Journal of Physics* (September 1976). Alvarez also conducted experiments to determine whether the motion of Kennedy's body after the head wound fit with physical laws of reacting to a shot fired from behind.

41. Martin Shackelford, "Listening to the Zapruder Film," *The Third Decade* 3 (March 1987): 19–20.

42. *Report of the President's Commission on the Assassination of President John F. Kennedy,* Chief Justice Earl Warren, chairman (Washington, D.C.: U.S. Government Printing Office, 1964), 109.

43. Meagher, *Accessories After the Fact,* 34. The diagram to which Meagher is referring is that constructed by Salandria and Fonzi based on their projection of Zapruder slides. See also Gaeton Fonzi, "The Warren Commission, the Truth, and Arlen Specter," *Greater Philadelphia* 57 (August 1966): 12–15, 73–86.

44. Thompson, *Six Seconds in Dallas*, 115–116. In a footnote Thompson mentions that commission critics Ray Marcus and Harold Weisberg, working independently of each other and himself, also discovered the double movement. See Harold Weisberg, *Whitewash II* (Hyattstown, Md.: Harold Weisberg, 1966), 221.

45. Thompson, *Six Seconds in Dallas*, 121.

46. Groden, "A New Look," 36.

47. The HSCA findings were not based solely on their reading of the film. They did entertain the Thompson-Groden thesis of a double hit but concluded that it ran contrary to the dictabelt evidence. Also, analysis of the bullet said to be responsible for Kennedy's death linked it with the rifle found on the sixth floor of the Depository. For this bullet to have eliminated any trace of a previous bullet fired from the knoll, a previous bullet fired at frame 312, the killing bullet would have to have been fired at frames 328–329, and according to the committee the film gives evidence of no such shot.

48. "CBS Reports: Who Killed Kennedy," 19 November 1993.

49. Gerald Posner, *Case Closed* (New York: Random House, 1993), 317.

50. In addition to this little girl's reaction, Posner cites as evidence for a frame-160 first shot Connally's reaction and an analysis of the film that suggests certain frames are blurry at this point in the film as a result of Zapruder's reacting to a shot. By locating the first shot at frame 160, Posner expands the time available for a shooter to get off three shots with the last one still at frame 313. Posner, *Case Closed,* 322. It is worth noting that, in his analysis of the film, Groden also located a shot between frames 157–161.

51. Posner 322.

52. Ibid., 321.

53. Ibid., 328–329. Here Posner is citing the work of Dr. John K. Lattimer. Lattimer puts forth the Thorburn's position thesis in *Kennedy and Lincoln Medical and Ballistic Comparisons of Their Assassinations,* (New York: Harcourt Brace Jovanovich, 1980), 240–245.

54. Ibid., 329.

55. Ibid., 333–335. Posner's readings of the film are based on computer work done by two sources. The first was that of a medical examiner and a journalist; the other, of a firm called Failure Analysis Associates, which he says specialized in "computer reconstructions for lawsuits." His fullest description of the details of the computer test come on page 334.

56. Thompson, *Six Seconds in Dallas,* 7. In fairness to Thompson, he does acknowledge the repeated viewings necessary for and the difficulty incurred by interpreting this imagery. Still, two pages after this statement above he remarks, "the Zapruder footage contained the nearest thing to 'absolute truth' about the sequence of events in Dealey Plaza." Not all critics insisted the film revealed the truth of the case. Sylvia Meagher noted, "It is frustrating and ironic that the Zapruder film does not enable the viewer to pinpoint the exact moment of impact of the bullet in the President's back or of the bullet (or bullets) that struck the Governor." *Accessories After the Fact,* 29.

57. Quoted in Trask, *Pictures of the Pain,* 116.

58. Gerald Posner, "The Magic Bullet," *U.S. News & World Report,* 30 August–6 September 1993, 88.

59. The phrase "painstaking analysis" is taken from *Life,* 2 October 1964, 42.

60. Thompson, *Six Seconds in Dallas,* 121.

Chapter 2 **The Body**

1. The individual to whom these remarks most specifically apply is Dr. Cyril Wecht, the long-time critic of the Warren Commission who was granted

access to autopsy material in 1972. Wecht's observations led him to agree that the wounds appeared to be inflicted by shots coming from the rear, but he disagreed with the location of the wounds cited by the official autopsy doctors. Wecht would later sit on the medical panel for the House assassinations committee and frequently offered the sole dissenting voice during its interpretations.

2. Cyril H. Wecht, M.D., "A Critique of President Kennedy's Autopsy," in Josiah Thompson, *Six Seconds in Dallas* (New York: Bernard Geis Associates with Random House, 1967; Berkeley Publishing, 1976), app. D, 361.

3. Michel Foucault, *The Birth of the Clinic: An Archeology of Medical Perception*, trans. A. M. Sheridan Smith (London: Tavistock Publications, 1973; New York: Vintage Books Edition, 1975), 125.

4. Ibid., 129.

5. Ibid., 140–141.

6. Ibid., 144.

7. For a brief summary of these journalistic accounts and a sampling of newspaper article citations, see Sylvia Meagher, *Accessories After the Fact: The Warren Commission, the Authorities and the Report,* with an introduction by Peter Dale Scott, preface by Richard S. Schweiker (New York: Vintage Books, 1976), 134–135. Meagher also provides perhaps the most reliable overview of the criticism aimed at the official autopsy report over the four years following the assassination.

8. Meagher, *Accessories After the Fact,* 146–147. The myriad questions and contradictions suggested by research into the JFK autopsy are obviously too wide ranging to catalogue fully here. As with my discussion of the motorcade film, my interest is not in compiling a checklist of discrepancies, but in suggesting the grounds on which to argue for a struggle with and a crisis of interpretation.

9. Quoted in Thompson, *Six Seconds in Dallas,* 252.

10. Defenders of the Warren Report have responded to the bullet hole discrepancy by claiming that the shirt and coat rode up on Kennedy's back while he sat in the limousine. Photographs taken earlier in the motorcade do appear to show the coat buckling up in back, but in one such picture, from the *Dallas Times Herald,* the fold in the back of the coat seems pronounced enough that a bullet piercing it might cause two holes in the material. The shirt and coat do not contain double holes. Humes suggested that the coat may have bunched up due to Kennedy's physique. Dr. John Lattimer suggests that JFK's position in the car caused a roll of the excessive tissue Kennedy had along that part of his back. Dr. John K. Lattimer, *Kennedy and*

Lincoln: Medical and Ballistic Comparisons of Their Assassinations (New York: Harcourt Brace Jovanovich, 1980), 200. Because JFK may have been behind the freeway sign at the moment this bullet struck, it is hard to tell from the film the position of his coat.

11. Weisberg makes these points next to his reprinting of the Clark Panel report in *Post Mortem: JFK Assassination Cover-up Smashed* (Frederick, Md.: Harold Weisberg, 1975), 580–595.

12. Lattimer, *Kennedy and Lincoln*, 192–219.

13. The doctor referred to is Robert McClelland. For more on his testimony and a diagram he drew of the head wound, see Thompson, *Six Seconds in Dallas*, 140. For a discussion of how the Dallas doctors responded to McClelland as of 1993, see Gerald Posner, *Case Closed: Lee Harvey Oswald and the Assassination of JFK*, (New York: Random House, 1993), 312–313.

14. Robert J. Groden and Harrison Edward Livingstone, *High Treason: The Assassination of President John F. Kennedy and the New Evidence of Conspiracy* (New York: Berkley Books, 1990), 82. Posner rebuts Groden's point by simply quoting the head of the HSCA medical panel as saying Groden doesn't know how to read x rays.

15. Richard B. Stolley, "What Happened Next," *Esquire*, November 1973, 135.

16. Lattimer, *Kennedy and Lincoln*, 193.

17. For a sampling of assassination literature in soft-core pornography, see *Playboy*, June 1965, November 1965, February 1967, October 1967, January– May 1976, November 1978; *Penthouse*, October 1981; *Gallery*, October 1975, February 1978, April 1978, June 1978, July 1979; *Playgirl*, August 1975.

18. Walter Kendrick, *The Secret Museum: Pornography in Modern Culture* (New York: Viking Press, 1987).

19. For an example of such catalogues and a sampling of the marginal topics that share sites of distribution, see Rev. Ivan Stang, *High Weirdness by Mail* (New York: Simon & Schuster, 1988).

20. "The Parts That Were Left out of the Kennedy Book," *The Realist* 74 (May 1967), 18.

21. The pornographic implications of Krassner's article were reinforced in this issue of *The Realist* by a center-spread illustration depicting Disney characters enjoying a "Disneyland memorial Orgy." For more on this, see Paul Krassner, *Confessions of a Raving Unconfined Nut: Misadventures in the Counter-Culture* (New York: Simon & Schuster, 1993), 126–144.

22. Jean-Louis Comolli, "Machines of the Visible," in *The Cinematic Apparatus,* ed. Teresa de Lauretis and Stephen Heath (New York: St. Martin's Press, 1980).

23. Ibid., 122.

24. Ibid., 123.

25. Serge Daney, "Sur Salador," *Cahiers du Cinema* 122 (July 1970): 39. The translated quote is taken from Comolli, "Machines of the Visible," 126.

26. Linda Williams, *Hard Core: Power, Pleasure and the Frenzy of the Visible* (Berkeley and Los Angeles: University of California Press, 1989), 37–48.

27. Ibid., 45.

28. Williams discusses this point throughout her book, and the phrase "involuntary convulsion" is taken from her discussion of pornography's money shot. *Hard Core,* 113.

29. Williams, *Hard Core,* 48.

30. Ibid., 49.

31. Ibid., 192.

32. Ibid., 193.

33. Ibid., 194. William's reference here is to the film *Snuff,* a commercial narrative from 1976 about the making of snuff films, in which the final reflexive scene implies that this film will end with the mutilation of one of its actresses.

34. Is it too speculative to suggest that, placed within the pages of soft core, the images of Kennedy's "involuntary spasm" substitute for the thoroughly concealed but often discussed spasms of sex for which he was well known? Having no access to the sight of JFK with Marilyn Monroe, the Zapruder film provides a record of an involuntary performance by the glamorous president, the only one a gossip-hungry public is likely to get, assuming that home movies of JFK with Marilyn, supposedly shot by Peter Lawford, never make it into public view.

Chapter 3 **Images of Oswald**

1. Quoted in Dan Carmichael, United Press International, "Efforts to open Oswald's grave blocked by his brother," *Minneapolis Tribune,* 15 August 1980, 5A. Oswald had been the focus of FBI and CIA attention well before the assassination.

2. A British assassination critic, Michael Eddowes, maintained that a Soviet agent had replaced Oswald and impersonated him in the states. After ob-

taining the approval of Oswald's widow Marina, Eddowes pressed for exhumation of the body. Dental and medical records confirmed that it was the body of Lee Harvey Oswald.

3. Images picturing Oswald handing out pro-Castro literature on a street corner or living with Marina in Minsk were used to situate him amidst a murky political background or to suggest his unstable past. Without supplying evidence that Oswald was directly involved in the assassination, they still functioned as arguments for his guilt. See Thomas Thompson, "Assassin: The Man Held—and Killed—for Murder," *Life*, 29 November 1963, 38; and "Oswald Called It my 'Historic Diary'—And It Is," *Life*, 10 July 1964, 28–29.

4. "A Big Sale," *Newsweek*, 2 March 1964, 80.

5. *Hearings Before the President's Commission on the Assassination of President John F. Kennedy* (Washington, D.C.: U.S. Government Printing Office, 1964), vol. 21, 449–451. From here on citations from these hearings will be abbreviated *WC Hearings* followed by volume number and pages.

6. *WC Hearings*, 21, 452–453.

7. Ibid., 456–458.

8. Exactly what Oswald told Dallas police before he was killed is unknown, because (quite remarkably) there was no record of the interrogations kept. For a paraphrasing of Oswald's remarks, see Meagher, *Accessories After the Fact: The Warren Commission, the Authorities and the Report*, with an introduction by Peter Dale Scott, preface by Richard S. Schweiker (New York: Vintage Books, 1976), 207.

9. A third backyard photo was discovered among the possessions of George DeMohrenschildt, a former CIA operative and acquaintance of the Oswalds, after DeMohrenschildt's suicide in 1977. For more on this third photo, see Groden and Livingstone, *High Treason*, 204–206.

10. For more on the critics' suspicions concerning the backyard photos, see Robert Sam Anson, *"They've Killed the President!": The Search for the Murderers of John F. Kennedy* (New York: Bantam Books, 1975), 78–80; and Meagher, *Accessories After the Fact*, 202–207.

11. Sigmund Freud, "The Uncanny," in *The Standard Edition of the Complete Psychological Works of Sigmund Freud*, ed. James Strachey (New York: Hogarth Press, 1953–1974), vol. 17, 219–252. Reprinted in Sigmund Freud, *On Creativity and the Unconscious* (New York: Harper & Row, 1958), 122–161. Citations below from this essay refer to this reprinted edition.

12. Freud, "The Uncanny," 129.

13. Ibid., 136

14. Freud in fact goes on to warn against the move I will make next; that is, arguing for an understanding of uncanny fear separate from castration anxiety and based solely on the loss of the eyes. With respect to the Sand-Man story and its analysis, Freud quite rightly points out how the Sand-Man is closely associated with the figure of Nathaniel's father as well as Nathaniel's attempts at love and thus would appear integrally linked to castration complex. Still, in what follows, I hope at least to suggest that the fears motivated by the Sand-Man need not and should not be conflated with castration anxiety.

15. Freud, "The Uncanny," 123.

16. Freud, "The Uncanny," 141.

17. Richard H. Popkin, *The Second Oswald*, with an introduction by Murray Kempton (New York: Avon and The New York Review, 1966).

18. For a detailed discussion of the Odio story and other examples of Oswald and his family being allegedly impersonated, see Popkin, *The Second Oswald*, 74–94, and Meagher, *Accessories After the Fact*, 359–387.

19. Robert Sam Anson, "The greatest cover-up of all," *New Times*, 18 April 1975, 26.

20. For more on Hidell, see Popkin, *The Second Oswald*, 67–73. Almost all the major authors on the assassination — Lane, Anson, and Meagher — give their own interpretations of the Hidell intrigue. Hidell may not have been an entirely fabricated identity. Oswald served in the Marines with a John Heindel who, according to testimony, had been referred to in the service as Hidell.

21. In fact, the double persists elsewhere throughout the case in ways that seem less directly traceable to the illegibility of images. Accounts of the arrival of JFK's body at Bethesda have suggested the presence of at least two caskets: one a polished bronze decoy which reportedly arrived in the naval ambulance escorted by a motorcade carrying Jacqueline and Robert Kennedy; the other, a plain grey metal casket containing the body, which arrived in a black Cadillac hearse. Lifton puts forth the multiple-casket theory in *Best Evidence: Disguise and Deception in the Assassination of John F. Kennedy*, 3d ed. (New York: Carroll and Graf, 1989), 569–652.

22. For a good example of the media's construction of Oswald along these lines, see Donald Jackson, "Evolution of an Assassin," *Life*, 21 February 1964, 68A–80.

23. Christopher Lasch, "The Life of Kennedy's Death," *Harper's*, October 1983, 34.

24. Dr. John K. Lattimer, *Kennedy and Lincoln: Medical and Ballistic Comparisons of their Assassinations* (New York: Harcourt Brace Jovanovich, 1980).

25. Freud, "The Uncanny," 132.

26. This theory is put forth in Lincoln Lawrence, *Were We Controlled?* (New Hyde Park, N.Y.: University Books, 1967).

27. The formal tropes and imaging technologies that conditioned and shaped this process were, of course, in place long before the shooting, but this project does not undertake a description of the history and formation of, say, the various news institutions or journalistic and historiographic tropes with which the assassination would become inextricably linked.

28. Michel Foucault, *The History of Sexuality*, vol. 1, *An Introduction*, trans. Robert Hurley (New York: Random House, 1978; Vintage Books, 1980), 59.

29. See, for example, Lawrence Zelig Freedman, "Psychopathology of Assassination," in *Assassinations and the Political Order*, ed. William J. Crotty (New York: Harper & Row, 1971), 150–160.

30. Priscilla Johnson McMillan, *Marina and Lee* (New York: Harper & Row, 1977).

31. "Oswald Called It My 'Historic Diary' — And It Is," *Life*, 10 July 1964, 26–31.

32. Thomas Powers, "The Heart of the Story," *New York Times Book Review*, 30 October 1977, 46.

33. Ira Progoff, "The Psychology of Lee Harvey Oswald: A Jungian Approach," *Journal of Individual Psychology* 23 (May 1967): 45–46. This essay appears as one of three essays in a symposium, "Lee Harvey Oswald in Freudian, Adlerian, and Jungian Views."

34. Lasch, "The Life of Kennedy's Death," 34.

35. *True* magazine outlined a generic psychological profile of the assassin in 1968. He was, in their words, "slight, straightlaced, resentful of authority, a failure with women, a chronic outsider." Edward Linn, "We Already Know the Next Assassin," *True*, November 1968, 25–29, 69–73.

36. For an example of this tendency in the (mostly) mainstream press, see James McKinley, "Playboy's History of Assassination in America," *Playboy*, January–May, 1976.

37. *Assassination and Political Violence: A Report to the National Commission on the Causes and Prevention of Violence*, ed. James J. Kirkham, Sheldon G. Levy, and William J. Crotty (Washington, D.C.: U.S. Government Printing Office, 1969).

38. Kirkham et al., *Assassination and Political Violence*, 73.

39. See Jacob Cohen, "Conspiracy Fever," *Commentary*, October 1975, 33–42.

40. Joseph Bensman, "Social and Institutional Factors Determining the Level of Violence and Political Assassination in the Operation of Society: A Theoretical Discussion," in Kirkham et al., *Assassination and Political Violence,* 349.

41. The literature produced by sociologists foregrounds how prepared the sociological community was to undertake its postassassination data gathering. For more on this, see Bradley S. Greenberg and Edwin B. Parker, *The Kennedy Assassination and the American Public* (Stanford, Calif.: Stanford University Press, 1965).

42. In "The Life of Kennedy's Death," Lasch makes a similar point with respect to the National Commission on Violence. For him the issue comes down to an endorsement, on the part of both the Warren and the violence commissions, of the legitimacy of government institutions. "Both reports," he notes, "placed far more emphasis on legitimacy than democracy."

43. Michel Foucault, *Language, Counter-Memory, Practice* (Ithaca: Cornell University Press, 1977), 138.

44. For specifics on how the commission was organized and how its report was composed see Edward Jay Epstein, *Inquest* (New York: Viking, 1966).

45. Even before the HSCA report, various buffs were lent some legitimacy by the mainstream press. Even as staid a publication as the *Saturday Evening Post* ran an article on the case accompanied by minibiographies of nineteen assassination critics. See *Saturday Evening Post,* September 1975, 51–53.

46. Edmund Aubrey, *The Case of the Missing President* (New York: Congdon & Weed, 1980).

47. For more on this suggestion and a good example of the multiplication of authorship, see *fact:* 3 (November/December 1966).

48. Ibid., 14.

49. This was the goal of the Citizens' Commission of Inquiry as articulated by Mark Lane in the introduction to the 1975 edition of *Rush to Judgment* (New York: Dell Publishing, 1975), xxxvii.

50. Harold Weisberg, *Photographic Whitewash* (Hyattstown, Md.: Harold Weisberg, 1967), 7.

51. Lane, *Rush to Judgment,* xxxviii.

52. Some critics assign Kennedy a liberal identity and insist that things would have been different almost as a reflex. However, some detailed analysis of Kennedy's Vietnam policy does appear in the literature. See, for example, Peter Dale Scott, "The Death of Kennedy and the Vietnam War," in *Government by Gunplay: Assassination Conspiracy Theories from Dallas to To-*

day, ed. Sid Blumenthal and Harvey Yazijian, with an introduction by Philip Agee (New York: Signet, 1976), 152–187. The position that JFK was preparing to withdraw from Vietnam and was breaking with a hard-line cold war policy in Southeast Asia found its most thorough expression around the time Stone's *JFK* was released, in John M. Newman, *JFK and Vietnam: Deception, Intrigue and the Struggle for Power* (New York: Warner Books, 1992). This position is thoroughly critiqued in Noam Chomsky, *Rethinking Camelot: JFK, the Vietnam War, and U.S. Political Culture* (Boston: South End Press, 1993).

53. Anson, *They've Killed the President,* 14.

Part Two

1. Michael McClure, "On Semina," interview by Eduardo Lipschutz-Villa, in *Wallace Berman: Support the Revolution* (Amsterdam: Institute of Contemporary Art, 1992), 62. For more on Semina and Berman in addition to this collection of essays, see Rebecca Solnit, *Secret Exhibition: Six California Artists of the Cold War Era* (San Francisco: City Lights Books, 1990).

2. Michael McClure, *Star* (New York: Grove Press, 1970), 31.

Chapter 4 **The Warhol Silkscreens**

1. Andy Warhol and Pat Hackett, *Popism: The Warhol '60s* (New York: Harper & Row, 1980), 274.

2. Part of the problem posed by these works is the difficulty of stabilizing the series. Since the key formal characteristic for these works is repetition, there are many variations. It should also be noted that many of these pieces are composed of individual silkscreens set together to form multiple panel grids. Some of the titles mentioned here were arranged by curators for exhibition, in particular *Three Jackies,* the panels of which were not originally intended by Warhol to form a triptych.

3. Thomas Crow, "Saturday Disasters: Trace and Reference in Early Warhol," *Art in America,* May 1987, 130.

4. Crow, "Saturday Disasters," 130–132.

5. Gertrude Stein, *Lectures in America,* with an introduction by Wendy Steiner (Boston: Beacon Press, 1985), 177.

6. This raises the question of whether insistence requires a narrative of some form, be it the history of the individual whose portrait is being constructed or some history into which the individual can be inserted. For example, the Marilyn portraits certainly reference a history, whether Marilyn's or that of

Hollywood's uses of the star. But the sources of these images are clearly more detached from a specific narrative than the Jackie silkscreens and thus are less infused with the dynamics of reception or reading, which are part of the concept of insistence. The Marilyn images, characterized more by repetition than the Jackies, which are subjected to reversals and alternations, fall more distinctly on the side of surface, atemporality, and replication — what I will later describe as the axis of crisis.

7. John Coplans, "Early Warhol: The Systematic Evolution of the Impersonal Style," ARTFORUM, March 1970, 59.

8. See *Life,* 29 November 1963, 23–39, and 6 December 1963, 38–52F. For an explicit example of this interpretive frame, see Paul Mandel, "End to Nagging Rumors: The Six Critical Seconds," *Life,* 6 December 1963, 52F. By some wonderful Warholian coincidence the advertisement on the page across from Mandel's article is for Campbell's soup, complete with a small reproduction of the can: Bean with Bacon.

9. Andrew Ross, *No Respect: Intellectuals & Popular Culture* (New York: Routledge, Chapman and Hall, 1989), 149.

10. Warhol, *Popism,* 60.

11. Ross notes, for example, that "in fact, Pop's doctrinal rejection of the elitist past was best played out, not with dadaist zeal, but with an attitude of pure indifference." Ross, *No Respect,* 150.

12. As Peggy Phelan has suggested to me, Warhol's indifference is at least in part a pose, a performance which insists on its opposite emotion: that one actually care about the tragedy.

13. Crow, "Saturday Disasters," 133.

14. Ibid., 134.

15. Ibid., 135.

16. Ibid., 133.

17. Ibid., 136.

18. Rosalind E. Krauss, *The Originality of the Avant-Garde and Other Modernist Myths* (Cambridge, Mass.: MIT Press, 1985), 8–22.

19. Ibid., 10.

20. Ibid., 18–19.

21. James writes, "the ideals of the sixties were always tempered with their opposites, and, from the constructivism of perpetual revolution to the irreverent debunkings of the mass media, the cults of authenticity were always conducted through the cultures of fabrication." David James, *Allegories of*

Cinema: American Film in the Sixties (Princeton, N.J.: Princeton University Press, 1989), 28.

22. Peter Gidal, *Andy Warhol: Films and Painting* (London: Studio Vista, 1971), 32–33.

23. Gidal, *Andy Warhol,* 33–34.

24. Gidal, *Andy Warhol,* 58.

25. Benjamin H. D. Buchloh, "Andy Warhol's One-Dimensional Art: 1956–1966," in *Andy Warhol: A Retrospective,* ed. Kynaston McShine (New York: Museum of Modern Art, 1989), 50.

26. Ibid.

27. See, of course, Kenneth Anger, *Hollywood Babylon* (New York: Dell Publishing, 1975). For a discussion of the relationship between the Jackie silkscreens and those of Monroe and Taylor concerning the theme of celebrity tragedy, see Thomas Crow, "Saturday Disasters," 133–135.

Chapter 5 **The Pop Camp**

1. For a concise but well-illustrated discussion of pop art's use of political iconography and the values of commercial culture, see Sidra Stich, *Made in USA: An Americanization in Modern Art, the 50s & 60s* (Berkeley: University of California Press, 1987), 15–44.

2. Congress, Senate, House, Committee on Public Works, *John F. Kennedy Center for the Performing Arts: Hearings Before the Joint Session of the Committee on Public Works,* 88th Cong., 1st sess., 12 December 1963, 8. Jessie Payne was instrumental in helping me focus on the congressional hearings and their construction of the JFK image.

3. Ibid., 6.

4. Ibid., 5.

5. Stich, *Made in USA,* 119.

6. The biographical information in my discussion of Ed Paschke is derived from Neal Benezra, *Ed Paschke* (New York: Hudson Hills Press and the Art Institute of Chicago, 1990), 15–39. My thanks to Melinda Barlow for bringing to my attention several references on Paschke's work.

7. Stich, *Made in USA,* 185.

8. Ed Paschke, *Violence in Recent American Art* (Chicago: Museum of Contemporary Art, 1968), quoted in Stich, *Made in USA,* 185.

9. Quoted in Warren I. Susman, *Culture as History: The Transformation of American Society in the Twentieth Century* (New York: Pantheon Books, 1984), 185.

10. By "Warhol signature" I mean any of the three identities outlined by Thomas Crow at the beginning of "Saturday Disasters." According to Crow, the well-rehearsed Warhol persona that claimed an affinity for machines and declared that "he and his art were all surface," has come to overshadow other, more interesting inscriptions of the man and his work. I would suggest that this dominating persona has also had considerable influence on readings of the assassination silkscreens.

11. Andrew Ross, *No Respect: Intellectuals & Popular Culture* (New York: Routledge, Chapman and Hall, 1989), 137–138.

12. For the latter, see any of the catalogues available from the Collector's Archive, Box 2, Beaconsfield, Quebec H9W 5T6.

13. Ross, *No Respect,* 139.

14. According to the terms laid out in his essay, Ross suggests that the notion that something is both camp and pop is a contradiction because, as he notes, "camp is the 'in' taste of a minority elite, while Pop, on the other hand, was supposed to declare that everyday cultural currency had value, and that this value could be communicated in a simple language." *No Respect,* 150. Although he is right to make distinctions between the two categories, my combining them to double-label this aspect of the debate is meant to suggest that tendencies of both are operating on assassination discourses.

15. Ross, *No Respect,* 155.

16. Ibid., 147.

17. For an example of assassination imagery treated as free-floating post-modern signifiers, see Derek Pell, *Assassination Rhapsody* (Brooklyn: Autonomedia, 1989).

18. "Bruce Conner," *Film Comment* 5 (Winter 1969): 18.

Chapter 6 **Bruce Conner**

1. Bruce Conner, "The Warp and Woof of Bruce Conner," interview by Thyrza Goodeve, *Idiolects* 14 (Spring 1984): 46.

2. I will elaborate on this last point later. The reader might anticipate, however, the linking of Conner's interest in images of the naked female body with Part One's discussion of the epistemology of the visible and the role of porn in the assassination debates. I am indebted to Teresa Podlesney for this insight concerning the ontological bond between filmic materials and the female body.

3. P. Adams Sitney describes Conner's attitude toward distribution and exhibition of his work as "ambivalent," in *Visionary Film: The American Avant-*

Garde 1943–1978 (New York: Oxford University Press, 1979), 305. For a discussion of Conner's ordeal with the New York gallery scene, see Stan Brakhage, *Film at Wit's End* (Kingston, N.Y.: Documentext, 1989), 136–138.

4. My thanks to Paul Arthur for his insightful comments on the depiction of the body in Warhol and Conner.

5. Quoted in Sidra Stich, *Made in USA: An Americanization in Modern Art, the 50s and 60s* (Berkeley: University of California Press, 1987), 180.

6. Scott MacDonald, *A Critical Cinema: Interviews with Independent Filmmakers* (Berkeley: University of California Press, 1988), 253.

7. Brian O'Doherty, "Bruce Conner and His Films," in *The New American Cinema,* ed. Gregory Battcock (New York: E. P. Dutton, 1967), 195. This is the only reference I have found to this piece.

8. Apparently only one print of this film was made. My description of it is drawn from Mitch Tuchman, "Kennedy Death Films," *Take One* 6 (May 1978): 20.

9. The point is underscored by a description of Conner given by Stan Brakhage: "Bruce was just alive and wracked on that day of the assassination, and he had to make his homage. . . . Alive and in a state of nervousness before that TV set, he took images charged with the immediacy of the actual event." *Film at Wit's End,* 133.

10. Conner, "The Warp and Woof of Bruce Conner," 45.

11. Brakhage, *Film at Wit's End,* 131.

12. David James, *Allegories of Cinema: American Film in the Sixties* (Princeton, N.J.: Princeton University Press, 1989), 158.

13. It is worth keeping in mind that throughout the sixties the graphic imagery of the Zapruder film was not exhibited to the general public as moving pictures. The images of the head wound were, however, published in *Life* magazine twice between November 1963 and November 1966 as well as in Volume 18 of the Warren Report.

14. Bruce Conner, "Bruce Conner," *Film Comment* 5 (Winter 1969): 18.

15. For a thorough discussion of the use of montage in *Report* and its function with respect to this point, see Leger Grindon, "Significance Reexamined: A Report on Bruce Conner," *Post Script* 4 (Winter 1985). Several points I will discuss are treated similarly and astutely by Grindon in his article.

16. James, *Allegories of Cinema,* 156–157.

17. This paradigm is nicely summarized by James at the end of Chapter 1 of

his book: "the ideals of the sixties were always tempered by their opposites, and, from the constructivism of perpetual revolution to the irreverent debunkings of the mass media, the cults of authenticity were always conducted through the cultures of fabrication." James, *Allegories of Cinema*, 28.

18. Ibid.

Chapter 7 **Assassination Video**

1. For a discussion of the formation and composition of Ant Farm and T. R. Uthco, see Patricia Mellencamp, "Video Politics: Guerrilla TV, Ant Farm, Eternal Frame," *Discourse* 10 (Spring–Summer 1988): 78–100.

2. The findings of this self-examination are found in the final report of the Senate Select Committee on Governmental Operations with Respect to Intelligence Activities issued in April 1976. The committee's investigation confirmed that the CIA had employed members of organized crime to participate in the assassination of foreign leaders and that the FBI had conducted a secret program dubbed COINTELPRO to harass and disrupt the work of liberal-left political activists, in particular elements within the black civil rights movement.

3. Mellencamp, "Video Politics," 92.

4. Ibid., 88.

5. Ant Farm and T. R. Uthco, *The Eternal Frame*, 1975.

6. "The Eternal Frame: A Nightmare Unfolds in Dealey Plaza," *National Lampoon*, January 1976, 44–48.

7. I want to underscore that what is revisionist here is not the specifics of this enemies list, the contents of which seem quite justified to me, but the way a school of assassination critics insisted that these were also the forces against which JFK was fighting and against which he would have succeeded had he not been murdered.

8. Al Andrien, "Jackie's Date with Destiny," *National Lampoon*, January 1976, 57.

9. Ant Farm's videos are undoubtedly a form of documentary. Here I want to distinguish between the group's documenting of spectacles they created for documentation and such vérité videos as TVTV's *Four More Years* or DCTV's videos documenting local or international social problems. For a brief discussion of these, see Deidre Boyle, "A Brief History of American Documentary Video," in *Illuminating Video: An Essential Guide to Video Art*, ed. Doug Hall and Sally Jo Fifer, with a preface by David Bolt, with a foreword by David Ross, with an introduction by Doug Hall and Sally Jo Fifer

(New York: Aperture, in association with Bay Area Video Coalition, 1990), 51–69.

10. CBS News was limited in the first several hours to Walter Cronkite in the studio with an occasional shot of the reception room of the Dallas Trade Mart where Kennedy was supposed to have spoken and where a camera was set up. On-camera NBC anchors Chet Huntley, David Brinkley, and Frank McGee somewhat awkwardly took a report from correspondent Robert McNeil over the phone. Images of the casket being unloaded from *Air Force One* at Andrews Air Force Base were broadcast live.

11. It is outside the scope of this project to detail the specific deployment of assassination imagery in the buff community's investigatory videos of the eighties and nineties. Their approach to representation still falls within the terms of faith and crisis I have laid out here. For a cataloguing of this work, see Anthony Frewin, *The Assassination of John F. Kennedy: An Annotated Film, TV, and Videography, 1963–1992,* with a forward by Martin Short (Westport, Conn.: Greenwood Press, 1993).

12. Pier Paolo Pasolini, "Observations on the Sequence Shot," in *Heretical Empiricism,* trans. Lawton and Barnett (Bloomington: Indiana University Press, 1988), 233–237.

13. Ibid., 233. At the beginning of this essay Pasolini defines the sequence shot as "subjective"; that is, as bounded by the subjective perspective of the individual who sees or hears the reality being filmed.

14. Ibid., 234.

15. Ibid., 235.

16. Ibid., 236.

17. Throughout this section I have assumed that Pasolini was not seriously involved in the assassination writing and research that was taking place in Europe almost as intensely as it was taking place in the United States. For example, he mislabels Zapruder's footage as sixteen millimeter at the beginning of his essay and, as has been mentioned, seems unaware of the existence of the other filmic evidence.

18. Gary Kibbons, *The Long Take,* 1988.

19. Pasolini, "Observations on the Sequence Shot," 237.

Part Three

1. Don DeLillo, *Libra* (New York: Viking, 1988), 370.

2. For critics who cite the *Suddenly* incident, see Priscilla Johnson McMillan, *Marina and Lee* (New York: Harper & Row, 1977), 380, and Robert G.

Blakey and Richard N. Billings, *The Plot to Kill the President* (New York: Times Books, 1981), 361.

3. In his annotated guide to assassination film, TV, and video, Anthony Frewin cites the work of Gary Mack who, in researching the TV listings for Dallas during the week of October 13 through 26, found no mention of *Suddenly*. Frewin acknowledges that Oswald may well have seen the film, but not at the crucial point reported by other writers. Anthony Frewin, *The Assassination of John F. Kennedy: An Annotated Film, TV, and Videography, 1963–1992, with a foreword by Martin Short* (Westport, Conn.: Greenwood Press, 1993), 93. It may also be worth noting that, in their reference to *Suddenly*, Blakey and Billings misidentify the year of the film as 1959.

4. In a promotional interview piece for the film's cablecast on Cinemax, Frank Sinatra discusses with director John Frankenheimer and screenwriter George Axelrod how Kennedy told him how much he liked the novel by Richard Condon and looked forward to the film version.

5. In his 1988 review of the film, Thomas Doherty reports that Sinatra did not know he held distribution rights to the film until he learned it in an interview with Richard Condon, author of the novel. Thomas Doherty, "A Second Look," *Cineaste* 16 (1988): 31.

6. In his chapter on *The Chase*, Robin Wood stresses the "topicality" of violence as rendered by Penn and specifically mentions the connection between Oswald's murder and the shooting of Bubber Reeves. Robin Wood, *Arthur Penn* (New York: Frederick A. Praeger, 1969), 70.

7. Arthur Penn, interview by Andre Labarthe and Jean-Louis Comolli, *Cahiers du Cinema* (December, 1967).

Chapter 8 **Executive Action**

1. Michael Ryan and Douglas Kellner, *Camera Politica: The Politics and Ideology of Contemporary Hollywood Film* (Bloomington: Indiana University Press, 1988), 95–105.

2. Ibid., 98.

3. Ibid., 99.

4. Ibid., 98.

5. Further examples of literature in this genre can be found throughout *High Weirdness by Mail*, cited in Chapter 1, a mail-order directory which testifies, in the words of its own introduction, to the "incredibly fertile fields for the sowing of superstition, cultism and pseudoscience." A film exemplifying postmodern conspiracy theory, which includes references to the JFK

assassination but should be considered distinct from the conspiracy literature I have discussed throughout this book, is *Tribulation 99*.

6. Richard Hofstadter, *The Paranoid Style in American Politics and Other
Essays* (New York: Vintage Books, 1967).

7. Ibid., 29. It is worth repeating, however, that neither of these characteristics describes the majority of assassination critics. In particular, the apocalyptic nature of the second tendency functioned more as a rhetorical device,
quickly becoming a rather tired one, than as a conviction that motivated
investigators.

8. Ibid., 14.

9. Christopher Lasch, "The Life of Kennedy's Death," *Harper's,* October
1983, 33.

10. It should be noted that most buffs kept their attention on the assassination and did not explicitly link their work with other sixties' movements.
Those critics who did seek such connections left themselves open to criticism by speaking of power only in terms of state secrecy and the operations
of governmental elites. Thus, when they included references to Vietnam or
the civil rights struggle, it was generally in terms of how the government
was waging war on protesters or how other political assassinations had affected these movements rather than in questions of economic injustice or
U.S. imperialism. This seems to spring from the critics' overvaluation of
JFK as civil rights advocate and opponent of the cold war.

11. Thomas Elsaesser, "Notes on the Unmotivated Hero, the Pathos of
Failure: American Films in the 70s," *Monogram* 5 (October 1975): 13. Some
of the films Elsaesser discusses in this context are *Five Easy Pieces, Two Lane
Bricktop, California Split, The Last Detail, Thieves Like Us, Bring Me the Head
of Alfredo Garcia, The Parallax View,* and *The Longest Yard*.

12. Ibid., 14.

13. Ibid.

14. Ibid., 18.

15. Ibid.

16. Ibid.

17. Ibid., 14.

18. Robin Wood, *Hollywood from Vietnam to Reagan* (New York: Columbia
University Press, 1986), 27.

19. Ibid., 28.

20. Ibid., 31.

21. Ibid., 49.

22. Wood's use of the term *incoherent* and his abbreviated references to the changes brought by the demise of the studio system are from his essay "The Incoherent Text: Narrative in the 70s," *Hollywood from Vietnam to Reagan,* 46–49.

23. Dominick LaCapra, *Soundings in Critical Theory* (Ithaca, N.Y.: Cornell University Press, 1989), 193.

24. Ibid., 194.

25. Most of the popular reviews for these films make reference to a cultural obsession with political intrigue and paranoia. George Wead assesses this attitude and then tries to establish the contours of a genre he calls filmnoia in "Toward a Definition of Filmnoia," *The Velvet Light Trap* 13 (1974): 2–6. See also Hendrik Hertzberg and David C. K. McClelland, "Paranoia: An Idée Fixe Whose Time Has Come," *Harpers,* June 1974, 51–60.

26. In one scene Foster hints to Farrington that JFK's death will allow important political strategies to proceed, such as limiting the population growth of peoples of color as well as of chronically poor whites. This more global motive for the Dallas shooting is mentioned only once and is subsequently abandoned.

27. In his semiparodic essay "Sixty Versions of the Kennedy Assassination," Edward Jay Epstein refers to this as the "Dallas Oligarchy Theory," its chief proponent being assassination critic Thomas Buchanan. Epstein writes: "According to Buchanan's theory, 'Mr. X,' a right-wing Texas oil millionaire, had to eliminate Kennedy and Khrushchev to gain world domination of the oil market. He decided to assassinate Kennedy in such a way that Kruschev would be discredited." *Smiling Through the Apocalypse: Esquire's History of the Sixties* (New York: McCall Publishing Co., 1969), 485. Although Ferguson clearly does not conform to this "Mr. X," his character signifies this presence in the assassination literature.

28. See Donald Freed and Mark Lane, *Executive Action: Assassination of a Head of State,* with an introduction by Richard H. Popkin, with special material by Stephen Jaffe (New York: Dell Publishing Co., 1973). Perhaps the most significant difference between the novel and the film concerns the former's concentration on the personal problems and psychological pressure endured by one of the assassins. The book therefore focuses on (or fictionalizes) the execution itself, allowing the reader psychological access to the plot and its implementation. Unlike the pulp novel, nothing in the film allows the spectator to become emotionally involved.

29. Joan Mellen, *"Executive Action:* The Politics of Distortion," *Cineaste* 6 (1974): 8–12.

30. Ibid., 12.

31. Ibid.

32. Ibid.

Chapter 9 **The Parallax View/Winter Kills/Blow Out**

1. In the novel on which the film is quite loosely based, those who have died mysteriously were captured on a short piece of amateur film. The murders are being carried out systematically from right to left as the witnesses appear in the frame. See Loren Singer, *The Parallax View* (New York: Dell Publishing Co., 1972).

2. The *New York Times* placed these two images side by side to accompany an article from August 1974. See Stephen Farber, "Movies That Reflect Our Obsession with Conspiracy and Assassination," *New York Times*, 11 August 1974, p. 11.

3. For an example of this, see Peter Dale Scott, "From Dallas to Watergate," in *Government by Gunplay*, ed. Sid Blumenthal and Harvey Yazijian (New York: Signet, 1976), 113–129.

4. Richard E. Sprague, *The Taking of America 1*2*3* (Woodstock, N.Y.: Rush Harp and Barbara Black, 1977). Sprague's book, of which only 500 copies were printed, argues for a rather opaque yet far-reaching theory which in some ways resonates with *The Parallax View*. Sprague suggests that a shifting cabal, which he calls the Power Control Group, has had power over the American political process since the early sixties.

5. For discussions of the Secret Team and related hypotheses, see Robert J. Groden and Harrison Edward Livingston, *High Treason* (New York: Berkeley Books, 1990), 403–446. The authors quote extensively from L. Fletcher Prouty, *The Secret Team: The CIA and Its Allies in Control of the United States and the World* (New York: Prentice-Hall, 1973). Prouty and other Secret Team theorists have been thoroughly critiqued for offering a reactionary theory about world domination which parallels the anti-Semitic theories of global conspiracy generated by the far-right fringe. For an overview of this criticism, see Chip Berlet, "Friendly Fascists: The Far Right Tries to Move in on the Left," *The Progressive*, June 1992, 16–20.

6. Michael Ryan and Douglas Kellner, *Camera Politica: The Politics and Ideology of Contemporary Hollywood Film* (Bloomington: Indiana University Press, 1988), 95.

7. Seymour Martin Lipset and William Schneider, *The Confidence Gap: Business, Labor and Government in the Public Mind* (New York: The Free Press, 1983), 36–37. For an example of an analysis of corporate power produced

around this time, see the essays contributed to Ralph Nader's Conference on Corporate Accountability, *Corporate Power in America*, ed. Ralph Nader and Mark J. Green (New York: Grossman Publishers, 1973).

8. For a shot-by-shot breakdown of the last several minutes of this montage, see Andrew Horton, "Political Assassination and Cinema: Alan J. Pakula's *The Parallax View, Persistence of Vision* 3 / 4 (Summer 1986), 66–67.

9. Ibid., 67.

10. Philip French, "The Parallax View," *Sight and Sound* 44 (Winter 1974–1975), 54.

11. Joseph Kanon, "The Parallax Candidate," *Atlantic,* August 1974, 86.

12. Robin Wood, *Hollywood from Vietnam to Reagan* (New York: Columbia University Press, 1986), 31. In this passage Wood is writing specifically about the films of Robert Altman, but his argument is that Altman's films are symptomatic of the seventies' American cinema in general.

13. Kanon goes on to suggest that the behavior of the film's characters "moves so effortlessly from real life to the sinister context on the screen that they remind us how unsettling everyday life has become." Kanon, "The Parallax Candidate," 86.

14. George Wead, "Toward a Definition of Filmnoia," *The Velvet Light Trap* 13 (1974): 5–6.

15. For a more detailed discussion of the film's bizarre production circumstances, see Richard Condon, "Who Killed *Winter Kills?*" *Harper's,* May 1983, 73–80. See also Aljean Harmetz, "Film Took a Gamble That May Pay Off," *New York Times,* 17 May 1979, p. 17.

16. Condon, "Who Killed *Winter Kills?*" 80.

17. Furthermore, as Condon points out in his article, the source of Goldberg's and Stirling's cash appeared highly suspect and was perhaps generated by cocaine sales. In 1979 Goldberg was murdered in his apartment, and two years later Stirling was convicted of narcotics distribution.

18. Robin Wood, *Hollywood from Vietnam to Reagan,* 50.

19. Ibid.

20. Linda Williams, *Hard Core* (Berkeley: University of California Press, 1989), 191.

21. Wood, *Hollywood from Vietnam to Reagan,* 155. For examples of the "other critics," see Beth Horning, "Blow Out: Fake Humanism," *Jump Cut* 27 (July 1982), 6–7, and Jacquelin Bautista, "Intent and Effect in Blow Out," 65–66, and Beth Horning, "Alienating Hopelessness," *Jump Cut* 29 (February 1984), 66.

22. Sigmund Freud, *On Creativity and the Unconscious* (New York: Harper & Row, 1958), 137.

23. Wood, *Hollywood from Vietnam to Reagan*, 160. The italics on *constructively* belong to Wood.

24. Chris Hugo, "Three Films of Brian De Palma," *Movie* 33 (Winter 1989): 58. Kellner and Ryan offer a similar critique of *The Parallax View*, labeling it "an exemplary rhetorical exercise in critique through negative representation," one that "lacks the elements required to draw an audience into the sort of sympathetic identification with character that permits political films to be effective or to have an impact." However, what those required elements are or how impact might be measured remain undefined. Kellner and Ryan, *Camera Politica*, 99.

Chapter 10 JFK

1. See George Lardner, "Dallas in Wonderland: Oliver Stone and JFK's Assassination," *Washington Post*, National Weekly Edition, 27 May–2 June 1991, 23–24. See also Richard Zoglin, "More Shots in Dealey Plaza," *Time*, 10 June 1991, 64–66. The assassination critic rumored to have leaked an early draft of the script is Harold Weisberg, whom *Time* quotes as labeling the script "a travesty."

2. From here on, references to Garrison will refer to Stone's Garrison as depicted within *JFK*. I will indicate in the text when I am referring to the real Jim Garrison.

3. Kenneth Auchincloss, "Twisted History," *Newsweek*, 23 December 1991, 46–49. For another editorial critical of Stone's representation of history, see Anthony Lewis, "'J.F.K.,'" *New York Times*, 9 January 1992. For a general discussion of the media attacks on *JFK*, see James Petras, "The Discrediting of the Fifth Estate," *Cineaste* 19 (1992): 15–17.

4. David Anson, "A Troublemaker for Our Times," *Newsweek*, 23 December 1991, 50.

5. Richard Corliss, "Who Killed J.F.K.?" *Time*, 23 December 1991, 68. See also David Denby, "Thrill of Fear," *New York*, 6 January 1991, 50–51.

6. Both *Newsweek* and *Time* gave Stone his say alongside their reviews: "What Does Oliver Stone Owe History?" *Newsweek*, 23 December 1991, 49; "Plunging into the Labyrinth," *Time*, 23 December 1991, 74–76; Gary Crowdus, "Clarifying the Conspiracy: An Interview with Oliver Stone," *Cineaste* 19 (1992): 25–27. This issue of *Cineaste* also reprinted Stone's address to the National Press Club. In addition to interviews, Stone was given considerable editorial space for longer defenses and explanations of *JFK*.

See Oliver Stone, "Oliver Stone Talks Back," *Premiere*, January 1992, 67–72. Oliver Stone, "Dallas in Wonderland: Seeking a Higher Truth . . . ?" *Washington Post*, National Weekly Edition, 10–16 June 1991, 24.

7. Stone, "Oliver Stone Talks Back," 72.

8. In April 1992 *The Village Voice* sponsored what was called "An Assassination Salon" at the Village Gate jazz club in New York City. It featured William Kuntsler, Jack Newfield, and Mark Lane. What was billed as the first annual Midwest Symposium on the Assassination of John F. Kennedy was held in Chicago in June 1992, and a second symposium, this time including the deaths of Robert Kennedy and Martin Luther King, Jr., was held in April 1993.

9. The relatively "upscale" audience at this forum was surprisingly diverse and seemed confined neither to college-age students coming to the debate for the first time nor to celebrity seekers there to see Stone and Mailer.

10. This clash was carried out in the pages of *The Nation* during March and April, primarily between Stone and John Newman, author of *JFK and Vietnam* and a consultant to *JFK;* Alexander Cockburn, outraged at the image of JFK as peacemonger; and Wesley Liebler, former assistant counsel to the Warren Commission. See, in particular, *The Nation*, 18 May 1992, 650, 676–680.

11. *Tikkun,* March/April 1992, 37.

12. Erwin Knoll, "Conspiracy," *The Progressive,* March 1992, 4.

13. John M. Newman, *JFK and Vietnam: Deception, Intrigue and the Struggle for Power* (New York: Warner Books, 1992).

14. For a good account of how Stone came to be interested in the assassination and his relationship to Newman's research, see Robert Sam Anson, "The Shooting of JFK," *Esquire,* November 1991, 93–102, 174–176. Newman's research could be labeled "credible" in that, previous to its use, Stone had relied on the theories of L. Fletcher Prouty, former Air Force colonel and aide to the Joint Chiefs of Staff. Prouty's reputation had come under attack primarily because of his association with the reactionary Liberty Lobby. The character X in *JFK* is based on Prouty. For an important critique of the position put forth by Newman and used by Stone in *JFK,* see Noam Chomsky, *Rethinking Camelot: JFK, the Vietnam War, and U.S. Political Culture* (Boston: South End Press, 1993).

15. Geraldo Rivera devoted yet another of his shows to the assassination on December 23, 1991, and Oprah Winfrey did the same a month later. The "Today" show devoted a week to reviewing the major conspiracy theories, from February 3 through February 7. The news divisions of the major net-

works also paid some attention to the assassination after the release of *JFK*. ABC's "Nightline" devoted a show to the KGB file on Oswald on November 22, 1991, a report that turned up little beyond the Soviet intelligence opinion that Oswald was too incompetent, physically and mentally, to pull off the assassination. See Bill Carter, "ABC Finds K. G. B. Fickle on Oswald," *New York Times,* 21 November 1991, C26.

16. See "'J.F.K.' May Elicit Action on Files," *New York Times,* 12 January 1992, 6.

17. On the Hoffa contract, see Jack Newfield, "Hoffa Had the Mob Murder JFK, *New York Post,* 14 January 1992, 4–5. On the tapes, see Jack Newfield, "Secret Tapes May Hold Key to JFK Plot," *New York Post,* 28 January 1992, 2, 16.

18. Lawrence K. Altman, "Doctors Affirm Kennedy Autopsy Report," *New York Times,* 20 May 1992, A1, B7. Just what else their "seven year effort" produced went unannounced by the association. However, Dr. George D. Lundberg, editor of the journal, did call upon the government to open the Kennedy archives. See Dennis L. Breo, "JFK's Death — The Plain Truth from the MDs Who Did the Autopsy," *Journal of the American Medical Association,* 267 (27 May 1992): 2794–2807.

19. "Two Shots, from the Rear," *New York Times,* 20 May 1992, A22.

20. Ibid.

21. Tim Weiner, "Papers on Kennedy Assassination Are Unsealed, and '63 Is Revisited," *New York Times,* 24 August 1993, A1, A11. "New Files on JFK Assassination Offer Gore but Few Revelations," *The Star-Ledger,* 4 May 1994, 5.

22. Richard Lingeman, *Don't You Know There's a War On?* (New York: G. P. Putnam's Sons, 1970), 242–243.

23. Stone, "Oliver Stone Talks Back," 69.

24. Pat Dowell, "Last Year at Nuremberg: The Cinematic Strategies of JFK," *Cineaste* 19 (1992): 10.

25. Quoted in Bob Fisher, "The Whys and Hows of JFK," *American Cinematographer,* February 1992, 45.

26. Auchincloss, "Twisted History," 47.

27. For details about that visual quilt and the range of film stocks, shooting ratios, and lighting techniques employed, see Fisher, "The Hows and Whys of JFK," 42–52.

28. There are several good analyses of the gender and sexual orientation politics of *JFK,* the arguments of which overlap with but also extend well

beyond the points I make here. See Michael Rogin, "AHR Forum JFK: The Movie," *American Historical Review* 97 (April 1992): 500–505; Roy Grundman and Cynthia Lucia, "Gays, Women and an Absent Hero: The Sexual Politics of JFK," *Cineaste* 19 (1992): 20–22; David Ehrenstein, "JFK — A New Low for Hollywood," *Advocate,* 14 January 1992, 78–80.

29. Rogin, "AHR Forum *JFK:* The Movie," 502.

Index

259